Unveiling the Color Line

A VOLUME IN THE SERIES

African American Intellectual History

EDITED BY

Christopher Cameron

Unveiling the Color Line

W. E. B. DU BOIS ON THE PROBLEM OF WHITENESS

LISA J. MCLEOD

University of Massachusetts Press
AMHERST AND BOSTON

Copyright © 2024 by University of Massachusetts Press
All rights reserved
Printed in the United States of America

ISBN 978-1-62534-793-0 (paper); 794-7 (hardcover)

Designed by Sally Nichols
Set in Freight Text Pro
Printed and bound by Books International, Inc.

Cover design by adam b. bohannon
Cover photo by Carl Van Vechten, *W.E.B. Du Bois*
(William Edward Burghardt), July 18, 1946.
Digital photo provided by
Beinecke Rare Book and Manuscript Library,
Yale University. © Van Vechten Trust.

Library of Congress Cataloging-in-Publication Data

Names: McLeod, Lisa J., author.
Title: Unveiling the color line : W.E.B. Du Bois on the problem of whiteness / Lisa J. McLeod.
Other titles: W.E.B. Du Bois on the problem of whiteness
Description: Amherst : University of Massachusetts Press, [2024] | Series: African American intellectual history | Includes bibliographical references and index. |
Identifiers: LCCN 2023046506 (print) | LCCN 2023046507 (ebook) | ISBN 9781625347947 (hardcover) | ISBN 9781625347930 (paper) | ISBN 9781685750695 (ebook)
Subjects: LCSH: Du Bois, W. E. B. (William Edward Burghardt), 1868-1963. | White people—Race identity—United States. | African Americans—Social conditions. | United States--Race relations.
Classification: LCC E185.97.D73 M434 2024 (print) | LCC E185.97.D73 (ebook) | DDC 305.800973--dc23/eng/20240214
LC record available at https://lccn.loc.gov/2023046506
LC ebook record available at https://lccn.loc.gov/2023046507

British Library Cataloguing-in-Publication Data
A catalog record for this book is available from the British Library.

Contents

Preface vii

Acknowledgments xiii

Introduction
1

CHAPTER 1
Early Interventions
18

CHAPTER 2
The Souls of Black Folk
31

CHAPTER 3
The Riddle of John Brown
47

CHAPTER 4
Darkwater's Faith in Humanity
63

CHAPTER 5
Black Reconstruction
81

CHAPTER 6
Dusk of Dawn and the Triumph of Unreason
97

CHAPTER 7
The Postwar Collapse of Whiteness
118

CHAPTER 8
The Promise of the Black Flame
134

CHAPTER 9
Moral Reconstruction
Du Bois's Legacy for a Critical Theory of Whiteness
157

CONCLUSION
171

Notes 175
Index 201

Preface

I began thinking about this book in the early days of Barack Obama's first term. Like many white Americans, I hoped that the election of a Black president (regardless of the complexity of his racial identity) meant a new era in the history of race in the United States. I did not think that racism had been defeated, but I did believe that some critical mass of white voters was able to recognize excellence, or at least competence, in an African American candidate.[1] Moreover, the willingness of at least as many white Americans to be represented globally by a man of color seemed new. I had students who worried that Obama would be assassinated, and that certainly seemed possible. I nevertheless thought that white supremacy had become a primarily a feature of American and world systems and institutions rather than conscious minds, and that most—or nearly all—white people would deny holding racist or white supremacist beliefs, at least for appearances' sake. In workshops and papers, race theorists used the phrase *white supremacy* to refer primarily to these systemic and unconscious forms of white supremacy—reassuring varied audiences that they did not mean the Klan.[2]

By 2016, though, we had learned that the Klan, or conscious racists, were more numerous, more unashamed, than we had previously believed. Of course, most white voters had not voted for Obama, despite a clear message that his commitment to racial justice was as abstract and fair-minded as it was possible to be. As months and years passed, white Americans revealed that Obama's election had signaled to them an existential threat.[3] Someone was taking the country away from "us," the real Americans, and it was time to "take it back." Finally, with the election of Donald Trump and ensuing events, it became clear that many white Americans were prepared to defend a white supremacist vision of the United States with violence.

This was not the first time that white Americans had reacted with fear and rage to substantive gains for people of color: just consider white southerners' violent response to *Brown v. Board of Education* in 1954 and white northerners' vicious response to busing and school integration in the 1970s. Many white Americans were, in a word, *challenged* by the election of a Black president and beside themselves with worry. The subsequent election of Donald Trump—who had falsely and shamelessly claimed that Obama had not been born in the United States and thus was not eligible to be president— and his open support for white nationalists only demonstrated the depth and fervency of this white panic.

Trump, who had seemed clownish in his racist denials of Obama's fitness to be the leader of the free world, has relegitimized all that white liberals and even leftists cannot face about white American identity. Those of us who identify as progressives still benefit from our white identity, of course, and cannot escape it. We do, however, wish to be recognized as not like *that*: not racist. Perhaps in this moment, rather than in 1877, 1954, or 1974, white Americans will begin to interrogate our identity and come to grips with our complicity in the ongoing horror show that is American whiteness. We have a long and sordid past, and there is less difference that we think between the young white couple who are choosing the best school for their child in 2024 and the white parents who were carrying "Keep Our Schools White" signs in Little Rock in 1957—because we simply do not think enough, or think well enough, about white supremacy. We white liberals and progressives who were concerned or even stunned by the depth of this white reaction now face the prospect that Trump and his ideologues will summon sufficient power to turn the electoral tide again in 2024.[4] Keep in mind that however horrified we were by his behavior before or during his presidency, we did not engage in anything that could be called mass resistance. As usual, that was left to people of color.

The resurgence of explicit white supremacy, of "saying the quiet part out loud," operates alongside the systemic, structural, and unconscious white supremacy that theorists have been discussing for decades. According to this view, the framework of American race talk—even when the talk is an effort at antiracism—has traditionally taken whiteness as the norm; it is the lens through which "the race problem" is viewed. People of color are seen as biased, overly sensitive, and thus imperfect witnesses to racism. We whites see ourselves as objective, neutral observers who can determine when race is and is not relevant socially or politically. Because we see ourselves as untainted by the issue of race and as more or less raceless, we have appointed ourselves to be the arbiters of racial justice. It is no accident that activists of color regularly point out the asymmetry between white and nonwhite racial groups in U.S. society: white people can walk away from the awareness of racism and reliably fail to recognize its pervasive harms.

As a result, whites often locate the problem of racism in Black individuals and the Black community. Consider, for example, the historical practice of attributing retrograde character traits to Africans and their descendants, which has persisted into the twenty-first century. Given this framing of the race problem, white Americans (and many Americans of color) view African Americans and other people of color as flawed. But the problem extends to even more progressive conceptions of racism, wherein people of color and their communities are perceived as damaged and in need of repair. Let me be clear that I am not trying to argue that people of color are unaffected by white supremacy; rather, I want to emphasize the point that W. E. B. Du Bois made as early as 1896: that white supremacy significantly warps whites' perceptions and behaviors.[5] White folk cannot accurately evaluate the capacity of people of color, at least not without significant effort, and are likely to "solve" racial injustice in ways that continue to privilege those racialized as white and harm people of color. Clearly, white efforts at remediation and inclusion have done considerable damage. For example, school integration, effected in the 1950s through the 1970s, resulted in the closing of Black schools, the firing of Black principals and teachers, and, initially, the inclusion of small minorities of Black children in white-dominated schools. As a result, schools remain racially segregated due to white flight from urban neighborhoods, and children of color not only have disproportionate suspension and expulsion rates but are also the primary players in the phenomenon known as the school-to-prison pipeline.[6]

Naomi Murakawa demonstrates that American institutions and structures are shot through and through with white supremacy, and this includes ostensibly reformative projects for at-risk youth.[7] White teachers, counselors, and social workers crowd the world of students of color. White college professors and staff keep an eye on students who were admitted provisionally and are seen as particularly at risk. Murakawa's work is part of what seems to me an important movement among theorists away from the liberal notion of racism as an unfortunate variation on a universal xenophobia and toward a historically informed and theoretically sophisticated conception of white supremacy as a structure that has a particular genealogy in European colonialism and more recent adaptations in a neoliberal, continuously evolving form of capitalism. Good white children in the United States grow up wanting to help the less fortunate, unaware that their own lifestyles create the conditions of abjection for those seen as unlucky. Further, they are unaware that their desire to help people of color and their inability to do this effectively are influenced by the same white supremacy that they condemn when it takes different shape in others.

Du Bois worked from the assumption that dominant cultural modes in the majority of the world support racial injustice; thus, any evaluation of people of color or their plight from the stance of this dominant worldview is corrupt. White misperception is nevertheless advantaged by a system of white supremacy. Although their epistemic and moral capacities have been deeply damaged by this complex, white people are supported in their worldview by dominant background assumptions. For Du Bois, the worldview and the self-conception of whiteness come fully furnished, as it were, as white folk grow into white racial identity. As the center of the universe, whiteness is not amenable to stepping outside of that center. As Aldon Morris notes, the white psyche that results from the system of white supremacy is not healthy or desirable. Rather, it is "scarred," and Du Bois was a virtuoso observer of that psyche.[8]

In *Living a Feminist Life*, Sara Ahmed writes, "When you become a feminist, you find out very quickly: what you aim to bring to an end some do not recognize as existing."[9] As Ahmed knows, antiracism work faces this challenge. Even white liberals who believe that racism exists see white supremacy as a relatively discrete (if recently more visible and powerful) problem. Many whites are convinced that the end of racism is just a matter of time. In this book I do not work to make skeptics believe in the ongoing overwhelming influence of white supremacy in the United States or global systems more generally. Rather, I take for granted that there is a substantial group of white scholars and activists who would like to see the end of white supremacy but are stymied by the sense that they cannot undo it because their own whiteness continues to influence their cognitive capacities and behavior.[10] For these comrades, Du Bois has a great deal to offer.

Thus, while I hope this book is a helpful contribution to critical race theory and whiteness studies in particular, the better result would be if more white scholars and activists were to engage with Du Bois himself. There is a wealth of insight to be found beyond *The Souls of Black Folk*, or even "The Souls of White Folk"; and as we find ourselves in a time that begins to resemble the 1950s in terms of open racism and political repression, we may turn to Du Bois as an example of one who paid a steep price for honesty yet was able, through his own fortitude and the support of friends, to thrive. He knew that his skills as organizer and leader of the masses were limited, but his ability to synthesize the social and political trends and ideologies of his own time was unmatched, even when his conclusions were imperfect (but less so than many). As I hope will become clear, Du Bois has a great deal to teach us, if we will pay attention.

Acknowledgments

A NUMBER OF PEOPLE and institutions have helped in ways large and small. Many thanks to the philosophical regulars of the California Roundtable on Philosophy and Race (CRPR), who heard various versions of parts of this project, beginning in 2010. Special thanks go to Falguni Sheth and Mickaella Perina for organizing and running such a generative, friendly space, and for being there. Gratitude forever to Charles Mills, who gave me encouragement at that conference, and continued to do stunning, courageous, and crucial work until his untimely death. Many thanks to Devonya Havis, Michael Monahan, and Michael Ng, regulars at the CRPR who have offered support and have held me up more than they know.

Thanks to Guilford College for a semester sabbatical in spring 2012 and for a year-long sabbatical in 2017–18, during which I was able to do a great deal of reading and to write the first draft.

So much gratitude to Whitney Battle-Baptiste, the brilliant director of the Du Bois Center at the University of Massachusetts, Amherst. As a Du Bois fellow in the summer of 2018, I worked on a different project there but mooted the idea for this book to several of the other fellows, including Phillip Luke Sinitiere and Camisha Scruggs. Phil, I guess it's done, and I thank you. Thanks to Adam Holmes of the Du Bois Center for great chats and support. And thanks also to the late Rob Cox and to other archivists at UMass Amherst's special collections, where most of Du Bois's papers are held, as well to the archivists at Fisk University's special collections and the Schomberg Center.

Many thanks to Eric Bayruns-García and Avery Smith for their generous and expert commentary at our session at the 2022 Eastern American

Philosophical Association meetings as well as to Linda Martín Alcoff for her engagement and her crucial reminder about Charles and Du Bois.

Writing can be a lonely business, and this book came together during an especially challenging time: political instability, a global pandemic, and professional upheaval as much of higher education faced COVID-19 by having a general breakdown. Many thanks to my colleagues in Guilford College's AAUP chapter for real solidarity and to the alumni who came together to help save the school. Thanks also to those who rallied to help my partner and me find a friendly berth in Boston.

I want to thank especially the editorial and production staff at the University of Massachusetts Press. I have heard nightmare stories of scholars battling editors et al. on their first book. My story is quite different, and much better. Thanks to Mary Dougherty, Matt Becker, and Sally Nichols, and to Dawn Potter, who took on the Byzantine prose of my draft and made it readable and clear. All thanks as well to the two anonymous readers who provided encouragement and loads of helpful observations and recommendations.

I owe tremendous thanks for support and distraction to found family. Love always to Maria Rosales and Tiffany Holland and their brilliant kids, and to Christian and Isaac for community and Community. To Laura Smith for monthly check-ins. To Anderson Hawthorne, Jr., for his patience and understanding above and beyond reasonable expectations. To my sister Hallie for support and excellent parcels arriving by post, even though we walk in different worlds. And above all to Vance Ricks who has made the space and fed the animals and cleaned the litterboxes while I grouched around like a world-class impostor: all my love and thanks.

Unveiling
the Color Line

INTRODUCTION

> I still believe that some day this nation will become a democracy without a color-line.
>
> —W. E. B. Du Bois, *In Battle for Peace* (1952)

W. E. B. Du Bois was an arch observer of white people. If his primary aim was the uplift of Black people and other people of color, his efforts were frustrated by the ignorance, arrogance, and intransigence of white people and their power—political and otherwise—in the United States and worldwide. Du Bois implicated the white world and its moral failings in every piece in which he took up the struggle for racial justice. His diagnosis of the wrongs of white supremacy and, by extension, of how white people could think and act differently to serve justice runs throughout his writings. Crucially, for Du Bois, the problem of the color line affects white people as well as those who are oppressed by it. Those of us who are white, who benefit from whiteness—who created it, who tolerate it, who profit from it, and are corrupted by it—must recognize how white supremacy shapes all of our lives if we want to understand the conditions of our existence. Yet we are less likely to take up this task. As I hope to make clear in these pages, we neglect this project at the risk of our humanity.

In this book I trace Du Bois's conception of whiteness as developed over time in his major published volumes, including his final trilogy of novels. My ambition here is not merely to understand this account—although reading Du Bois is always edifying—but to understand how white people can work to dismantle the color line and help to unmake the white supremacist world we have constructed. I focus on his published books, assuming that his anticipated audience for these (as compared with, say, his work in *The Crisis* or in his columns for the Pittsburgh *Courier*) would explicitly include white readers. To trace the development of his thinking, I address these works in roughly chronological order, beginning with his early days as a student, as a historian, and then as a social scientist hoping to change white beliefs by documenting clear evidence of Black humanity. As he approached middle age and then passed it, a period that roughly spans 1910 to 1945, Du Bois's faith in the humanity of whites, especially American whites, appears to have waxed and waned, as did his continuing efforts to bring down the color line with evidence, rhetoric, and what he sometimes called propaganda. Finally, I will examine Du Bois's least-read later works, arguing that they are less doctrinaire and more consistent with the development of his lifelong antiracist agenda than much Du Bois scholarship suggests.

My approach to Du Bois's work is neither critical (in the sense of engaging in a sustained critique) nor recuperative—at least not intentionally. As well known as some of it is, his work has been undervalued and needs greater attention, particularly from white scholars and race theorists. It is not my aim to evaluate any particular work or even his body of work. I do, however, take seriously the principle of charity: when engaging with Du Bois's writing, I assume that he is saying something coherent and that what he is saying about whiteness in particular is worth understanding. I am indebted to Eric Porter's *The Problem of the Future World* for, among other things, his discussion of Adolph Reed Jr.'s "generative approach" to Du Bois's thought.[1] Like Reed and Porter, I think we can make good use of Du Bois's work in our efforts to investigate the time in which we find ourselves. Reading Du Bois carefully for the key components of whiteness allows us to generate new and useful strategies for defeating white supremacy. Thus, while my project here is primarily exegetical, I also hope to demonstrate how Du Bois's account can elucidate contemporary examples of whiteness as a problem and fight its harmful effects.

In my view, Du Bois's conception of whiteness is best summarized with the umbrella concept of *arrogant, irrevocable license*, which includes three identifiable elements simultaneously constitutive of such license and supportive of it:

* A *heedless comportment*, where whites act as if they were the center of the universe, stomping and flailing about with little awareness of the racially disparate impact of their actions, even when those actions take an easily quantifiable form such as in voting legislation, employment practices, or public health policy

- An *epistemic opacity*, which is a form of ignorance that resists all available evidence of (1) the humanity of people of color and (2) the unremarkable nature of white persons and accomplishments and, conversely, the deeply horrific historical wrongs committed by whites

- A *resilient presumption of innocence*, so basic to white self-conception that any suggestion of race-related wrongdoing triggers extreme defensiveness based, as I will explain, on an existential fear that white supremacy is false and on the profound moral guilt that would follow from recognition of those white historical wrongs

In its combination of heedless comportment, epistemic opacity, and the presumption of innocence, whiteness plagues the majority population of the globe in ways that should be clear to all but remain opaque to most white observers and to those people of color who have themselves absorbed the worldview and the shortcomings of whiteness. As Du Bois's work demonstrates, breaking through this complex of self-protective strategies to convince white people to change not only their treatment of people of color but also their perceptual habits and, indeed, their entire orientation to the world around them would be a project akin to the Copernican Revolution. Du Bois did not make the reorientation of the white moral compass his central project, and we can surely understand why, given how white Americans would have responded to an African American giving them advice for becoming better people. Yet from his earliest writings to the end of his career, he saw the transformation of whiteness and white people as a necessary condition of racial justice.

The persistence of white supremacy and its catastrophic yet rarely acknowledged effects on the global population suggests the structural complexity of whiteness, even if this connection is easily perceived by many people of color. As a group with more access to resources and structural power, white people are clearly obliged to understand and begin, in whatever way possible, to undo white supremacy. My driving assumption has been that the lifetime work of W. E. B. Du Bois offers us a rich curriculum for the attainment of racial justice, if we have the fortitude necessary to see beyond the veil constructed to keep white people not just ignorant but ludicrously and culpably so.

ARROGANT, IRREVOCABLE LICENSE

My particular use of the word *license* to capture Du Bois's conception of whiteness as a problem trades on John Locke's description of the state of nature in his *Second Treatise on Government*, where he importantly emphasized that it is not "a state of license."[2] Locke insisted that humans living without government would, despite the absence of external authority, generally behave according to "the natural law" of reason and thus recognize each other's rights to life, liberty, and property.[3] A state of license, then, could be understood as one in which individuals do not respect the rights of others, even their right to life, and certainly not their liberty or property. (In fact, it is unlikely that property would be recognized in the state of license.) For Locke, the state of nature was nothing like Thomas Hobbes's conception of a wilderness in which human life is "solitary, poor, nasty, brutish and short"; we are not free to destroy ourselves or other humans, as this would violate the natural law, to which we all have access. For my purposes, then, license involves acting toward other human beings as if they share none of the natural rights to which natural law entitles them. Du Bois does not use this term in the way I've employed it, although in the first chapter of *The Souls of Black Folk*, he describes white perceptions regarding Black Americans as based, among other things, in "distortions of fact and wanton license of fancy."[4] That white people are constrained neither by facts nor reasons in their interactions with Black folk captures just the air of untethered lawlessness I mean to invoke with my use of license.

Du Bois's report of the lynching of Sam Hose and its effect on him grimly illustrates this sense of license (see chapter 6). Hose was a grocer near Atlanta who was lynched in 1899 for a supposed crime. Du Bois, then a professor at Atlanta University, had heard of the crime and was on his way to deliver an editorial in an attempt to prevent the man's lynching when he learned that it had already happened and that Hose's knuckles were on display in a shop just a few city blocks from the office of Atlanta's world-class newspaper, where Du Bois had been headed. Lynchings continue to be the epitome of white violence and depravity vis-à-vis people of color. The transformation of a human being into so much refuse is more than homicide and indicates a level of depredation that is difficult to contemplate. Du Bois realized, on hearing the news of the lynching, that his efforts as a social scientist would not change the worldview of whites who were capable of such depravity. The capacity of white Americans to tolerate such crimes, let alone commit them, meant that they were not to be moved to change by more and better data underlining Black humanity: reason alone would not save anyone. White people were not simply ignorant of Black humanity—not ignorant, at least, in a way that could be cured by information.[5] Their ignorance had its foundation in a different lacuna entirely. It was a moral lack, and Du Bois repeatedly had to come to terms with not only whites' capacity for brutality but also their presumption that such behavior was theirs by right, or license.

This license is arrogant because whites grant it to themselves without any basis for doing so. Clearly, whites as a group and as individuals have been responsible for many of the greatest crimes against humanity in recorded history, and many of the achievements we claim are contested. But even if this were not true, the human beings identified as white have not distinguished themselves in a way that could come close to justifying the advantages and dispensations that we have historically assumed for ourselves. Moreover, having arrogated this license, whites do not recognize any conditions under which they might lose it. Thus, the license is irrevocable in that, even when a white person is deemed a race traitor by other whites, they retain white racial identity and, especially among unfamiliar people, the privileges attached thereto.

Heedless Comportment

According to Du Bois's account, white folk individually and in groups demonstrate heedless and often destructive comportment, whether that means assuming that non-white people will yield space on an Atlanta sidewalk or requiring that fully grown adults overturn their entire existence and become, on pain of maiming or death, unpaid laborers in colonial Africa, Asia, and the Americas. Du Bois portrayed this tendency with a deceptively light touch in a famous passage in *Dusk of Dawn*. His fictional character Roger Van Dieman is ignorant of many things, including his own ignorance, but nevertheless acts with an assurance that he knows all that he needs to know. He takes himself to be the expert, superior in intelligence and taste to Du Bois himself and to any other person of color imaginable. He suggests that he and Du Bois repair to a restaurant in midtown Manhattan and must be reminded that such places will not serve Du Bois.

His manner, after this reminder, is absolutely without apology or regret, as if it is a mere peccadillo to thoughtlessly underline an acquaintance's second-class status by forgetting that Jim Crow segregation exists. Neither does Van Dieman give any indication that he objects to racial exclusion and would change it if he could.

Du Bois's best-known work begins with a less obnoxious but no less alienating example of such comportment. In the opening of *The Souls of Black Folk*, the author imagined a white interlocutor who is aching for connection but wants his Black acquaintance to act as something like a "native informant," who will share his perspective on "the Negro problem" when slyly prompted with remarks such as "I know an excellent colored man in my town; or I fought at Mechanicsville; or Do not these Southern outrages make your blood boil?"[6] For Du Bois, the underlying question was really "How does it feel to be a problem?" And while we might applaud such curiosity in a long-time friend who is willing to engage in a genuine exchange of intimacies, the obtuseness of a casual acquaintance who picks at a scab is neither admirable nor appropriate. Du Bois revealed a different form of heedless comportment in his 1947 book *The World and Africa*, describing the piano-playing daughter of a wealthy British family, whose insistence on ivory keys for her instrument requires not only the slaughter of elephants but also intolerable labor practices that distance hides from her sight.[7] We could add the British habit of tea consumption, the American devotion to coffee, and the increasing demand for sugar and cacao to a list of apparently innocent delights that result in global inequities along the color line.

To be clear, what makes this comportment so remarkable is the lack of awareness that characterizes widespread but specific white behavior. We don't expect a toddler to understand that harming others requires an apology and the effort to improve, but adults should know and act with more consideration. Racial segregation was and is a moral wrong when imposed by those who are powerful upon those who consequently lack opportunity and access to key resources. Yet the controversy around anything like reparations or even a spoken apology for decades of Jim Crow or centuries of slavery suggests that more recent and subtle (perhaps from a white perspective) racist harms will go unacknowledged. As a matter of course, the white sense of entitlement often prevents whites from effectively understanding racially inflected historical or contemporary wrongs.

White Epistemic Opacity

Like very young children, whites in Du Bois's work seem to think of themselves as the reason for the universe and as welcome to whatever is necessary to satisfy their whims, even if the desired item is obviously someone else's property, livelihood, or life. Du Bois traced the repetitions of this behavioral pattern well into postwar colonialism, when whites' insistence that they were benefiting the natives was simply indefensible—to any reasonable observer. He argued that whites are *not* reasonable observers in the face of such questions. Their capacity to perceive and interpret human affairs is deeply compromised, especially when people of color are present or race is otherwise relevant, and race is relevant often, given that white people carry their racial identity about with them at all times, whether or not they explicitly acknowledge it.

The philosopher Charles Mills discussed the cognitive failings of white people at length, powerfully elucidating their inability to absorb evidence of the humanity of people of color.[8] Focusing on the concept of white ignorance, he inspired a growing body of work on epistemologies of ignorance aimed at explaining both the prevalence of systemic injustice and the lack of attention to such injustice from those thereby advantaged. As he suggested, whites are primed by their own expectations either to fail to recognize the depth of racial inequalities, or to see them as appropriate given the subperson status of nonwhite people. As Mills wrote, "part of what it requires to achieve Whiteness, . . . is a cognitive model that precludes self-transparency and genuine understanding of social realities." Inhabitants of foreign lands are read as fictional beings, as "Calibans and Tontos, Man Fridays and Sambos" rather than as the human beings they are, and those people of color closer to home can be viewed as lazy, stubborn, or otherwise deserving of their misfortune.[9]

As I have noted, Du Bois began to engage with this conception of whiteness as early as the 1890s. In *The Souls of Black Folk* (1903), he used the metaphor of the Veil to capture whites' inability, not yet perceived as a refusal, to recognize the truth of Black Americans' daily lives. He thereafter portrayed white Americans as variously greedy, cruel, oblivious, or pathetic. By *Darkwater: Voices from within the Veil* (1920) he was explicitly alert to and much less patient with the inability of otherwise competent white persons to recognize the humanity of people of color or the scale of injustice constituted by white supremacy. This incapacity was particularly hard to tolerate given the increasing tendency of white people to seize large swaths of land and resources belonging to others before and during the wars and "police actions" of the twentieth century.[10] By *Black Reconstruction* (1935), Du Bois specifically identified the "blindspot in the eyes of America, and its historians" that prevented the courage and ingenuity of Black activists during slavery and Reconstruction from being widely recognized, to say nothing of their efforts gaining traction.[11]

In a passage from *Dusk of Dawn*, Du Bois offered an uncharacteristically personal account of the difficulty of explaining to white audiences "the full psychological meaning of caste segregation."[12] As such an audience seems unable to respond to or even notice what the narrator is saying, his attempts become more and more extreme until he seems to break through a thick pane of dark glass, emerging bloody and tattered. The onlookers, now astounded by what seem to be the hysterical gesticulations of an overwrought storyteller, infer that the crimes described can have nothing to do with them and are made insensible by fear. Charles Mills referred to Du Bois's account of white innocence as a kind of "white self-veiling": "The veil is a cognitive barrier to whites' veridical apprehension of the situation of blacks, a barrier erected not merely by particular white individuals but by a white society willfully ignorant in general."[13]

A Resilient Presumption of Innocence

The connection between ignorance (regarding the nature of people of color as well as the harm done by white supremacy) and obtuse comportment is not difficult to imagine, and the damage done by this complex is visible everywhere to those who will recognize it. In Du Bois's analysis, perhaps the greatest obstacle to whites' recognition of the wrongs in our history and our present is the resilient presumption of our own innocence. Of course, this presumption exists only in the white mind, but it has in some fashion been built into social and political institutions via a sort of shared delusion of whiteness: that white people are incapable of the actions that they have repeatedly, over centuries, performed. The presumption of white innocence is flexible enough to take in the entire United States—racialized as white in almost every context, as Toni Morrison and others have noted—whenever any party suggests that the U.S. prosecution of a war or other international action requires investigation. The white worldview does not allow for the evaluation of whites as moral monsters regarding crimes against people of color. Similarly, neither the United States nor Europe can commit crimes against nations of color on an international scale. As I will discuss in chapter 7, Du Bois was horrified by Hitler's crimes against Jews and other minorities in Europe. He noted, however, that Germany and other nations had committed comparable atrocities against Africans decades before World War II and that the world had not taken notice.

The neglected question of Confederate reconciliation after the Civil War also reveals this asymmetry. In *Black Reconstruction* and elsewhere, Du Bois highlighted what most white Americans have never considered: that white northern power prioritized the repatriation of treasonous white southerners over support for freed and newly recognized African American citizens. In doing so, northern whites abandoned the emancipated to the murderous violence of former Confederates throughout the South.[14] This welcoming attitude toward the former traitors continued well into the beginning of the twentieth century, despite reams of evidence that southern states were acting—as states—to circumvent the postwar constitutional amendments requiring voting rights and equal protection of the law for all, regardless of race.

One of Du Bois's first public addresses was his Harvard University commencement speech in 1890. While I will engage at some length with this talk in chapter 1, it is useful to note here that, in this speech, given to a predominantly white audience, the twenty-two-year-old Du Bois grappled head on with the reputation of Jefferson Davis, who had recently died. As president of the Confederacy, Davis had represented the effort to defend the rights of white Americans to own other human beings for the purpose of exacting from them, at the very least, unpaid labor and forced breeding. Nonetheless, he served only two years in prison and then was allowed to return home and travel freely until his death. He never admitted that his actions were illegal or wrong.[15]

Davis was hailed throughout the South as a hero and representative of "the Lost Cause." When he died, former Confederate states vied to become his final resting place. After his widow finally chose Richmond, Virginia, to be his permanent gravesite, his corpse was disinterred from Metairie, Louisiana, and, under military escort, carried through numerous southern capitals, where it lay in state and received plaudits from local officials. At times the cortege swelled to tens of thousands of people.[16] Young Du Bois was one of the few to speak plainly about Davis's actual legacy, although it is unclear how many in the audience heard all that he said. This sort of white national amnesia has reappeared with regularity throughout American history. In his writings during the mid- to late 1940s, Du Bois noted that the United States seemed to have an ethical carte blanche in its engagement with "the darker races." He emphasized the assumption by the Allied powers following World War II that, despite their own history of colonial atrocities, they were the obvious candidates to direct the redistribution of African and Asian territories forfeited by Axis nations.[17]

Individual whites, of course, are infamously attached to our own innocence vis-à-vis racist acts. White defensiveness and fragility are prominent phenomena that support this dynamic. Du Bois's remarkable passage in *Dusk of Dawn*, in which the Veil creating the color line is now a thick, dark pane of glass over the entrance of a cave, is an incisive illustration of the power of the white commitment to innocence (see chapter 6). White passersby who witness the emergence of a bloody and disheveled figure through that glass are so disturbed by its implications as to fear for their lives. This passage allows for multiple interpretations, but I contend that this moment reflects the too-frequent reaction of white audiences to expressions of pain by Black, Indigenous, and other people of color.

For Du Bois, then, whiteness is constituted by a tangle of traits that should be disastrous to the holder: heedless comportment, accompanied by a presumption of moral innocence, maintained by a robust epistemological opacity. If the damage flowing from these traits were to redound more obviously on whites, they might be moved to change. Instead, because of the systemic power constituted by white supremacy, the external costs of our behavior are borne by exactly those who are least able to avoid them. The damage done to whites by white supremacy is profound but not obvious to them; to a great extent, it amounts to a lack of self-knowledge and a consistent moral failure that plays out as a particularly blameworthy form of cluelessness. Most white Americans, and whites around the world, would not recognize themselves in Du Bois's conception of whiteness. Du Bois, however, gleaned his evidence regarding white folk from what they did rather than from what they said about themselves.

A NOTE ON USAGE

Racial categories are notoriously fragile in both logical and biological terms, even as they remain sociopolitically robust.[18] Du Bois's metaphysics of race was briefly a popular topic in the philosophical world, but it is not my subject here. Nevertheless, my discussion will no doubt benefit from a brief clarification of the vocabulary I use in exploring his work. With the term *white*, I take him to refer to those human beings who trace their known ancestry all and only to European regions, exclusive of Asia, beginning with the so-called modern era.[19] Du Bois, born in the United States, wrote that whiteness was a modern invention; and as far as I can tell, he maintained this definition of whiteness in his published writings.

Regarding the language used to refer to other racial identities, I strive for accuracy and transparency and work to stay consistent with the practices of the nonwhite writers on whom my work relies. I use *nonwhite* to indicate the broadest possible category of those who identify themselves, or are socially identified, as having non-European ancestors—in other words, those who do not identify as white or would not be so identified by social custom.[20] As a general matter, I use more specific terminology where it is appropriate. Du Bois's early work is most often concerned with racial justice for African Americans (those with American residence or citizenship with recognizable African ancestry—often but not always those whose ancestors were enslaved in the United States). However, he sometimes, even quite early in his career, focused on the impact of white supremacy on those whom he called "the darker races," by which he generally meant Africans, Asians, and their descendants. I will thus use *African American* to refer to Americans (by residence or citizenship) with African ancestry and *people of color* when referring to the larger category of those oppressed by white supremacy, especially in the American context. As I move away from exegesis, I will make use of the newish acronym BIPOC, which refers to Black, Indigenous, and other people of color in the United States.[21] In a more global context or where efforts to specify seem more fraught than usual, I will fall back on the extremely generic *nonwhite*.

OVERVIEW OF THE BOOK

The opening chapters engage with the first ten years or so of Du Bois's public career. Chapter 1 examines two public speeches: his Harvard commencement speech, which reveals that the young man was not shy about describing the problematic behavior of white individuals, even those often labeled as heroes; and "The Conservation of Races," delivered at the first meeting of the American Negro Academy, which offers a vision of global racial difference that insists on human equality and the duty of white Americans to work against racism. Chapter 2 delves into Du Bois's best-known book, *The Souls of Black Folk*, a masterpiece of prose that works to persuade minds and hearts to recognize Black humanity. Together, these three pieces demonstrate that Du Bois saw "the Negro problem" as (in Robert Gooding-Williams's words) a "concrete test of a great republic" and an anomaly in a nation dedicated to liberty and democracy.[22] They also display his conviction that careful scientific work to document the nature of racial oppression and the equality of "the Negro" was necessary for racial justice. As Du Bois wrote, he perceived this work as an effort to correct an error: "The world was thinking wrong about race, because it did not know."[23]

As the prose in *The Souls of Black Folk* makes clear, Du Bois hoped that his use of rich, vivid descriptions might evoke sentiments that would, in turn, awaken reason. The carefully wrought volume thus offers a view of the Black South to which a white reading public had little access. Its painstaking melding of social science with rhetoric was, in Eric Porter's words, "motivated in part by the hope that careful social scientific research would disprove assumptions about black inferiority and provide a path toward equality through scientifically planned uplift strategies and reasoned discussion of black contributions to and marginalization from the fabric of society."[24] I emphasize, however, that white readers of *Souls* cannot fully apprehend the significance of the volume unless they remember that they themselves are intimately implicated in the circumstances that frustrate and even defeat Black humanity. Du Bois makes this plain by bookending the text with notes beseeching the reader to tarry with him and not dismiss his words out of hand.

Chapter 3 examines Du Bois's only biographical work, *John Brown*. Though it is often summarily dismissed as flawed, he insisted that it was among the best of his books.[25] In it, there are indications that Du Bois had begun to suspect that white folk in the main supported white supremacy not because they lacked sufficient information about Black Americans but for more complex reasons. The abolitionist John Brown was not unique in his experiences or in his intellectual gifts; yet, surrounded by other whites, he was nearly unique in his commitment to the humanity of African-descended people and their need to be free. As a man, he thus presented a sort of riddle about white morality. The biography, which was written during Du Bois's first period at Atlanta University, following the dreadful lynching of Sam Hose in 1899 and the bloody Atlanta Riot of 1906, offers white readers an opportunity for self-reflection. Du Bois condoned not only Brown's aim but also his use of violence in pursuit of slavery's abolition; in doing so, he implicitly challenged white readers to face their obligation to end white supremacy. Nahum Dmitri Chandler's scholarship on this biography is crucial to my analysis, as he emphasizes Brown's alienation from his society and calls into question Brown's whiteness, given his actions and worldview.[26]

In chapter 4, I consider *Darkwater*, an essay collection that contains some of Du Bois's most direct challenges to white readers. Following World War I, Black American soldiers and their families struggled to come to terms with a war in which they seemed to have defended democracy for everyone but themselves. On the heels of this disappointment, hundreds of Black Americans were murdered by white rioters in violent race riots that erupted across the nation, from St. Louis to New York.[27] Published in 1920, *Darkwater* addresses this dark climate. The collection includes the searing essay "The Souls of White Folk," which, along with several other pieces, suggests that Du Bois was losing patience with white Americans. Each essay is accompanied by a poem, sometimes despairing, sometimes raging, but always aiming to convince white readers that life within the veil is not merely misfortune but injustice. Many of Du Bois's white readers were put off by this work, calling it bitter or angry. Although this is not surprising, it is nevertheless disappointing; as one of Du Bois's most revealing works, *Darkwater* was a worthy successor to *Souls*. But the collection appeared during a wave of explicitly white-supremacist publications drenched in pseudo-science. This timing ensured that most white readers would dismiss it but also demonstrates Du Bois's rare and courageous brilliance in context.[28]

By the mid-1930s, Du Bois, in his mid-sixties, was moved by his social and political milieux to consider the role of capitalism in human suffering as well as its undeniable role in maintaining white supremacy.[29] In chapter 5, I examine *Black Reconstruction*, the work of long years, in which Du Bois—newly self-taught on the work of Karl Marx—explicitly considered a potential dictatorship of the U.S. proletariat and the role of white supremacy in preventing that triumph of labor. His discussion of white supremacy in this work is groundbreaking in its recognition of the epistemic incapacity that supports loyalty to whiteness. As Joel Olson wrote, both the promise of democracy and the promise of socialism are hampered by whiteness, which Du Bois frames here as "the American Blindspot."[30] It is, he says, "the American Assumption" that the misery of African-descended people and the stranglehold of whiteness are both destined by nature. As Porter notes, this brilliant volume "theorize[s] the centrality of racial exclusion to democracy" in the United States.[31]

Just five years after composing *Black Reconstruction*'s careful blend of history as social science and antiracist advocacy, Du Bois published *Dusk of Dawn: An Essay toward an Autobiography of the Race Concept*. At age seventy-two, he could be forgiven for believing that this book might cap off the series of semi-autobiographical, multi-generic collections that he had begun with *Souls* and continued in *Darkwater*. *Dusk of Dawn* does often read as if Du Bois had gained some equanimity with age. But in chapter 6, I will demonstrate that *its* extended contemplation of whiteness lays bare the twisted and virtually willful ignorance of white Americans to the damage they have done and continue to do. *Dusk*'s attention to the complex psychological and social mechanisms maintaining whiteness—in particular, whites' attachment to innocence—is revealed in Du Bois's unusually personal account of the pain involved in the effort to make white Americans attend to what it means to be Black.

Two of Du Bois's lesser-known works appeared swiftly at the end of World War II: *Color and Democracy: Colonies and Peace* (1945) and *The World and Africa* (1947). In chapter 7, I explore how they add richness to his analysis of white supremacy, which he had expressed as global even at the beginning of his professional life. Here, he explicitly addressed the difficulty of communicating to a white audience the depth of destruction caused by European and American colonialism in Africa, Asia, and Latin America. As Porter argues, "additional work on Du Bois's midcentury writing helps open up the usable past of his intellectual history and the radical possibilities in mid-twentieth century black intellectual life more generally."[32] It also reveals Du Bois's great optimism: he'd hoped that the defeat of Hitler's white supremacy and fascism's territorial ambitions would motivate white leaders in the United States and Europe to rethink their sense of entitlement to global leadership—or domination. Instead, these nations continued to express their right to police the world and control which nations were and were not ready for independence.

In chapter 8, I consider the three novels of the *Black Flame* trilogy, which have received little serious attention due to the common assumption that

Du Bois's age and ideological dogmatism had affected his worldview as well as his capacity for quality work. While these works certainly lack the precision of his midcentury nonfiction, all of his novels, even the earlier ones, are deeply romantic and overly ambitious in scope. Certainly, the *Black Flame* trilogy would have benefited from more revision and a committed editor—but one can forgive Du Bois for his hurry to publish, given that he wrote the three novels during the decade straddling his ninetieth birthday. I argue that Du Bois's increasing internationalism at midcentury did not detract from his concern with American white supremacy. As he had been doing since *Darkwater*, he continued to illustrate that white supremacy in the United States has always existed alongside European and American colonialism. Meanwhile, the arrogant license of the white characters in these novels dogs the steps of the protagonist, Manuel Mansart, and his family from the death of Reconstruction through the midcentury McCarthy era. Du Bois demonstrated how the social and political systems created by white supremacy undermine the life chances of talented and sensitive individuals from Alabama and Georgia to India and Vietnam. Mansart tries to comprehend people's revolutions in Eastern Europe and Asia even as he faces the consequences of school desegregation and the tragic impact of this apparent victory on Black teachers and Black education.

While the development of Du Bois's conception of white supremacy was not neatly linear, an overall arc displays an increasing degree of complexity in his analysis of the problem of whiteness. Following his early work, which clings to the faith that white people need only be shown the truth of their greed and violence in order to change, he grappled with the realization that white folks' capacity not only to conceive of Black people as human but to imagine that they themselves might not be the sole arbiters of the good and the right was severely compromised. His efforts to tease apart and bring to light the deeply embedded psychological and structural systems supporting whites' epistemic opacity and their illusion of innocence were necessarily subordinated to his activist projects of racial uplift, but careful analysis reveals his insight regarding the barriers presented by the devotion of white Americans to the advantages of whiteness.

Du Bois predicted that race would be not only *the* problem of the twentieth century but also, as Porter reminds us, the problem "of the future world."[33] Here, in that future world, the development of Du Bois's conception of whiteness over time still reveals a wealth of insight. From his youthful insistence that white supremacist ideology absurdly creates heroes of murderers and cowards to his description of complex white characters in his fiction and from his life, he tugged at the threads of white moral psychology and behavior to unravel the puzzling knot at the center of white supremacy. His perception of the structural elements of whiteness not only anticipated the insights of critical race theory several decades hence but maintained a commitment to the basic humanity of white individuals. I agree with Porter that Du Bois's work offers "a moral and epistemological orientation from which future analysis and activism against racism may be launched."[34]

Finally, in chapter 9, I place Du Bois's diagnosis of whiteness and its ills in conversation with philosophers of race who have taken on this challenge at the turn of the twenty-first century. Here I hope to summarize Du Bois's challenge to the readymade habits of thought that are embedded in a white supremacist society and show how they are echoed in contemporary critical work on race. Du Bois's analysis of whiteness in this context makes significant resources available to those who seek to deconstruct, in Manning Marable's words, "both whiteness as a social category . . . and its hierarchy of oppression."[35] As I have noted, his early optimism gave way over time to a conception of whiteness as multifaceted, psychologically entangled, and deeply lodged in human-created political and economic structures, especially nineteenth- and twentieth-century capitalism. By the time he moved to Ghana at the age of ninety-three, Du Bois may not have concluded that white America was incorrigible, but he had certainly concluded that neither whiteness nor racial oppression was susceptible to change through the use of reason and evidence alone and that they were also cunningly resistant to carefully crafted propaganda and even some carefully crafted threats of force.

Throughout my work on this book, I have been committed to the principle that whiteness never shows up as whiteness *only*. Anyone with a racial identity also has some gender identity, an experience of social and economic class, is disabled or nondisabled, and may or may not experience their sexual orientation as central to their identity. Our group-based, socially constructed identities are, in life, ever cross-constructed and influenced by social context. For more than thirty years my politics has been, in theory, intersectional.[36] But in reading Du Bois for his conception of whiteness as an oppressive phenomenon, I have most often interpreted his analysis as fundamentally genderless. Of course, as a male-identified person writing about his experience, what seems gender-free is often recognizably gendered as masculine, in the sense that both his conception of the oppressor and his presumption of the oppressed code them as *male*. In a patriarchal society in which, certainly during Du Bois's lifetime and even today, the public sphere is dominated by male-identified people, this presumption would be difficult to avoid.

This is at best a tentative conclusion for me, and there are some outstanding exceptions to this rule. As I will indicate too briefly in chapters 3 and 8, his fiction often includes gendered characters and offers nuance regarding the varieties of white supremacy. For instance, *Darkwater*'s "The Comet" and "Of Beauty and Death" present white women as something like foils to Black men. Likewise, in the *Black Flame* trilogy, the character of Clarice Breckinridge, who appears only briefly, unmistakably plays out her whiteness as an upper-class woman, and her gendered behavior as well as her gender in context lead to tragedy. While I hope to write more on this topic in his fiction, and trace it back to my analysis here, I simply could not find time or space for that work in this volume. This is not the book's only shortcoming, I know, but it is one I regret strongly.[37]

Nonetheless, in tracing Du Bois's understanding of the structure and vulnerability to change of whiteness and white supremacy, I do intend (to borrow words from Eric Porter) to contribute to ongoing efforts to "address race and racism as multilayered, protean, global phenomena in the present."[38] To this end, I identify throughout the book and especially in its final chapter the resources against white supremacy that Du Bois's work on whiteness offers us all. Perhaps for white readers in particular, Du Bois gives us a wealth of material with which to engage as we set about the crucial work of saving our own humanity and learn, slowly and carefully, to respect the humanity of others. We ignore his insights at our great peril. As Martin Luther King Jr. insisted at the memorial service held in New York on the hundredth anniversary of Du Bois's birth:

> Dr. Du Bois confronted this powerful structure of historical distortion and dismantled it. He virtually, before anyone else and more than anyone else, demolished the lies about Negroes in their most important and creative period of history. The truths he revealed are not yet the property of all Americans but they have been recorded and arm us for our contemporary battles.[39]

CHAPTER 1

Early Interventions

There are formidable challenges to reading Du Bois adequately.
—Nick Bromell, *The Political Companion to Du Bois*

Du Bois in his early career is often portrayed as a dapper and somewhat dour gentleman-scholar, determined to lift up his people by demonstrating that they—at least many of them—were capable of excellence as defined by Eurocentric ideals. He later admitted that he had been, in these early years, "blithely European and imperialist in outlook," having absorbed the omnipresent message that white society was superior to anything found in any nonwhite culture.[1] Why would a person, especially one with the mind of Du Bois, not jump at the chance to join the world of Goethe, Wordsworth, and Hegel? His early strategy for overcoming racism, for himself and for his people, was apparently to convince white America that African Americans were perfectly capable of conforming to the expectations of the culture and, in many cases, excelling.

Ibram X. Kendi has captured this early Du Bois nicely, calling his strategy "uplift suasion": achieving inclusion in a white-dominated society by behaving within the narrow bounds defined as acceptable by that society. Uplift suasion emphasizes the assumption that failing to behave within these bounds will impugn all members of the group, thus giving all individuals a keen interest in the behavior of other Black Americans.[2] Kendi is rightly critical of this strategy; it panders too much to oppressors, for a start. Ultimately, it is ineffective, primarily because white supremacy is impervious to evidence that human talents and virtues are distributed evenly among all groups. As will become clear, the goal of white supremacy is precisely not to consider whether its worldview is accurate.

At the beginning of Du Bois's career, however, he felt it was perfectly rational to assume that presenting evidence of Black Americans' abilities and fundamental humanity would be the best strategy for achieving acceptance after centuries of exclusion from society. To a great extent, his earliest works are concerned with offering such evidence, assuming that white Americans would absorb it and rationally change their misperceptions regarding Black inferiority.[3] *The Souls of Black Folk* is a perfect example of this sort of persuasion (see chapter 2). Yet as a portrait of Du Bois's initial approach to the problem of the color line, this is an incomplete assessment. Even in his earliest writings, where he emphasizes the need for Black self-improvement as a means of racial uplift, he identifies white biases and other failings that would have to change if Black racial uplift were to succeed.

It is not surprising that Du Bois's project of racial justice required white people to change. After all, white people had built the white supremacist systems that he was determined to end, and they controlled the greatest share of the social and material capital that was keeping those systems in place. However, the logic of white supremacy has always portrayed white individuals and white culture as the gold standard and the color line as stemming from shortcomings among the nonwhite. Changing white perceptions of people of color would thus be the obvious first step in eliminating the color line; if there were more complex white failings to be diagnosed, communicating them to the white community would be a delicate task. Du Bois's early recognition that white shortcomings were central to the problem of racism nevertheless counts as a significant intervention in the racial theorizing of the late nineteenth century, which was overwhelmingly concerned with cataloging the perceived inferiority of nonwhite races.[4]

In this chapter, I focus on two of Du Bois's earliest works, with an eye toward highlighting his remarks on whiteness as *the* problem of the color line: his Harvard University undergraduate commencement speech (1890) and his speech to the American Negro Academy (1897). Despite his obvious admiration for European culture, his perspicacity about its flaws is evident in both of these speeches. Here his critiques of white supremacy fall into two categories. First, they assert that white individuals and civilizations wrongly comport themselves as if people of color are morally negligible, though sometimes useful. This tendency was so obvious and widespread that it was hardly worthy of remark; yet, on reflection, it is notable that a young scholar would offer this diagnosis to a white audience. Second, they argue that whites must learn how to live meaningful, ethical, human lives in a world that would make them monsters, even as it holds them up as paragons. Though this idea is more explicitly communicated in his earliest published books, it is astounding that, in these early days, we already see the nascent elements of whiteness as arrogant, irrevocable license.

JEFFERSON DAVIS AND THE BRUTALITY OF WHITE CIVILIZATION

In his 1890 Harvard commencement address, Du Bois spoke on "Jefferson Davis as Representative of Civilization."[5] The speech exudes an arch skepticism that is probably attributable to the arrogance of youth; it is a far cry from sorrowful evocation of human tragedy in *The Souls of Black Folk*, published more than a decade later. At the ripe age of twenty-two, Du Bois took careful aim at the recently deceased president of the Confederacy before an audience of Harvard fellows and American notables. In his posthumously published *Autobiography*, he recalled the glowing commentary that followed the oration. A white Harvard professor noted how surprising it was "to hear a colored man deal with [Jefferson] so generously."[6] Yet while Du Bois did characterize Davis as "passionate, ambitious and indomitable," fiery as a young soldier but cool and determined as a senator, his ultimate point is less generous: there was something missing, something "fundamentally incomplete" about Davis's character and the civilization he fought for as "judged by every canon of human justice."[7]

According to the *Autobiography*, Du Bois's speech "made a sensation."[8] Still, even though the audience was by all accounts impressed, they were likely unable to absorb more than a general impression of its themes. As David Levering Lewis reports, the young scholar was a striking figure, "with an almost unmistakable self-possession." He had memorized his speech, as was the custom of the day, and wasted little time in presenting it. "As Du Bois shifted quickly into high gear, it was as though the audience had been instantly hitched to a fast, new-model locomotive. Astonished applause exploded when he finished in less than ten minutes."[9] Certainly an audience in 1890 would be capable of greater auditory comprehension than a similar audience today, but one still wonders just how much detail they were able to grasp, for Du Bois was not merely pointing out the shortcomings of

Davis as an individual or even as a representative of Confederate culture. The nearly all-white audience had listened to a twenty-two-year-old African American diagnose white American civilization as warlike in service of murderous goals, including violent domination over peoples of color. Most likely, as Shamoon Zamir claims, his audience "heard only the plea for moral rehabilitation, not the sharper ironies."[10]

Du Bois's critique of Jefferson Davis in this setting is remarkable, because, as I will discuss in chapter 5, the mood of white America toward the Confederacy was unambiguously conciliatory. Davis had been the leader of an indubitably treasonous faction but had suffered little in the way of retribution. After spending two years in prison under indictment for treason, he was pardoned by President Andrew Johnson and survived to become a celebrated author and a mascot of the romantic Lost Cause mythology that was spawned before his death.[11] If Harvard in 1890 was not rife with Jefferson Davis fans, neither was it bothered by his violent treason in support of human slavery. Neither the university nor the nation viewed "the white race" as flawed or imperfect despite the brutal practices attendant to slavery in the Americas. Whiteness, rather, was synonymous with the most civilized of tendencies. Louis Agassiz, who had come to Harvard in the early nineteenth century, had been converted to the pseudo-scientific racism of Charles Morton and Josiah Nott, despite being one of the most famous and respected scientists in the world.[12] Pseudo-scientific racism was up, condemnation of the Confederacy was down: into this environment Du Bois arrived with his pointed but reasonable evaluation of Jefferson Davis.

Du Bois's brief speech couched a critique of Davis and his self-satisfied civilization within a narrative of heroism. He noted that Davis had been raised to accept wholeheartedly the romantic lesson that military service was proud and noble, despite requiring brutal violence against vulnerable people. Du Bois must have known that his almost entirely white audience revered military service. He also knew that the conflicts in which Davis cut his teeth were morally ambiguous at best. Regarding his first experience of combat in the "Indian wars" in Michigan and Illinois territories, Du Bois bluntly opined that young Davis had "advance[d] civilization by murdering Indians." Moreover, he deconstructed Davis's next military success as "a national disgrace called, by courtesy, the Mexican War."[13] Du Bois could not have believed that his audience would be sanguine about either characterization, even though his claims could be easily defended.[14] He was speaking to the winners; but even if the doctrine of Manifest Destiny were still gospel among these establishment thinkers, he was able to appeal to their hubris by turning his scornful attention to Davis's presidency of the Confederacy. This, Du Bois insisted, was the "crowning absurdity" of his career, making Davis "the peculiar champion of a people fighting to be free in order that another people should not be free."[15]

With his surgical sketch of Davis's moral failure, Du Bois also indicted the willingness of white northerners (including many in his audience) to reconcile with their southern counterparts after the war. As I will discuss in chapter 5, Du Bois was by turns perplexed and outraged by northern whites' forgiveness toward the treason of those who had fought for the Confederacy, especially its leaders. He concluded—correctly, I think—that the war's aftermath in the United States was dictated as much by white supremacy as by any other single factor. For this reason, the South would never be forced to pay reparations, neither to the North nor, more significantly, to those they had held in bondage. Quite the contrary: by the time white Americans had conspired to kill the appropriately ambitious postwar program known as Reconstruction, those freed from bondage, and their children as well, were once again reduced to subhuman status by institutions such as sharecropping and convict leasing and by the legislative fiat known as Jim Crow. As subsequent chapters make clear, Du Bois would become all too aware that the nation and its heroes had abandoned Black southerners to the depredations of those who had lost the war but were nevertheless governing the peace. For the moment, the undergraduate was not properly armed to confront his audience with this sort of fire, yet his speech was a powerful indictment of Jefferson and the culture that both produced and supported him.

The audience may have absorbed Du Bois's speech as a mild rebuke to a departed hero, but it should have landed with the force of a lightning bolt, for the young man was arguing that the causes Davis championed did not flatter either him or the Teutonic race.[16] By implying that Davis's early campaigns had revealed his tendency to bully, Du Bois was highlighting a particular psychological malformation: that white people's sense of vast superiority had allowed them to do whatever they liked to those who were constructed as beneath them—such as murder and dispossess beings who were ill-equipped to defend themselves—and then to emerge from such slaughter with the conviction that good had triumphed.[17] Du Bois's thinking in this historical moment was influenced by the Hegelian notion that, by failing to recognize the humanity of the other and engage them as an equal, Anglo-Saxon behavior is characterized by "the overweening sense of the I and the consequent forgetting of the Thou."[18] Du Bois absorbed from G. W. F. Hegel the idea that such a nation, because of its inability to properly recognize others, value their contributions, or even allow them to exist, is an obstacle to true civilization. In *The Phenomenology of the Spirit*, Hegel asserted that the world spirit is moved forward only by the interaction of differing cultural ideals to produce new and better ones on the way to its perfection. Du Bois here echoed Hegel's insistence that an individual or culture must be able to recognize the *thou*, or other, and be recognized in turn, in order to attain subjectivity, or true self-consciousness. The tendency of the strong man or nation to ignore the interests and even life of the other is a failure that stands in the way of the development of the human spirit. Such a nation will not be changed by its interaction with others, which is the Hegelian basis of all historical progress.[19]

Du Bois's analysis of the strong man's "overweening sense of the I" anticipated what I take to be one of the primary components of his account of white supremacy: a heedless comportment. In this early speech, he characterized the attitude of the strong man as "short-sighted national selfishness," marked by "moral obtuseness and refined brutality."[20] The strong man's comportment, premised on "superiority" and shaped by its failure to recognize the other as a being like himself, is a moral disaster. The Teutonic nation, Du Bois contended, has historically risen upon the ruins of other nations; such a civilization will never contribute to the betterment of humanity "until checked by its complementary ideas."[21] These, Du Bois claimed, come from the southern hemisphere in the form of the African man. Two more opposed races, he said, are hard to imagine: "The Teutonic met civilization and crushed it—the Negro met civilization and was crushed by it."[22]

Readers may find Du Bois's conception of the African character as submissive to be odd (at best), but its rhetorical value is clear: as ironic as the characterization may be, in light of the late-twentieth-century mythology of Black folk as inherently violent, he hoped to convince white Americans that the need to change their character was not premised on the benefit to the so-called "Submissive Man" but to "the advance of all—not in mere aimless sacrifice, but recognizing the fact that, 'To no one type of mind is it given to discern the totality of Truth.'"[23] Their duty to humanity required a change in their ideals as well as in their behavior.

Du Bois, I imagine, hoped that his audience would recognize their alignment with Davis and his shortcomings. In the closing paragraph of the speech, he suggested that the uplift of Black Americans ("the rise of the Negro people") might be of more than sentimental interest to "you whose nation was founded on the loftiest ideals, and who many times forgot those ideals with a strange forgetfulness."[24] The intention was clear: white people, as characterized by the "hero" Jefferson Davis, must not continue their single-minded, heedless march forward. They and all future generations of humanity would benefit from the betterment of white people; this in turn required the contribution of the "African," whose virtues included patience and submission.[25] Approaching African-descended people as partners in the new nation would not only temper the lesser angels of Teutonic nature but align with America's stated ideals.

By naming the "strange forgetfulness" of those idealistic Americans and emphasizing the rightful moral demands of those "crushed" by the momentum of Teutonic civilization, Du Bois made what might have been his first public attempt to hint at the moral shortcomings peculiar to whiteness.[26] He was not suggesting that hypocrisy afflicts only the strong man. Rather, he was pointing out that European-American culture is noticeably attached to claims about respect for the inalienable rights of man while simultaneously constructing schemas of human value that minimize the reason and morality of the other.[27] I will delve more deeply into the epistemic elements of this failure in future chapters. Here, with Du Bois, I want to emphasize the destructive comportment that implicitly claims all available space and resources for its use, despite the presence and manifest needs of others.[28] Whether those others are merely ignored or become the stated targets of exploitation or genocide, the comportment of the white/strong man denies that they deserve moral consideration. In sum, Du Bois urged whites to recognize that, however superior white civilization appears to be, "it must receive the cool purposeful 'Ich Dien' [I serve] of the African for its round and full developement [sic]."[29]

"THE CONSERVATION OF RACES" (1897)

Seven years after his Harvard commencement address, Du Bois spoke at a gathering that could hardly have been more different: the founding of the American Negro Academy. After earning his Ph.D. from Harvard, Du Bois spent an unhappy two-year stint at Wilberforce University before finding a research position at the University of Pennsylvania, where he embarked on the groundbreaking study of the Seventh Ward that would become *The Philadelphia Negro*.[30] While he was, with good reason, unsatisfied with his professional situation (the university refused to let him teach classes or list his name in the catalog), he remained committed to an academic career and, with Alexander Crummell and others, founded the Negro Academy, which positioned itself as the intellectual center of Black America. Like his Harvard commencement address, Du Bois's speech at the opening celebration, "The Conservation of Races," insists that Black people have a vital contribution to make to humanity, especially as a complement to European cultures. However, given that he was delivering this lecture to a select Black audience, Du Bois focused less on the supposed characteristics of African and African-descended peoples than on their duty to create and maintain separate institutions in order to develop their group-specific excellences. The speech apparently caused some consternation among the attendees, and Du Bois himself later found it more than a bit embarrassing—perhaps wincing at the excess of youth.[31]

A great deal of philosophical writing has grown out of the attempt to understand the metaphysics of race on display in "The Conservation of the Races." Not surprisingly, it is difficult to determine from this speech if Du Bois believed in 1897 that race was a biological, social, or cultural matter.[32] Thinkers during this era often floundered in a conceptual muddle regarding human tendencies, and Du Bois naturally did not feel compelled to state a position on the issue. However, what is clear from the text is that he believed that every racial group could contribute to the betterment of humanity. He noted that many of these groups *are* difficult to define clearly; in fact, he said, "the term Negro is, perhaps, the most indefinite of all" because it includes many groups on at least two different continents.[33] In a move demonstrating that Hegel was always a greater influence on him than Louis Agassiz or Charles Davenport was, he argued that racial differences "transcend" physical ones and are primarily "spiritual, psychical."[34]

This, combined with his invocations of history and ideals of life, echoes Hegel, especially given the overall thrust of his argument that development of the separate groups in line with their own inherent ideals would lead to "one far off Divine event."[35] Like the argument in his Harvard speech that Teutonic culture might learn from Black Americans, Du Bois's argument in this very different context supports the value of cultural exchange and challenges the wider social milieu of racial deprecation.

Often neglected in studies of this speech is Du Bois's insistence that Black and white Americans should be able to share the United States without "fatal collision." Between white and Black folk there is "substantial agreement in laws, language, and religion," he explained; thus, two or even three different "national ideals" could develop and thrive together. To this end, Du Bois laid out a creed for the American Negro Academy, a plan for its work toward the preservation and support of African American ideals. The "first and greatest step" centered around the need for Black Americans to improve themselves in a clear and unambiguous display of what Kendi has since called "uplift suasion."[36] Crucially, however, Du Bois made it clear that the good of the nation also depended upon the improvement of the white race:

> The second great step toward a better adjustment of the relations between the races should be a more impartial selection of ability in the economic and intellectual world, and a greater respect for personal liberty and worth, regardless of race. We believe that only earnest efforts on the part of the white people of this country will bring much needed reform in these matters.[37]

Du Bois's modest assignment for white America was twofold. The first, "a more impartial selection" in jobs and academia, could have been perceived as an epistemic critique or an impugnment of the integrity of white value judgments: either whites were falling prey to their own perceptual biases, or they were disregarding actual ability and choosing white candidates; in any case, neither was fair to Black Americans or good for the nation. The second, however, clearly took aim at white comportment: the failure of whites to respect the liberty and human worth of African Americans. It is hard to overstate the audacity of these suggestions. In a different context, asking someone to respect the worth and liberty of others might seem reasonable and maybe a bit embarrassing, for it clearly implies that the person's behavior is less than good. Had Du Bois anticipated that white readers would one day obtain access to the record of his talk, one can only imagine how he thought they might respond. Despite the modesty of his suggestions, it is hard to believe that white Americans would have responded graciously to suggestions for character improvement from a young African American observer. (Du Bois was then just shy of thirty.)

Just a year earlier, in 1896, the U.S. Supreme Court had ruled, by a devastating seven-to-one majority, that laws requiring racial segregation in public transportation did not violate the Fourteenth Amendment's requirement for equal treatment under law.[38] Writing for the majority, Justice Henry Billings Brown went so far as to explain: "We consider the underlying fallacy of the plaintiff's argument to consist in the assumption that the enforced separation of the two races stamps the colored race with a badge of inferiority. If this be so, it is not by reason of anything found in the act, but solely because the colored race chooses to put that construction on it."[39] Of course, neither Justice John Harlan in dissent nor any Black citizen was convinced by this bit of rhetorical tripe, but certainly there was some level of self-deception on the part of Justice Brown that was shared by some of his colleagues and by many white Americans who were convinced of their own goodness. Du Bois's suggestion that white Americans could work harder to be impartial thus seems reasonable in context, setting the stage for his eventual diagnosis that whiteness is marked by an epistemic opacity that helps to explain its persistence in the face of so much evidence that gainsays white supremacy.

According to Nahum Dmitri Chandler, "Conservation" and other early essays document the way in which Du Bois grappled with the challenge of constructing meaningful forms of Black American life in the narrow spaces offered to them—especially considering the apparent gap in meaning between *Negro* and *American*. This tension is first articulated in "Strivings of the Negro People" (1897), an essay that formed the foundation of the first chapter of *The Souls of Black Folk*.[40] Chandler argues that Du Bois was struggling in these early essays with the simple question of how to *be, and be African American—a virtually impossible conjunction, given the color line* in the world that whiteness had made. That question came to haunt not only *The Souls of Black Folk* but also several of Du Bois's twentieth-century publications.

It also offers a concomitant challenge to white Americans, if only we can recognize it. Just as Du Bois faced the problem of how to be Black and

American in a nation that despised him, white Americans need to consider what sort of human life they can build as the heirs and caretakers of a monstrous regime. Du Bois's agenda for white Americans may seem modest, but that does not mean that he saw it as easy or even believed they would accept the challenge. Likely, members of the Negro Academy did not have much hope that white America would take up the challenge laid down during that small meeting in Washington, D.C., but Du Bois's occasional project of explaining the breadth and depth of their responsibility had just begun.

THE SUPPRESSION OF THE AFRICAN SLAVE-TRADE AND THE PHILADELPHIA NEGRO

In both his Harvard commencement speech and his speech to the American Negro Academy, Du Bois emphasized that Black flourishing required white folk to change their behavior. This made perfect sense, of course. So long as white folk remained dominant in the United States and their perceptions were unreliable, no amount of Black self-improvement would convince them of Black humanity. With social, cultural, and political power firmly in white hands, the strivings of Black folk toward uplift would be insufficient. Nevertheless, his statements challenged an ideology that had been dominant in the United States since the end of slavery: that the race problem was the problem of people of color, and they were responsible for fixing it, primarily by becoming even less visible.

Du Bois's book-length writings during this era included two highly academic studies, one in history, the other in sociology. Shortly before his speech to the Negro Academy, his doctoral dissertation was published as the first volume in the prestigious Harvard Historical Studies series. Despite its title, *The Suppression of the African Slave-Trade to the United States of America, 1638–1870* was, in fact, a history of the *failure* of white efforts to suppress that traffic. The volume remains an early classic in the field of modern history, primarily due to Du Bois's integration of data from countless original sources in support of his powerful narrative. Nevertheless, its final chapter ends with a section titled "The Lesson for Americans," which states clearly that slavery became a problem for the nation primarily because of "the cupidity and carelessness of our ancestors."[41] Here Du Bois generously and accurately included himself among the descendants of those white ancestors who were too greedy to abolish slavery in the eighteenth century. Arguing that this generation of revolutionaries should have stamped out the institution at the nation's beginning so as to prevent it from growing more complex and difficult, he "conclude[d] that it behooves nations as well as men to do things at the very moment when they ought to be done."[42]

With a similar directness, Du Bois closed *The Philadelphia Negro* (1899), written during what was effectively a poorly paid postdoctoral stint at the University of Pennsylvania, with a straightforward statement about the duty of white Americans to end racial discrimination. Keeping Black Americans out of the workforce due to race prejudice or avoiding those who are presumed to be ignorant "is morally wrong, politically dangerous, industrially wasteful, and socially silly."[43] What's more, he insisted, whites must stop discriminating "for their own sakes." Quite against the expectations of those who had funded his research, Du Bois concluded that the rates of crime, idleness, lewdness, and poverty among the Black residents of Philadelphia were rooted in racial prejudice, not in an inherent moral weakness.[44] White Philadelphians might have been resistant to working alongside Black Americans; but as Du Bois pointed out, doing so was far preferable to the degradations that resulted from Black unemployment, which in turn resulted from white racism. In an echo of *Suppression*, he noted that the longer it took for whites to improve, the greater the problem would become. It is difficult to overstate the courage and perspicacity of Du Bois's claims at this point in his career, though to our eyes they may seem relatively modest: he made it clear that white Americans' behavior is morally deficient and deeply implicated in the experience of African Americans. He had not quite intimated that the entire problem of the color line is whiteness itself, but he had laid the groundwork.

CONCLUSION

> No American can study the connection of slavery with United States history, and not devoutly pray that his country may never have a similar social problem to solve, until it shows more capacity for such work than it has shown in the past.
>
> —W. E. B. Du Bois, *The Suppression of the Atlantic Slave Trade to the United States, 1638-1870*

In his earliest works, Du Bois offered white America a gift: a mirror to show that their behavior was causing not just the suffering of Black Americans but the dreadful social results of racism that harm whites and the nation as a whole. By failing to act in accordance with their moral duty or even to recognize their wrongdoing, white Americans were creating conditions in which Black folk could barely survive, let alone thrive.[45] Du Bois urged white America to consider the Black talents and skills that were being daily smothered by racial discrimination—talents and skills that could lead to industrial innovation and scholarly discovery. In the final decade of the nineteenth century, Du Bois laid out a set of propositions and supported them with both quantitative data and philosophically rigorous value claims. Yet white America was so convinced of its own excellence that it failed to note the need to change course, at a time when it could have done much good.

Du Bois's early works were a significant intervention in the racial theorizing and taxonomizing of his day. In them, he asserted that African-descended people are fully human and capable of participating on equal terms with other races in the construction of the United States. With great idealism, he insisted that every race on earth would necessarily be part of that one "far off Divine event."[46] While he had not completely escaped the tendency of classically trained scholars to view Africa and Africans as essentially different from and "behind" Anglo-Europeans and their civilization, he had, in the era of Joseph Conrad's *Heart of Darkness* and *Lord Jim* and fully fifteen years before publication of Edgar R. Burroughs's *Tarzan the Ape Man*, managed to sustain an argument before a white audience that white civilization was imperiling the progress of humanity and must make room to receive the benefits of African peoples as indubitably *human* peoples.[47] His attempt to prompt soul searching in white audiences could have had only a limited effect, given the context, but it tells us quite a bit about the development of his conception of whiteness.

CHAPTER 2

The Souls of Black Folk

> Your country? How came it yours? Before the Pilgrims landed we were here.
>
> —W. E. B. Du Bois, *The Souls of Black Folk*

In his early speeches, Du Bois set before relatively small, select audiences his conviction that African-descended peoples had much to offer humanity. Those pieces and the arguments supported by the massive data troves of his first two published books, *The Suppression of the African Slave-Trade* and *The Philadelphia Negro*, showed that the accomplishments of white Americans in founding the United States must be considered in the context of the moral catastrophe of their subjugation of Black people. *The Souls of Black Folk*, Du Bois's best-known volume, was aimed at a wider audience, many of whom would be white. *Souls* offers a depth of sentiment and personal exposure unusual fur Du Bois (though five of these essays had previously appeared in various forms in periodicals).[1] Containing some of the most powerful imagery in Du Bois's oeuvre, it "rewards," in the words of David Blight and Robert Gooding-Williams, "an attentive, chapter-by-chapter perusal."[2]

Du Bois's aims in *Souls* required a new rhetorical style. In *The Suppression of the African Slave-Trade*, he had argued that the primary driver of racism was simply ignorance; thus, "the recitation of facts with a dose of moralism might be sufficient to bring about change."[3] In *The Philadelphia Negro*, a tour-de-force combination of sociological data and insight, he again worked to correct white misperceptions. But as the century drew to a close, Du Bois became increasingly pessimistic. Not only was he appalled by the ongoing violence against people of color, but he was unable to land an academic position appropriate to his credentials. By now, he could reasonably conclude that persuasive evidence had not "sufficiently compelled white America to confront its own image in the mirroring gaze that [he] had exposed."[4] So, in *Souls*, he chose a tone and style that might work differently on its audience. Rather than relying on the scholarly presentations of his sociological publications or the dialectic of his speeches, he spoke directly to human sentiment. As Blight and Gooding-Williams write, "*Souls* is an example of style that is not mere decoration in the place of argument. Images become explanation in many chapters.... [Du Bois] saw the mutual infection of narration and analysis as a good thing."[5]

While the book is primarily remembered for its impact on the Black intellectual community, it is equally incisive about white supremacy. *Souls* chronicles Black Americans' efforts to make meaning under post–Civil War white supremacy, emphasizing the dynamic by which whiteness bolsters itself: the construction of Blackness as the subhuman other for which the fully human have no responsibility. Du Bois meant to destabilize this dynamic by integrating a more expressive style with the presentation of the interior lives of Black Americans, in joy and tragedy. The aim of *Souls* was to put white readers into authentic relation with the world "behind the Veil," by communicating "the strange meaning of being black."[6] Striving to reach the sympathetic hearts of his readers, especially his white readers, required him to offer fully realized portraits of individuals and families in their joys and their sorrows as well as necessary detours into the social and political context in which those lives were lived.

Du Bois composed and edited the essays in *Souls* between 1897 and 1903, a historical moment that was, in Rayford Logan's famous phrase, "the nadir of American race relations."[7] The hope that African Americans had felt during Reconstruction was dashed by what became known, tellingly, as "the Redemption," white southerners' brutal and deadly determination to restore antebellum social and political arrangements. After stripping African Americans of their newly granted civil and constitutional rights via a combination of local legislation, federal inaction, and terrorist violence, white supremacists retook political and economic control of the South.[8] Convict leasing, tenant farming, and Jim Crow legislation combined to impoverish and disenfranchise the recently emancipated and their children, cementing a racial hierarchy that constituted both written and unwritten law well into the twentieth century. Within this miasma, *Souls* offered, according to Blight and Gooding-Williams, a "poignant but often biting dissent from the racist and nationalist ideologies animating post-Reconstruction political culture."[9] Du Bois therefore had the perfect, terrible background against which to portray the demonstrably human sorrows of his subjects: their pain and their joy stand out in relief from the palpable indifference of the whites who were responsible for their suffering, and, as a matter of civil rights, for ameliorating it.

For members of the Black community, writes David Levering Lewis, *The Souls of Black Folk* felt like "fireworks going off in a cemetery," a burst of "sound and light" that rekindled a flame that had been dying since Reconstruction's end in 1877.[10] Dolan Hubbard describes it as "a single candle in the dark—a testament of hope" during this dolorous era.[11] It spoke directly of the perversity of reviving social structures that had flourished under the Confederacy. Du Bois's slight book continues to reward interpretation—a mark of his genius and of his capacity for editorial sorcery. Recent writings on *Souls* persuasively argue that it should be read as a primer on Black political theory in the context of white supremacy and as a work of philosophy that presents Black Americans as a world-historical people crucial to the final realization of Hegelian world spirit.[12] Consistent with these projects, my more or less straightforward reading of *Souls* emphasizes the rhetorical tools that Du Bois used to take aim at white epiphany. In this light, I read the book's various portraits of whiteness as illustrating *the* problem of the color line. Whites' neurotic obsession with racial hierarchy and their contemptible exploitation of Black people's poverty and desperation are woven into the background of the book, and I will highlight a few such cases to demonstrate the implicit argument.

In a 2015 letter to "white America" printed as part of a series in *The New York Times*, George Yancy asked white readers to "tarry, to linger, with the ways in which you perpetuate a racist society, the ways in which you are racist."[13] Du Bois, in the Forethought" of *Souls* is making a similar request, much less explicitly. He knew how the white world would typically explain the economic and social difficulties that characterize Black lives, and he recognized that he must not only offer readers compelling evidence of the humanity of Black folk but also motivate white America to overcome its apathy toward African Americans' pain. The effort he made in *Souls* to engage white readers was unprecedented in his work and may help to account for the fact that the book has never been out of print since its appearance in 1903.

THE ARROGANT AND IRREVOCABLE LICENSE OF WHITENESS

The essays in *The Souls of Black Folk* are nearly all preceded by epigraphs that pair a line of traditionally exalted verse from the European American canon with a few measures of melody from an African American spiritual. In this way, the two pieces become mirror expressions of longing, celebration, despair, and other powerful emotions. By way of this simple but easily overlooked device, Du Bois emphasized that Black American art is as powerful and complex as the best works of European culture.[14] Charitably assuming the humanity of white folk, he extended the hand of an equal and invited his readers to engage with these powerful excerpts in the sort of reflection that leads to transformation.

After the first of these epigraph pairings, Du Bois opened chapter 1 with a glimpse into his personal experience: "Between me and the other world there is ever an unasked question." This haunting, evocative sentence demonstrates the metaphysics that makes the book necessary. Du Bois and his people were confined to a world separated by a vast gulf from the other, more powerful world of whiteness. His unasked question, "How does it feel to be a problem?," is intimated in awkward conversational gambits, some of which will feel familiar to Americans today: "I know an excellent colored man in my town; or I fought at Mechanicsville; or Do not these Southern outrages make your blood boil?"[15] There were many reasons why white Americans did not ask him the real question. Perhaps it seemed rude or prurient: they weren't sure how to ask it or were afraid to receive an answer. The answer may have told them something they would rather not know or require something that they were unwilling to give. Perhaps it would reveal that they had asked the wrong question. Whatever the case, their substitute questions and comments revealed a certain obliviousness to the terrible situation in which Du Bois was placed. At very least, interrogating a stranger on the intimate details of his suffering or disadvantage is a breach of etiquette; and as he listed these conversational gambits, Du Bois began to hint at the arrogance and license of white Americans who grant themselves permission to investigate what is not, given their explicit worldview, their business.

Even as an implication, "How does it feel to be a problem?" assumes that the African American population *is* a problem. It is tempting to read *Souls* as an answer to that question because each of its fourteen pieces provides a glimpse "behind the Veil" to explain how it feels to be a Black American. However, none of them suggests that "the Negro" is in fact the problem.[16] Despite Du Bois's occasional, infamous cataloging of Black shortcomings, he always made it clear that the problem lies with white Americans, whiteness itself, and the way in which white people continue to make Black lives difficult or impossible.[17]

To understand the "souls of Black folk," we must understand that they live in a context of white supremacy and white ignorance: their lives are lived in relation to white supremacy, often explicitly: "Despite compromise, war, and struggle, the Negro is not free. In the backwoods of the Gulf States, for miles and miles, he may not leave the plantation of his birth; in well-nigh the whole rural South the black farmers are peons, bound by law and custom to an economic slavery, from which the only escape is death or the penitentiary."[18] Du Bois wisely did not reveal the identities of the plantation owners, the enslavers—the very human causes behind the Black workers' inability to earn enough to escape peonage or avoid the arbitrary but enforceable "rules" by which whites exerted capricious power over them. White overseers, legislators, and jailers thrived on the system of dehumanization that followed the abolition of slavery. White readers who did not see themselves as part of that system no doubt felt powerless to do anything about it, but Du Bois aimed to overcome that sense of powerlessness by way of *Soul*'s style and content.

Of course, had those white readers been fully educated and alert to the nature of socioeconomic systems, they would have seen that, even (perhaps especially) in the North, they were benefiting from the exploitative nature of agriculture and industry in the South. Moreover, they would have understood the power of organizing with others to object to and end such exploitation. In this light, we might see the continuing popularity of *Souls* as indicating that white readers have remained resistant to, or, at best, unaware of, the connection between the pain and struggle it describes and their own behavior.[19] That is, for the work to be effective, white readers must understand that Du Bois was not merely relating a distant human tragedy. If they conclude that the pain and struggle portrayed in *Souls* are merely inevitable facts of Black life, a distant tragedy, then they are appreciating the pathos of the work but missing the point that the actions and omissions of white Americans created that fate and that many of us benefit from the exploitation the book depicts.[20] If the book's millions of white readers had always seen *Souls* as an indictment of their own way of life and of their apathy toward the misery that such a life had created, they might well have refused to buy or open it. Of course, I cannot prove this claim, but I suspect that the popularity of *Souls* indicates that white American readers have long been able to separate themselves from the world it portrays.[21]

In relation to Black Americans, white people in Du Bois's early works are blithely unconcerned with key facts about the world that they have made and often uncurious about situations in which they or people like them have certainly played a part. In the first essay, "Of Our Spiritual Strivings," Du Bois outlined how emancipated people turned first to political power and then to education to "attain . . . [their] place in the world."[22] The goal of political power had been foreclosed by the white supremacist defeat of Reconstruction. Similarly, access to education was determined by white preferences, continually held out of reach by "that nameless prejudice . . . the distortion of fact and wanton license of fancy." Here, *Soul*'s use of *license* is not precisely the same as my attempt to capture Du Bois's mature account of whiteness within the term *arrogant license*, but what is consistent is the sense in which white supremacy is often displayed in caprice. White folk, Du Bois noted, perceive "everything black, from Toussaint to the devil," as inferior and subhuman and hold fast to that perception, regardless of its merit.[23]

The essays in *Souls* demonstrate that Black American despair stemmed primarily from trying simply to live human lives while being repeatedly defeated by white Americans acting on their own delusions. In the essay "Of the Training of Black Men," he reminded readers that the United States is "a Nation naturally skeptical as to Negro ability," not disposed toward "careful inquiry and patient openness to conviction" on the topic: "We must not forget that most Americans answer all queries regarding the Negro *a priori*, and that the least that human courtesy can do is to listen to evidence."[24] With his habitual understatement, he accused white Americans of lacking "courtesy," but of course the results of this are catastrophic. Recall the well-meaning whites who want to awkwardly interrogate him about "being a problem." Even if we can credit them with the desire to connect to another human being, they appear stunningly obtuse about just what they are asking. Surely it is a painful topic, perhaps *the* painful topic, in a life marked by frustration and suffering (as well as by connection and joy). The white stranger somehow is both entitled to ask the question and oblivious as to its cost to the subject of their investigation. Less abstractly than in his critique of "the Teutonic" in his Harvard graduation speech, Du Bois's portrayal of the white stranger here illustrates heedless comportment.

DOUBLE CONSCIOUSNESS, THE VEIL, AND THE OBLIVIOUS PERFORMANCE OF WHITENESS

In Du Bois's work, most white Americans are embedded in a socioeconomic system that ensures that their benefits come reliably at the expense of Black Americans. Despite the predictability of this connection, white Americans show little curiosity about the pattern. This heedlessness is thrown into significant relief when *Souls* introduces the concept of double consciousness. The phrase appears just once, in the third paragraph of the first essay, but has become one of the most renowned concepts in Du Bois's writings. For my purposes, double consciousness is the mirror image of what we might call the *null-consciousness* of white Americans. When whites do not fully understand their own behavior or its impact on African Americans, their nonwhite counterparts are driven to exquisite lengths in their search to comprehend the dynamic that white supremacy creates in the human world.

Following is the passage in which Du Bois introduced double consciousness and other key metaphors:

> After the Egyptian and Indian, the Greek and Roman, the Teuton and Mongolian, the Negro is a sort of seventh son, born with a veil, and gifted with second-sight in this American world,—a world which yields him no true self-consciousness, but only lets him see himself through the revelation of the other world. It is a peculiar sensation, this double-consciousness, this sense of always looking at one's self through the eyes of others, of measuring one's soul by the tape of a world that looks on in amused contempt and pity. One ever feels his two-ness,—an American, a Negro; two souls, two thoughts, two unreconciled strivings; two warring ideals in one dark body, whose dogged strength alone keeps it from being torn asunder.[25]

The exhaustion produced by this dynamic is palpable. Crucially, double consciousness results in an asymmetry between Black and white persons, not only in the care that must be taken in public behaviors but also between Black and white epistemic capacities. Black Americans are required to measure their own souls "by the tape" of that other world, but they also must view the entire social world as white people see it so that they can meet its expectations. White Americans, however, are never required to understand the perspective of Black Americans. Similarly, they fail to understand that their experience of themselves as "normal" Americans, as *white*, necessarily depends on the existence and exclusion of nonwhite people. In his explication of Du Bois's attempt to destabilize white readers just enough to make them receptive to the possibility of Black humanity, Keith Byerman notes, "There are few ways for the powerless to change circumstances unless those who dominate are willing to change."[26] But if white readers can be gentled or humbled into a realization of their shortcomings, they may be more willing to consider such changes. Byerman considers this in relation to "The Forethought" of *Souls*, in which Du Bois wrote:

> I pray you, then, receive my little book in all charity, studying my words with me, forgiving mistake and foible for the sake of the faith and passion that is in me, and seeking the grain of truth hidden there.
>
> I have sought here to sketch, in vague, uncertain outline, the spiritual world in which ten thousand thousand Americans live and strive.[27]

While its humility can be read as serious and sincere, an invitation to white Americans to view life within the Veil with something like a native guide, Byerman suggests that we read it as a touch of parody, one that paints the white reader as unable to enter the world of Blackness without careful preparation. In doing so, he argues, Du Bois "reverses the act of racial definition" by depicting "the 'master' race as bumbling, sentimental, and incapable of facing the truth about themselves and about the so-called inferior race."[28]

I am not convinced that Du Bois's tone is parodic, for he had every reason to draw white readers carefully into the world of the book, though he may have been enraged by their inability to exhibit even the simplest human connection. He wanted the book to be an invitation, not mockery, whatever his private feelings were. Du Bois knew that when white folk run up against their bumbling inability to confront the truth about themselves, the results can be deadly for African Americans. Byerman is nevertheless correct that Du Bois must have seen the irony, even the comedy, involved in having to take such care of the "superior" race.

By the time he published *The Souls of Black Folk*, Du Bois was facing a kind of Gordian knot regarding white supremacy. Its dismantling would require sustained and difficult work by white people, but how could he motivate them to do this when they could not see that they were the problem? Obviously, Du Bois was engaged in more than a moralistic hectoring of guilty white folk.[29] Rather, he believed that recognizing the humanity, the subjectivity, and the agency of Black folk would enhance the white American soul and humanity more broadly. The book's focus on the benefits to white Americans was surely a wise move; it was not his fault that it failed to move many of them to action.

As I have noted, Du Bois's methodology in *Souls* was rooted in his growing doubts about whites' capacity to take in the truth about Black people. Having learned that scientific data could not move them, he now took up a poetic tone in his quest to engage their humanity. Commenting on *Souls* in a 1904 essay, he refused to regret his choice to employ a "tone of self-revelation" and cast off "English restraint," though he found himself at times thinking poorly of that tone.[30] While he had sacrificed the appearance of objectivity, he had been able to present "some revelation of how the world looks to me" with "vividness."[31] Whatever the response, he had done what he could to evoke a sympathetic reaction in readers. He had been willing to make himself vulnerable if this meant that white America, if addressed in just the right way, could change. The hope and despair that are so evident in *Souls* reflect Du Bois's continuing faith in humanity's gifts of reason and emotion and the power of art to bridge chasms of misunderstanding.

At the turn of the century, Du Bois believed that white supremacy was motivated by greed and sustained by ignorance.[32] The initial mechanisms allowing white men to dehumanize the people of color they had encountered during the periods of exploration and colonial extraction had, by the late nineteenth century, cemented the menial status of Black Americans. As a result, white children had grown up believing that the world was as it was meant to be: that the diminished status of Black Americans was appropriate. In short, white Americans did not know or wish to know about the souls of Black folk. To counter this, Du Bois tried to portray Black lives in all of their diversity, thereby offering a primer on the Black World. He was no longer able to hope that, as Eric Porter writes, "careful social scientific research would disprove assumptions about black inferiority and provide a path toward equality."[33] Now he paired empirical evidence with deeply affecting accounts of Black families in the South, filling gaps in opportunity with love and longing. Working to unsettle the prejudice of whites, he portrayed individuals—from bright, hardworking Josie in rural Tennessee, the dedicated young teacher in the short story "Of the Coming of John," to the distinguished Reverend Dr. Alexander Crummell. His portraits worked to shatter every stereotype that Jim Crow was inscribing on the public consciousness.

The legacy of slavery, the cornerstone of the house of whiteness, was heightened by the white South's vicious undoing of Reconstruction. This legacy appears on every page of *Souls*. In particular, Du Bois's rendering of his son's death in "Of the Passing of the First-Born" reveals the horror of living in the world that whiteness had made, for that loss is figured also as a reprieve: the child will not have to grow up to discover the injustice of life within the Veil. It is difficult to imagine a more heartbreaking instance of white supremacy's disastrous impact. David Levering Lewis suggests that "the elegiac prose ... verges on bathos today," yet this essay must have been extraordinarily difficult to sculpt.[34] The careful balance of science and sentiment in the rest of the book is understandably (and perhaps appropriately) absent in Du Bois's reflections on his son's brief life and difficult death.

Du Bois's careful portrayal of African American life was a clear effort to overcome rampant ignorance in the white world. With the metaphor of the Veil, he offered white readers a rare opportunity: a window not only into the damage they were doing as white folk but also a view of how African Americans were looking at whites from the other side. These descriptions are, for the most part, indirect. For example, in depicting Josie's squandered promise, the lynching of the brilliant John Jones, and the death of his toddler son, Du Bois showed white readers the consequences of Reconciliation.[35] He challenged them to understand that they were connected to these narratives, to recognize that they and people like them had created the conditions for those tragedies and were benefiting from them in ways large and small. Moreover, those white readers had helped to build the social barriers and expectations that were allowing them to hide from the tragedies that were endemic to Black life. At best, whites Americans were left believing that sadness was unavoidable for those behind the Veil.

Stephanie J. Shaw provocatively considers *The Souls of Black Folk* as a Hegelian account of the development of African Americans as a world-historical group.[36] She reads the Veil as an echo of the caul that covers the faces of some infants at birth, a sign of supernatural ability. This reading is supported by Du Bois's first mention of the subject (quoted above), which describes Black Americans as being "born with a veil" that provides second sight. The importance of the various talents that accompany Black racialization in his work is key, for Black folk must not only survive in a nation wasted by civil war, but also help to realize its full recovery. The second sight of Black folk, suggested by the Veil or caul, can be read as a kind of higher understanding born, as Shamoon Zamir argues, of alienation.[37] This makes sense, even in the absence of the supernatural. Those who are comfortable in the world, who have the opportunity for satisfaction, are not compelled to investigate or criticize the way things are. In contrast, folk to whom the world consistently offers disappointment have tremendous motivation to examine, observe, and consider alternate ways of understanding the phenomena they witness.

This reading is also consonant with Robert Gooding-Williams's interpretation of the Veil, which initially seems to be quite different from Shaw's reading. Gooding-Williams primarily focuses on Du Bois's theory of Black political leadership in *Souls*. In this light, the "veil of Jim Crow engenders tragedy . . . for it keeps men from apprehending the character of each other's lives, and thus from sympathizing with each other's work and striving."[38] Alexander Crummell, for example, was affected by the Veil in two ways. First, his work was concealed from the greater world because of the color line, so Du Bois sought to "'sweep the Veil away'" and expose his work to the white world.[39] Second, Crummell himself could not fully escape the distorted perception wrought by the Veil. While the white world lacked sympathy for him, he, in turn, lacked sufficient sympathy for both the enslaved and the emancipated masses. Du Bois was urging an increase of sympathy, a piercing of the Veil, in Black leaders and in white readers. *The Souls of Black Folk* is not only an unprecedented document of, in David Levering Lewis's words, "the primordial condition" of Black folk as "scorned and exploited" but also an exposé of the white Americans who are ultimately responsible for that condition.[40]

Du Bois is frequently cited as a pioneer in whiteness studies, primarily because of his explorations in "The Souls of White Folk" (included in *Darkwater*) and *Black Reconstruction in America*.[41] But David S. Owen also reads *Souls* as a critique of whiteness.[42] Owen was one of the first philosophers to read the book this way, pointing out that the mediated self-consciousness of Black Americans (as double consciousness) is a product of the social order of domination and subordination that serves whiteness, making the

Veil that obscures Black life from white viewers a continuing function of whiteness. White Americans do not lack *all* curiosity about those who live behind the Veil. As Owen suggests, Du Bois implicitly turned around the famous "What is it like to be a problem?" question, noting that the question becomes meaningless outside of the norming of whiteness. Owen argues convincingly that, for Du Bois, whiteness is the problem of the color line and the underlying mechanism of the Veil.[43] Whiteness in the United States and elsewhere in the so-called developed world normally has such hegemonic authority as to be invisible, especially to white people. Thus, the ways in which that construction warps the white self are, to white folk, also invisible. Having generated a white self whose being is hidden from itself, the white American finds only the ostensibly warped African American an object of interest. Once Du Bois made plain the role of white misperception in the necessity of Black double consciousness, whiteness and its power were made visible. While he did not, in *Souls*, comment at length on the flaws built into the white self in this process, the fact that white superiority depends upon a fictional Black inferiority makes its status always ontologically precarious and in need of constant reinforcement.

As Owen notes, Du Bois referred to the white world as "the other world" because his explicit focus was the Black experience. Once the reader comes to understand that it is possible to center Black subjectivity—or allow for Black subjectivity at all—the typical centrality of the white experience should come into question. Whiteness then becomes a possible object of inquiry, one that Du Bois challenged us to investigate in *Souls* (and more explicitly in later works).[44] Whiteness is not simply a way of being human in some unremarkable, organic human society but a toxic and unnecessary component of human relations in the society into which Black Americans have been born, and in which they must make their way.

White folk are therefore epistemically untrustworthy agents, unable to take up or evaluate evidence about themselves or others (and perhaps much else), unable to properly comport themselves in community with others. Rather, they see themselves as the community that matters. Others who may inhabit it are perceived only instrumentally, as useful objects rather than human subjects.[45] In this regard, Byerman's reading of the opening paragraphs of *Souls* comes to mind. Here, Du Bois first recounted the infamous incident during his primary school days when a young white girl, a newcomer, shunned him during a new game of exchanging greeting cards with classmates. As Byerman points out, the event is often noted as Du Bois's first taste of racism in Great Barrington, Massachusetts, but it may more usefully be read as an indictment of the teachers and schoolmates who knew young Du Bois yet did not advise the girl that her behavior was unacceptable. The white students also learned a lesson that day, Byerman implies, and not one they should have learned.[46] Yet white folk are not apt to see this situation as requiring intervention.

THE PESSIMISM OF *SOULS* AND ITS AMBITION

The only fictional piece in *The Souls of Black Folk*, "Of the Coming of John," portrays a lynching as the inevitable result of the collision of human dignity with the white supremacist patriarchy. John Jones, the most promising son of his Georgia community, goes north for a good education—the inverse of Du Bois's own path. When he returns to his community, he convinces white leaders to allow him to start a Black school. A white judge agrees, hiring John to lead it. But when he learns that John is teaching the children to think and to believe in their own humanity, he promptly fires him and closes the school. John is devastated, unable to imagine a future for himself in his hometown. While he is wandering through the woods, despondent, he comes across the judge's white son, who is attempting to assault John's sister. John kills the son and is then murdered by a vengeful mob. Though Du Bois resists detailing that scene, the lynching nonetheless lingers as a horror in the reader's mind.

In his stunning memoir *Just Mercy*, Bryan Stevenson writes of meeting a client's family and then reflecting on the implications of John Jones's fate to the larger community:

> I had never before considered how devastated John's community must have felt after his lynching. Things would become much harder for the people who had given everything to help make John a teacher. For the surviving black community, there would be more obstacles to opportunity and progress and much heartache. John's education had led not to liberation and progress but to violence and tragedy.[47]

As Stevenson points out, there is no justice, or even comfort, available in Du Bois's fictional town—a crime that echoes in the failures of the U.S. criminal justice system today. It must have grieved Du Bois terribly to write of his fictional character's efforts to return home and lift up his community. He knew all too well that real Johns were common, that white supremacy's avenues for enrichment usually ended in horror.

Souls is bookended by the short pieces "The Forethought" and "The Afterthought," which speak directly to the reader, pleading for understanding, for patience, for "vigor of thought and thoughtful deed" so that the result of his effort would "be not indeed / The End."[48] Yet the very first words of "The Forethought" suggest that the work is already dead: "Herein lie *buried* many things."[49] This intimation of the Veil echoes in "The Afterthought," which prays to "O God the Reader" not to let the book "fall . . . still-born into the world-wilderness."[50] Perhaps Du Bois feared that his effort in *Souls* would be pointless: after all, he had already produced unrivaled works in history and sociology that had failed to move white America to confront its wrongdoings. Nonetheless, he explicitly (if parenthetically) sent forth this appeal to "the ears of a guilty people" that they might "tingle with truth."[51]

It's possible that Du Bois's pessimism was a performance: a challenge to the white world to be better—more receptive, more biddable—than he had reason to expect it would be.[52] I suspect, however, that he genuinely doubted that Black life would improve as a result of his book. Too often, white supremacy destroys those who are bright and full of promise—people like Du Bois's own son, like the character John Jones. Josie Dowell, one of several students Du Bois mentioned in chapter 4, "Of the Meaning of Progress," also falls prey to the ravages of life behind the Veil. Although the essay is vague about the details of her disaster, it offers a rich portrait of her bright essence: "the centre of the family: always busy at service, or at home, or berry-picking: . . . she had about her a certain fineness, the shadow of an unconscious moral heroism that would willingly give all of life to make life broader, deeper, and fuller for her and hers."[53]

If we compare this description of Josie to Du Bois's words about Jefferson Davis, we cannot doubt who was the finer person. Josie is, as Hazel Carby asserts, "a symbol for the desires and the struggles of the African American folk," especially through her longing for an education.[54] But when Du Bois returned to visit the Dowell family ten years later, she was dead—of overwork, sorrow, and disappointment. Thus, the "meaning of progress" in this little valley, in this family, becomes clear. As Carby notes, "Josie's life and death become a metaphor for what progress has meant for the folk," the inevitable sacrifice of Black lives when whiteness stands in the way of Black ambition, even if that ambition is simply reaching toward the everyday opportunities of white America.[55] Surely, any honest person would see these deaths as tragic, would share the grief that repeatedly lashes the Black community. Yet Du Bois knew that from experience that white Americans did not mourn them. We cannot be surprised, nor can we blame the author for his fears about the future of his work and the lives it chronicles.

Du Bois did not, in this moment, reflect on the peculiar pressures that would have weighed on Josie as the oldest girlchild in the house. In the essay, she denies herself fulfillment, spends too many hours a day working for family, and does not take time for rest or recreation. Du Bois lionized Josie and condemned the system of white supremacy that led to her death, but he did not connect the South's systemic racism to the burden of gendered ideals. Not until 1920 did he take up the general cause of supporting the advancement of African American women in his everyday dealings.[56]

CONCLUSION

> Whatever of good may have come in these years of change, the shadow of a deep disappointment rests upon the Negro people.
> —Du Bois, *The Souls of Black Folk*

Many agree that Du Bois's objective in *The Souls of Black Folk* was to use reason and sympathetic reflection to persuade white Americans of the humanity of Black Americans. According to this consensus, he intended white readers to be moved enough by the depicted virtues of African Americans so that they would want to change their beliefs and actions in the social and political realms. But I also perceive a more radical program in flatly stating that "most Americans answer all queries regarding the Negro *a priori*, and that the least that human courtesy can do is to listen to evidence."[57] I see *Souls* as more than an invitation to white readers into a lifeworld they have avoided. It also confronts them with their own accountability for the pain of that world, and it urges action.

Though *Souls* was certainly Du Bois's most commercially successful work, that doesn't mean it fulfilled its author's aims. From the first, white misunderstanding of "the Negro problem" and "the problem of the color line" drove his efforts to illustrate the impact of white supremacy. Thanks to white incapacity, the book has failed to prompt white self-examination on any scale in the years since its publication. Instead, tenderhearted white folk have perceived the suffering and death in the Black South as tragic but distant. Du Bois's favorite Harvard professor, William James, wrote to his former student after reading *Souls* to say that he found the work "too despairing."[58] This letter has not apparently survived; one is left to wonder if James found its despair out of proportion to the situation reported or, with typical liberal confidence, believed that life for Black folks in the United States would inevitably improve. Perhaps he meant only that it was too sad for white Americans to want to read. In any case, Du Bois reassured his mentor that he was, in fact, full of hopefulness.[59]

White Americans are in the habit of presuming that people of color are responsible for their own difficulties and for rising above them. At best, their suffering seems tragic but part of the natural order of things. It is certainly possible for white Americans to read *The Souls of Black Folk* and miss the crucial truth that the suffering of African Americans is neither their own fault nor the result of the deeply mysterious workings of a random universe. After finishing the book, they might decide that they now understand what it is like to be a Black problem; they might even wish that they could do something to enact change, completely unaware of their own proximity to the problem.

In about 1905, a recent immigrant we know only as D. Tabak managed this epiphany after reading *Souls*, and he wrote to Du Bois to thank him for the book: "Am 24. A Russian Jew. Adverse circumstances have brought me to this country where more than one eight [sic] of the entire population is being hated and persecuted and lynched and denied all rights a thousand times more cruel than we Jews are in Russia. Believe me, Mr Du Bois, that when I read your 'Coming of John' I was ashamed of being white colored."[60] No reply is recorded.

Tabak's letter is heartfelt and unpretentious. It does not propose a plan of action beyond hoping that Du Bois will keep up his "noble work" and one day live to see "those ghastly social injustices" abolished. Perhaps, among white people, only a recent immigrant could recognize that such injustices are not an inevitable social reality.

CHAPTER 3

The Riddle of John Brown

> When a prophet like John Brown appears, how must we of the world receive him?
>
> —W. E. B. Du Bois, *John Brown*

In *The Souls of Black Folk*, Du Bois offered a glimpse of the epistemic and moral problem at the heart of the United States: that white Americans are unable, in the normal course of events, to accurately perceive Black Americans and, when they do recognize suffering in that community, blame it on inherent tendencies of the group rather than on white racism.[1] However, understanding his next major publication requires a bit of context. As I've discussed, this fin de siècle moment witnessed tremendous blows to the cause of racial justice. Hateful white supremacist propaganda was rife, including Thomas Dixon's infamous romanticizing trilogy *The Leopard's Spots* (1902), *The Clansman* (1905), and *The Traitor* (1907).[2] Imagine Du Bois's frustration and despair as his efforts to convince white Americans of Black moral worth were countered by cartoonish potboilers supporting, in David Levering Lewis's words, the "national white consensus emerging at the turn of the century ... that African-Americans were inferior human beings whose predicament was three parts their own making and two parts the consequence of misguided white philanthropy."[3] White supremacist misinformation touched daily life everywhere in the United States. In 1896, Frederick Hoffman, an actuary for Prudential Insurance, published *The Race Traits and Tendencies of the American Negro*, in which he predicted the extinction of Black Americans based upon their declining life expectancy, especially vis-à-vis their white counterparts.[4] Even America's most famous scientist, Louis Agassiz, had become a public and devoted racist.[5]

In *Souls*, Du Bois had labored to build a small but sturdy rampart against a mighty enemy. Yet, unfortunately, while it was a tremendous inspiration to many African Americans, and surely graced the bookshelves of thousands of well-meaning white people, the book could not turn the tide of white supremacy. It would be nice to spin a tale about what happened next with Du Bois's work: to imagine that he made the purposeful decision to change white Americans via the narrative of one of themselves, the rare figure who had transcended white supremacy. His 1910 biography of John Brown—a white man who sacrificed his own life and the lives of several of his children in his quest to end slavery—would slot nicely into this invented tale. But the actual genealogy of *John Brown* is more complex.

Du Bois's editors at McClurg had suggested that a fictional account of the travails of Black southerners might be even more persuasive than the essays in *Souls*, so he began working on the novel that would eventually become *The Quest of the Silver Fleece*.[6] But when another publisher asked him to write the biography of a civil rights giant, he jumped at the chance. His plan was to write about Frederick Douglass, and the publisher agreed. However, they soon learned that Booker T. Washington had already expressed interest in writing about Douglass, so Du Bois swallowed his pride and suggested Nat Turner.[7] After some back-and-forth, his editor instead suggested that Du Bois write about John Brown.[8]

Du Bois's primary aim in the volume was to demonstrate Brown's moral vision and to argue that his strategy had been solid and not indefensibly violent, given what was at stake. In short, he meant to show that "John Brown was right."[9] Du Bois did not comb the archives for material to support this contention.[10] Instead, he turned to already published works, intent on "lay[ing] new emphasis" on existing material and "treat[ing] the facts from a different point of view."[11] He relied in particular on accounts by African Americans such as Osborne Anderson and Frederick Douglass (who had known Brown well at the time of the Harpers Ferry raid) as well as on contemporaneous documents such as Brown's own diary. He was not interested in uncovering new facts about his life or even adjudicating the question of whether Brown was sane—which today, more than a hundred years after his death, is still often historians' primary question.[12]

By all accounts, John Brown recognized the equal humanity of Black Americans and acted accordingly. Against white custom, he addressed Black adults by their surnames and maintained genuine friendships and working relationships with them. Ultimately, he raised a guerrilla army to try to force an end to slavery. Brown was not an anachronistic antiracist paragon: he was sometimes paternalistic toward the Black community.[13] However, he felt intense responsibility for the souls of *all* of his neighbors, so it is difficult to judge if his hectoring of Black Americans was different from his hectoring of whites.[14] In the biography, Du Bois made it clear that Brown was both an epistemic and active model for white Americans. He called Brown the man "who of all Americans has perhaps come nearest to touching the real souls of black folk."[15] He considered *John Brown* to be "one of the best books that [he] ever wrote," though it did not fare well with critics, due to minor factual errors and a sense that the author was too adulatory.[16] In my view, however, Du Bois fulfilled his purpose in the biography. While some of its dates may be unreliable, it explicitly and emphatically offers a new interpretation of Brown, one that counters the still widespread perception that his militant commitment to racial equality was evidence of mental instability or fanaticism.

JOHN BROWN'S LIFE IN BRIEF

Brown's life was intimately entwined with the lives of African Americans, and it was this dimension of his story and its aftermath that intrigued Du Bois. As Nahum Dmitri Chandler notes, Brown's narrative "is enigmatic and difficult of telling."[17] This makes it difficult to create a portrait that neither demonizes nor sanctifies him but maintains his humanity. Without doubt, John Brown's life was marked by extremism, but, as Du Bois contended, this was the morally proper position for him to take.

Du Bois wrote, "John Brown was born [in Connecticut in 1800] just as the shudder of Haiti was running through all the Americas, and from his earliest boyhood he saw and felt the price of repression—the fearful cost that the western world was paying for slavery."[18] In that same year, Gabriel Prosser died in a foiled uprising, and Nat Turner was born, who in 1831 would lead the greatest slave revolt in North American history. John Brown was reportedly a sensitive child, scarred by the early loss of his mother, who died when he was eight years old. His father, Owen, was a devout Calvinist, and John, too, maintained that rigorous faith. In his youth, he learned to tan hides, and for a while he supported himself as a tanner. He married and started a family in Pennsylvania, settling into his role as a civic and religious leader, until his finances were wiped out by the Panic of 1837. He then retreated to Ohio, where his father and siblings were living, and became a tenant farmer. Attempting to recoup his losses via land speculation, he soon became entangled in legal proceedings and was forced to declare bankruptcy.

Despite this dispiriting sequence of events, Brown was already taking a very public stand against racism. When his local church in Franklin, Ohio, relegated Black congregants—both free persons and fugitives from slavery—to seats in the rear, Brown declared that God was no "respecter of *persons*" and invited them to sit in his family's pew near the front, which they did. The Brown family then took the vacated seats in the rear.[19]

After this conflict, Brown moved his family from Franklin to Hudson, Ohio, a town founded by the white abolitionist David Hudson, who had been heard to exclaim, after reading about Nat Turner's uprising, "'Thank God for that! I am glad of it! Thank God they have risen at last!'"[20] In Hudson, a Black itinerant preacher lodged with the Browns, sharing "his story of persecution and injustice." Brown appealed to his older children and his wife: would they pledge to God that they would henceforth always work to end slavery? The family agreed (although we cannot know their level of enthusiasm), and Brown fell to his knees "and implored God's blessings on his enterprise."[21]

Before long, Brown and his family moved to Springfield, Massachusetts, where Brown planned to take up the wool trade. According to Du Bois, this triggered a period of relative stability for the family, and Brown took advantage of it to study New England's organized abolition movement, recent slave insurrections, and the various routes of the Underground Railroad—learning, among other things, about "the organized resistance to slave-catchers in Pennsylvania, and the history of Haiti and Jamaica."[22] According to Du Bois, however, the most felicitous event during this period was Brown's introduction to a range of Black Americans:

> He had met black men singly here and there all his life, but now he met a group. . . . He came to them on a plane of perfect equality—they sat at his table and he at theirs. He neither descended upon them from above nor wallowed with their lowest, and the result was that as Redpath says, "Captain Brown had a higher notion of the capacity of the Negro race than most white men."[23]

Springfield is where Brown first met Frederick Douglass, who spent the night at Brown's home on their first meeting. While Douglass was shocked that an apparently prosperous businessman would have such a plainly furnished house and even plainer food at table, he was even more amazed by Brown's nascent plans to take up arms against slavery. According to Du Bois, Brown "thought that slaveholders had forfeited their right to live; that the slaves had the right to gain their liberty in any way they could."[24] Douglass demurred as he still hoped that the movement might convert slaveholders. Yet Brown insisted that slaveholders would never be convinced through suasion; some threat of violence would be necessary to change their "proud hearts."[25] The two men never entirely agreed about the most effective way to end slavery, but they remained close until Brown's death.

Du Bois's biography is clear and insightful about the evolution of Brown's plans:

> Human purposes grow slowly and in curious ways; thought by thought they build themselves until in their full panoplied vigor and definite outline not even the thinker can tell the exact process of the growing.... Few Americans recognized in 1839 that the great central problem of America was slavery; and of that few, fewer still were willing to fight it as they knew it should be fought. Of this lesser number, two men stood almost alone, ready to back their faith by action—William Lloyd Garrison and John Brown.[26]

Brown and Garrison were at odds in many ways. Garrison was a nonviolent activist and writer who retained his faith in pacifism and moral suasion long after Brown had determined that violence was necessary to end slavery. But by placing these names side by side, Du Bois distinguished himself from those who had labeled Brown a militant fanatic and Garrison a man of principle. He believed that Brown's single-minded commitment to ending slavery was a logical extension of his belief in the humanity of enslaved people and in the divine commandment to act as if the enslaved were his own brothers. It is astonishing that Brown was able to resist the common wisdom of the day, exemplified not only by those who supported or accepted slavery but also by abolitionists who were willing to tolerate this great evil until it could be peacefully eliminated.

WHITENESS AND JOHN BROWN

If white Americans are to begin to experience themselves as white, they need to read works about whiteness and white supremacy written by people of color. Likewise, if we are to overcome, undermine, and dismantle the horror of whiteness as coextensive with white supremacy, then we must begin to understand lives such as John Brown's. Brown's life choices were his way of declaring, essentially, that Black lives matter; and studying Brown gave Du Bois the opportunity to consider what set him apart from most of his white contemporaries, who either supported slavery or were willing to tolerate it. In this way, Du Bois's biography allows us to see the life of a white person from the other side—as, perhaps, Brown himself sometimes saw it.

Chandler argues that Brown was the rare white American who could be described as having experienced double consciousness.[27] As a result of his genuine friendships with Black Americans, he had "died as a white man."[28] That is, he had moved beyond the epistemic failures of white Americans to see Black people as they were. His transformed perceptions inspired his outraged misery. How could he bear the knowledge that families were being separated and that children were suffering? As answer, Du Bois evoked Brown's motto: "Action, action ... for we have but one life to live."[29] He would ameliorate suffering where he could and pray where he could not.

In the biography, Du Bois explicitly located Brown within the tradition of Africa and Africans in the United States, certainly because of the role he played in Kansas and at Harpers Ferry but also because of his ability to live and work with Black Americans.[30] Chandler urges us to see that Du Bois's portrait of Brown reveals a white man who was "no longer white."[31] Though racial identities are socially constructed through practices, policies, and familial and cultural relations, this is not, I think, what Chandler has in mind. Rather, he is arguing that Brown's level of empathy for the experiences of the enslaved and the trust he inspired in Black abolitionist circles are evidence that he had rejected the racial script that was his birthright. Chandler urges us to see the terrible uncertainty within this approach to life. Despite Brown's reputation for fiery firmness, Du Bois portrayed him as a man of great melancholy. As Chandler notes, this portrayal differs greatly from that of other biographers, and even Du Bois's readers often do not mention it.[32]

As Chandler makes clear, John Brown experienced a "profound sense of disjunction" from the culture of whiteness in nineteenth-century America. Moreover, he was unusual among other abolitionists because he was willing to strike violently against slavery. Brown was not a violent man in general. Rather, he recognized that slavery was itself a state of war; and because it was so deeply and morally wrong, violence against it could be justified. Since its inception, American culture has been open to the notion that violence may be necessary in pursuit of a just cause. With that in mind, we might ask why more abolitionists were not willing to share Brown's stance, but the great majority of white Americans were aligned against him and his cause. As slaveholders continue to flourish, while poor white merchants were struggling, Brown was increasingly aware of the shortcomings of whites who refused to do their duty to humanity because material comfort lay elsewhere.

Brown, again, also transcended the demands of whiteness in his personal relationships. In the biography, Du Bois reported the testimony of Osborne Anderson, an African American who took part in the raid on Harpers Ferry. Before the incident, he had shared a house with Brown and some of his family and had witnessed

> no offensive contempt for the Negro while working in [Brown's] cause. . . . Each and every heart beat in harmony for the suffering and pleading slave. I thank God that I have been permitted to realize to its furthest, fullest extent, the moral, mental, physical, social harmony of an anti-slavery family, carrying out to the letter the principles of its antitype, the anti-slavery cause. In John Brown's house, and in John Brown's presence, men from widely different parts of the continent met and united into one company, wherein no hateful prejudice dared intrude its ugly self—no ghost of distinction found space to enter.[33]

Figures as diverse as Frederick Douglass and the novelist, lawyer, and abolitionist Richard Henry Dana Jr. remarked on the social equality that characterized interactions in Brown's home, where the sons and daughters served with their mother at table and Black guests were referred to by honorifics and surnames rather than by first names.[34]

Still, while I appreciate the rhetorical force of Chandler's reading of Du Bois's Brown as "no longer white," I think it is also important to see him as a white American who rejected the logic of whiteness. Brown's struggle against the endemic white supremacy of the United States illustrates many things, but I believe that Du Bois was most interested in him as a white American who had cast his lot with Black abolitionists. Brown's willingness to kill other whites and to sacrifice his children and himself in the fight against slavery was vehement testimony that white people could act in solidarity with Black people. Even today he continues to represent the possibility of antiracist whiteness. It may have been intolerable for Brown to live *as a white man was expected to live* in a nation in which whiteness meant the denial of Black humanity, for he understood American slavery as "the foulest and filthiest blot on nineteenth century civilization."[35]

"THE VISION OF THE DAMNED"

> Four things make life worthy to most men: to move, to know, to love, to aspire. None of these was for Negro slaves. A white child could halt a black man on the highway and send him slinking to his kennel.
>
> —W. E. B. Du Bois, *John Brown*

Chapter 5 of Du Bois's biography, "The Vision of the Damned," offers a brief sketch of antislavery activity on both sides of the color line. It begins with an epigraph, "Remember them that are in bonds as bound with them," a verse from the Book of Hebrews that John Brown chose as the motto for himself and his family.[36] The chapter's title speaks to the lived experience of slavery and to the hopelessness that was rife among people such as Brown, who could not be enslaved but nonetheless deeply empathized with the abandonment and despair of those who were.

In this section of the book, Du Bois recounted a vignette that he called a "foretaste and prophesy" of Brown's unusual destiny. During his first solo business trip, when he was about twelve years old, Brown made friends with a Black age mate who was a servant in a businessman's household. Even as the businessman praised young John for taking on the responsibility of an adult, he was cruel to this enslaved boy, at one point hitting him in the head with an iron fireplace shovel over some perceived shortcoming in the child's serving of dinner.[37] For Du Bois, Brown's reaction signaled his deep empathy with the enslaved: "He asked 'Is God their Father?' And what he asked, a million and a half black bondmen were asking through the land."[38] We are urged to understand that, for people who were convinced of the humanity of the enslaved, the system was a version of damnation.[39]

Most white Americans were inclined to see slavery as either justified or, at worst, a minor moral wrong. Slaveholders argued that it was a beneficial institution for the enslaved, as it gave them access to white civilization. Moreover, slavery itself had been ordained by God.[40] Many settlers believed that the agricultural economy in North America would collapse without the mass of free labor made possible by enslavement. Du Bois explained that, as slavery became the cornerstone of the cotton kingdom, "all the subtle moral adjustments which follow were in full action."[41] If we consider the intense physical and mental cruelty occasioned by North American slavery, including the regular yet unpredictable destruction of the bonds of family and friendship, we should recognize that Chandler's dictum—that Brown's space and time were nothing less than a "metaphysical horror"—is simple truth.[42]

Du Bois was familiar with the extreme pathology of a society in which recognizing and being moved by the suffering of another human being required rejecting a silent and perhaps unconscious compact. He recognized the alienation Brown would have experienced, rejecting the desensitization or repression that made it possible for white Americans to live in a society marked by the regular separation of children from their parents, by purposeful maiming and killing, and by the many other common, terrible practices of North American slavery. Even most northern whites went about their daily affairs without being too distracted by the suffering in the South, but as Douglass pointed out, slaveholding white Americans were particularly dehumanized by the practice.[43] Desensitization and compartmentalization may be convenient, but they damage one's humanity. The enslaved paid the highest costs of slavery; but, as Du Bois pointed out:

> To reduce the slave to . . . groveling, what was the price which the master paid? Tyranny, brutality, and lawlessness reigned and to some extent still reigns in the South. The sweeter, kindlier feelings were blunted: brothers sold sisters to serfdom and fathers debauched even their own dark daughters. The arrogant, strutting bully, who shot his enemy and thrashed his dogs and his darkies, became a living, moving ideal from the cotton-patch to the United States Senate from 1808 onward. No worthy art nor literature, nor even the commerce of daily life could thrive in this atmosphere.[44]

Witnessing "the horrors of slavery with unseeing eyes" requires extreme moral opacity.[45] This moral insensibility underlies the heedless comportment that appears consistently in Du Bois's portrayal of whiteness. John Brown was unable to achieve that opacity, a moral virtue that also contributed to an inevitable melancholy. This difficulty may have led him to his death, but as Chandler suggests, it was also a sign that he had attained double consciousness. Du Bois knew it was hard to accept one's Blackness and one's Americanness in an America that rejects Blackness. Likewise, it is hard to be a white person who rejects the key elements of whiteness that are demanded of whites in his society. In virtue of this suffering, Brown, too, was one of the damned. It may be fair to conclude that everyone in a society premised on chattel slavery is damned in one fashion or another.

"THE RIDDLE OF THE SPHINX"

In Sophocles' *Oedipus Rex*, the sphinx asks, "What animal walks on four legs in the morning, two at noon, and three at evening?" The answer is, simply, "a man."[46] Du Bois referred to this riddle repeatedly in his work.[47] However, in the biography he framed it as a specific question relevant to his subject: how did John Brown come to be the man that he was? Du Bois evoked the riddle as he wrote about a moment of despair: the passage in 1850 of the Fugitive Slave Act. At this time, a great stirring occurred, especially among the Black community and the abolitionists:

> A great unrest was on the land. It was not merely moral leadership from above—it was the push of physical and mental pain from beneath;—not simply the cry of the Abolitionist but the upstretching of the slave. . . . It came like some great grinding ground swell,—vast, indefinite, immeasurable but mighty, like the dark low whispering of some infinite disembodied voice—a riddle of the Sphinx. It tore men's souls and wrecked their faith. Women cried out as cried once that tall black sibyl, Sojourner Truth:
>
> "Frederick, is God dead?"
>
> "No," thundered Douglass, towering above his Salem [Massachusetts] audience. "No, and because God is not dead, slavery can only end in blood."[48]

As in *Oedipus Rex*, such questions must be answered on pain of death. In 1850, the question may have been "What are we to do?" It may have been "What does it mean to be human? What can it mean, when human beings, even children, are traded like chattel and trade one another? What can it mean when human beings are stolen, and returned, and stolen again, even in the supposedly free North?" The question that Du Bois attributed to Sojourner Truth echoes the question of young John Brown, who could not understand how, in a universe governed by a benevolent God, a young orphan could be brutally beaten on a whim.

Another invocation of the riddle appears in the penultimate chapter, titled "The Riddle of the Sphinx." Here it becomes a test of moral probity in a morally perilous time: "If we are human, we must thus hesitate until we know the right. How shall we know it? That is the Riddle of the Sphinx. We are but darkened groping souls, that know not light often because of its very blinding radiance. Only in time is truth revealed. Today at least we know: John Brown was right."[49] With this passage, Du Bois articulated the dreadful weight of wanting to act rightly when one can see no obvious way of doing so. John Brown knew what was right but faced a whole white world that refused to allow him to do so, and he could not wait for this world to change. He had solved the riddle because he had managed to cast off the Veil of ignorance imposed by white supremacy.

Slavery is an intolerable moral crime, but was Brown right to take up arms against it? Du Bois said yes. By what logic did he make this claim? Du Bois took the perspective of the enslaved. It is fair to say that most enslaved people were convinced of the wrongness of slavery.[50] They knew this not only because they suffered under it but because they had direct access to their own humanity and that of their mothers, fathers, siblings, and children. They experienced the ways in which enslavement had denied that humanity. Whites' actions suggested that they saw Black people as less than human, but Black people recognized the craven, self-deceiving mechanisms that allowed whites to live with the knowledge of what they were doing without confronting it. The resistance to slavery, as practiced by many enslaved people—even resistance that included violent uprisings against slaveholders—was morally justified. If I am being held against my will, especially if this condition endangers my life, then in self-defense I am justified in using violence against my captors.

In criminal law, the extension of this theory is known as *defense of others*: when a person finds other humans endangered by one or more wrongdoers, that person is permitted to take physical action, up to and including fatal action, against the wrongdoers.[51] For Du Bois, Brown was proof that it was possible for white Americans to answer the riddle correctly, to do what was right. Those who failed to confront this riddle killed their own souls. Thus, as Nahum Chandler infers, Brown's achievement of humanity necessarily entailed his death as a white man.

As Du Bois wrote, Brown was convinced that to "recognize an evil and not strike at it was ... sinful," and he lived his life accordingly.[52] He was an "exasperatingly simple" example of a blazing light in moral darkness:

"'Slavery is wrong,' he said,—'kill it.' . . . Was he wrong? No."[53] Mired in their attachment to whiteness, many abolitionists who objected to slavery on moral grounds could not bring themselves to sacrifice material well-being or reputation by joining his campaign.[54] For those who take an empathetic position that fully accepts the humanity of Black Americans and rejects whites' privilege to use others for their own advantage, his urge to strike a killing blow against slavery is not only sensible but admirable. Yet twenty-first-century white observers are unlikely to see Brown's militaristic campaigns in Kansas and at Harpers Ferry as admirable. They may laud his aims but remain puzzled by his methods. This gulf is not identical to his alienation in 1859, but some similarities are inevitable, and they become clear when one reads Brown's attempts to clarify his position during his imprisonment.

The penultimate chapter of *John Brown* recounts the days and weeks following the raid on Harpers Ferry. Brown survived the event; and his ongoing attempts to explain why he had done what he did, and why he did not regret it, were widely disseminated in the news. According to Du Bois, the following conversation took place after Brown was captured in the Engine House at Harpers Ferry, as his sons Oliver, age twenty, and Watson, age twenty-four, lay dead nearby. Several white leaders, including the generals J. E. B. Stuart and Robert E. Lee and Governor Henry Wise of Virginia, interrogated him:

"Upon what principles do you justify your acts?"
[BROWN:] "Upon the Golden Rule. I pity the poor in bondage that have none to help them. That is why I am here; not to gratify any personal animosity, revenge, or vindictive spirit. It is my sympathy with the oppressed and the wronged, that are as good as you and as precious in the sight of God."

. . . .

[INTERROGATOR:] "I think you are fanatical."
[BROWN:] "And I think *you* are fanatical. Whom the gods would destroy they first make mad, and you are mad."[55]

Brown's claim was more than a rhetorical flourish. Americans who supported slavery and were willing to give up their own lives and their sons' lives in its defense do seem to have been mad: either unaware of what they were doing or unable to distinguish right from wrong.[56] They failed to take humanity into account and to act appropriately. Enslaved people did laugh, cry, and seethe at injustice; they loved their children and often became experts at complex and delicate tasks. All of these facts were available to white Americans, although pseudoscientific propaganda may have obscured their clarity.

Du Bois was not naïve about the reasons for slavery's longevity in the United States. During his time at Fisk College, he had met families whose elders had been held as slaves. His research for *The Suppression of the African Slave-Trade* had revealed numerous explicit and implicit motivations for supporting slavery and resisting abolition. However, for thousands of white folk, rich and poor, who had daily contact with the enslaved and could be said to have had relationships with them—intimate and long-standing, in many cases—the explanation was not simple. If they had been unable to absorb the available evidence of Black humanity and act accordingly, their problem might have been framed in the terms of that archaic legal standard *They did not know what they were doing, and they did not know right from wrong*. The white denizens of Harpers Ferry would, of course, have believed Brown to be insane.[57] In fact, recent works discussing Brown still find it necessary to ponder his sanity, but none of these diagnoses move us toward moral wisdom.[58]

The raid on Harpers Ferry forced the nation to confront the moral status of slavery. Prominent abolitionists needed to distance themselves from Brown or, if they supported him, explain (even if only to themselves) why they had not taken part. "To be sure," Du Bois wrote, "the nation had long been thinking over the problem of the black man, but never before had its attention been held by such deep dramatic and personal interest as in the forty days from mid-October to December, 1859."[59] Enslaved revolutionaries such as Denmark Vesey, Gabriel Prosser, and Nat Turner had made white slaveholders aware of the dangers of enslaving human beings, but the willingness of white Christian men to shed blood for slavery (and not just their own blood) was a different sort of portent. Moreover, Brown's "strength, simplicity and acumen made his trial, incarceration and execution the most powerful Abolition argument yet offered."[60] His martyrdom is still seen as a key milestone on the way to the Civil War.[61]

John Brown was not exactly the man that Du Bois portrayed in his biography, but neither was he the deranged specter who appears in other works. For Du Bois, he was both a good person and a moral lesson for white America—and perhaps also for Black Americans who wondered if any whites were capable of real humanity. Du Bois may have overstated his strategic brilliance and courage in the face of danger, but the reasons for such overreach are clear: John Brown showed us that the white shortcomings entrenched in our racially diverse yet white supremacist nation are not inevitable. We can resist them and make that resistance the key principle for our lives.

CONCLUSION

As Chandler argues, Du Bois's project required him to interrogate the formation of a racial subject such as John Brown. How did he emerge from the white world with this peculiar orientation toward African Americans? Du Bois took him seriously as an antiracist abolitionist, and this approach might have caused some readers to mistake analysis for praise. But the point of the biography was to explain what made Brown stand apart from the white supremacist world, to feel or know the extent to which he was alienated from that world, which allowed Du Bois to circumvent the question of whether his subject was worthy of admiration.

As Chandler notes, Du Bois "situate[d] John Brown squarely within the folds of the productivity of Africa in America."[62] In fact, as many commentators have pointed out, he began the biography with a chapter titled "Africa and America." Du Bois wrote:

> The mystic spell of Africa is and ever was over all America. It has guided her hardest work, inspired her finest literature, and sung her sweetest songs....
>
> Of all inspiration which America owes to Africa, however; the greatest by far is the score of heroic men to whom the sorrows of these dark children called to unselfish devotion and heroic self-realization: Benezet, Garrison, and Harriet Stowe; Sumner, Douglass and Lincoln—these and others, but above all, John Brown.[63]

For him, the connection between Africa and North America would always be portentous: Africans were among the earliest of outsiders to arrive, coming "on the heels, if not on the very ships of Columbus."[64] In *The Souls of Black Folk* and then more explicitly in his work on pan-African congresses, Du Bois noted African Americans' special relationship with Africans. In his early writings, he seemed to believe that Africans had left the historical stage, giving it over to African Americans. Later, he recognized the arrogance of this stance and worked to convince the wider world of African nations' right to independence and self-determination. But in 1910, he still hoped that some spiritual connection between Africans and African Americans could be established. This viewpoint was appropriate to a study of John Brown, who himself referred to the American South as "Africa" and whose last home was a Black settlement that escaped persons had named Timbuctoo.[65]

In the final chapter of *John Brown*, Du Bois asked, "Was John Brown simply an episode, or was he an eternal truth? And if a truth, how speaks that truth today?" In 1910, his answer was not hopeful. Since Brown's time, scientific and economic advances had accompanied "distinct signs of moral retrogression in social philosophy."[66] Numerous whites were willing to read the findings of Charles Darwin and other scientists as a defense of white supremacy. While many people continued to work for progressive causes, the entrenchment (and healthy funding) of white supremacist ideologies had "made their voices falter and tinged their arguments with apology."[67]

Reviews of *John Brown* rarely discuss the last chapter, whose target is very much the "hegemony of the white races" since Brown's execution, especially during the first decade of the twentieth century—the "nadir" of racism in the United States.[68] Du Bois focused on developments in the United States, Australia, and South Africa, where whites, without subtlety or excuse, were excluding Black persons from property ownership, economic opportunity, and civic participation. His well-documented demonstration of white racial crimes and hatred reiterated Brown's message that "the cost of liberty is less than the price of repression."[69] Though slavery had ended, the cost to both whites and people of color remained high:

> We have come to see a day here in America when one citizen can deprive another of his vote at his discretion; can restrict the education of his neighbors' children as he sees fit; can with impunity load his neighbor with public insult on the king's highway; can deprive him of his property without due process of law; can deny him the right of trial by his peers, or of any trial whatsoever if he can get a large group of men to join him; can refuse to protect or safeguard the integrity of the family of some men whom he dislikes; finally, can not only close the door of opportunity in commercial and social lines in a fully competent neighbor's face, but can actually count on the national and state governments to help make effective this discrimination.[70]

The odds are against Black Americans, Du Bois mourned, in a situation skewed by wealth, tradition, learning, and guns.[71] Though he was writing in the early twentieth century, every one of these concerns continues to vibrate today. Now, as then, "on the [white] side heart-searching is in order. It is not well with this country of ours."[72]

According to David Roediger, Du Bois's *John Brown* opens inquiries into the "meanings and miseries" of white identity, and the writer would continue that work in the 1910 essay "The Souls of White Folk." But the biography does more than simply raise questions about white identity. For Du Bois, John Brown represented the potential of white Americans to become something other than twisted and benighted souls who risk "deteriorating from within."[73] We, too, can "die as whites" and continue to live as human beings.

Du Bois wrote *John Brown* at a time when the United States seemed to be abandoning any attempt to support racial equality. His first sojourn at Atlanta University, between 1896 and 1910, was similarly marked with disappointment: lack of funding, a dearth of civil replies to inquiries about federal and state collaboration on research projects. The 1906 Atlanta riot had forced him to sit on his front porch with a shotgun, his belief in the possibility of white racial progress shaken to the core.[74] John Brown must have seemed like a splendid (if not spotless) beacon.

CHAPTER 4

Darkwater's Faith in Humanity

What on earth is whiteness, that one should so desire it?
—W. E. B. Du Bois, "The Souls of White Folk"

MANNING MARABLE WROTE that "*Darkwater* takes the reader on a spiritual journey."[1] Compared to the approach of Booker T. Washington in this same era, Du Bois does not mollify or cajole; "instead, he insults, shocks, and denounces whites," trying to save "both them and world civilization from themselves."[2] *Darkwater* is a fascinating, brilliant collection. Like *The Souls of Black Folk*, it is composed of essays, stories, and poems; yet, as Marable notes, while its purpose is similar, it differs in overall tone and historical context. Published nearly ten years after *John Brown* and nearly twenty after *Souls*, *Darkwater* was released amid a frenzy of anti-Black violence during what became known as the Red Summer of 1919, an era marked by white nations' ongoing brutal imperialism and the rise of pseudo-scientific racist eugenics in popular culture.[3]

In *John Brown*, Du Bois had shown that whites themselves could resist the ideology of white supremacy, even with violence. The idea that it was possible for white Americans to devote themselves to Black liberation continued to be a key element of Du Bois's ongoing project, and contemporary reactions to *Darkwater* indicate that he had struck a nerve. Oswald Garrison Villard, his colleague and sometime rival at the National Association for the Advancement of Colored Persons (NAACP), described it as "tinctured with hate," and "bitter" seems to have been the liberal press's favorite adjective for the collection.[4] In a move that should surprise no one, a white reviewer in *The Times Literary Supplement* denounced *Darkwater* as racist.[5] Yet while its style is more insistent and less elegiac than *Souls*'s, the book is far from racist. The white response to *Darkwater* was a predictable function of the operation of whiteness: white interaction with an honest person of color virtually always results in the white person's conclusion that there is a problem with that person of color. According to such corrupt reasoning, Du Bois was responsible for his own dissatisfaction, his own bitterness. Thus does white cognition misfire in a predictable way—one that is common among those who are powerful enough to make their perceptions reality.

According to Marable, Du Bois had two aims in writing *Darkwater*. First, he wanted white readers to see and comprehend the world from the perspective of Black Americans. Second, he hoped to "offer white America a way out of its racial hatred, through the salvation of hope in humanity. In a sense, what Du Bois want[ed] to achieve [was] the deconstruction of both whiteness as a social category, and of its hierarchies of oppression. For this to be accomplished, Du Bois contend[ed] that white Americans must come to a new understanding and an appreciation of what it means to be black."[6] Thus, white Americans might, even if temporarily or fitfully, be able to see the world and themselves from the perspective of the other side of the color line—a more accurate viewpoint, a kind of reverse double consciousness.[7] The white psyche in *Darkwater* is portrayed as a knot of self-deception, fear, and the frantic shoring up of counterfeit superiority. Du Bois's growing recognition that white people were unwilling or unable to accept these home truths might explain why, along with unprecedented anger, he also expressed something like pity for their deep need to deceive themselves about themselves.

Marable contends that *Darkwater* represents Du Bois at the height of his political influence and intellectual maturity. His writing here displays confidence in his own abilities and impatience at the slow pace of racial justice since the Civil War. As David Levering Lewis writes, the book "was meant to be drunk deeply by whites."[8] Precisely because of those white pathologies, *Darkwater* has never matched the prominence of *The Souls of Black Folk*, though scholars often evoke two of its essays: "The Souls of White Folk" and "The Damnation of Women." Nonetheless, the book offers the frankest accounts of whiteness in Du Bois's published works and deserves more sustained attention than it has received.

HEEDLESS COMPORTMENT: "OWNERSHIP OF THE WORLD FOREVER AND EVER"

"The Souls of White Folk" is the second essay in *Darkwater*. To create this version, Du Bois reworked two previously published essays: "The Souls of White Folk," which appeared in *The Independent* on August 18, 1910; and "Of the Culture of White Folk," published in the *Journal of Race Development* in April 1917.[9] In the *Darkwater* version, he offered up the same question he had asked in the earlier essay of the same name: "But what on earth is whiteness, that one should so desire it?" Du Bois was one of the first writers to name whiteness as a racial identity and to articulate it as harmful.[10] Now he famously answered his own question with "whiteness is the ownership of the earth, forever and ever, amen."[11] He continued: "The discovery of personal whiteness among the world's peoples is a very modern thing—a nineteenth and twentieth century matter, indeed."[12] In this way, he clearly linked the worst tendencies of whiteness to the trans-Atlantic slave trade and to European-American colonial and imperial ventures. He focused particularly on the American hypocrisy of claiming to be a defender of democracy, even as the nation was annexing territories during the Spanish-American War and mistreating its own Black soldiers during World War I. The United States had revealed itself to be a bully, running roughshod over weaker nations and denying human freedoms to both Black Americans and people of color overseas.

In recounting the damage done by Belgium in Congo, Du Bois emphasized that the worst of the suffering was not, perhaps, the killing and the physical harm but "the invasion of family life, the ruthless destruction of every social barrier, the shattering of every tribal law. . . . in a word, a veritable avalanche of filth and immorality overwhelmed the Congo tribes."[13] Here, he highlighted white comportment vis-à-vis "darker peoples": whites behaved as if they did not need to follow the rules that normally governed war. Even amid the existential crisis of World War I, European nations observed various war conventions with one another, yet these conventions evaporated in their behavior toward the Congolese. In fact, they enacted almost unimaginable depravity in Congo and elsewhere; and, in doing so, they resembled the stereotyped image of Africans that was populating white supremacist tales in these years.[14]

Likewise, as Du Bois wrote, we have seen "right here in America, . . . cruelty, barbarism, and murder done to men and women of Negro descent."[15]

If whites truly felt that they were superior to Black people, why did they feel compelled to commit such violence, to revel in the basest desires humans have ever known? Du Bois recognized the dissonance and, despite his outrage and hurt, felt "a vast pity,—pity for a people imprisoned and enthralled, hampered and made miserable for such a cause, for such a phantasy!"[16] These horrific assertions of supremacy revealed not only whites' systematic inability to recognize the moral demands of humanity, even when its requirements were manifest, but also a shocking lack of moral imagination and human ambition that left Du Bois in despair.[17]

To emphasize the moral ignorance of whites in the first decades of the twentieth century, Du Bois turned to the poetry and prose produced by white artists in the postwar years, which often decried a world "gone mad." He described the European fronts where soldiers fought "under essentially equal conditions, equal armament, and equal waste of white wealth," supported by nurses, surgeons, and the Red Cross. While those fronts were a hideous nightmare, he insisted, they were orders of magnitude less awful than were East Africa, North Africa, Persia, Mexico, and dozens of other places where white Americans and Europeans had been slaughtering men, women, and children of color for decades. Those victims had no army medics, no Red Cross. To Du Bois and millions across the globe, the brutality of the Great War was "not Europe gone mad; this is not aberration nor insanity; this *is* Europe."[18]

Du Bois, in a now-famous editorial, had urged NAACP members to "close ranks" when the United States entered World War I.[19] By 1919, he was open in his belief that "competition for the labor of yellow, brown, and black folks . . . was the cause of the World War."[20] To him, the fact that nations were willing to fight over access to local labor and resources rather than, say, negotiate with workers for favorable employment contracts proved that white Americans and Europeans saw people of color as natural resources rather than humans who could and should exercise their own rights. The depth of this conviction and the lengths to which whites would go in order to profit from it said a good deal about whites' capacity to perceive humanity in unfamiliar places. Even white socialists "all but read yellow and black men out of the kingdom of industrial justice," bribed by their membership among the "lordly whites," who would share in the spoils of war with higher wages, paid for by slavery abroad.[21]

Du Bois acknowledged that "such degrading of men is as old as mankind."[22] Using skin color as a justification for degradation, however, and the resulting scale of the cruelty, was new in the modern era. Since *Souls* and *John Brown*, he seemed to have changed his views about reaching through the Veil to change white perceptions. *Heedless comportment* did not adequately describe the brutality of Americans and Europeans in colonial ventures during the second decade of the twentieth century. The license of whiteness could go further: toward a complete abnegation of western philosophers' attachment to the requirements of natural law. After the lynching of Sam Hose and its aftermath, after the 1906 Atlanta race riot and Belgian brutality in Congo, how could he believe that white folk might bow to reason?[23]

Europe's willingness to impress cheap labor rather than pay for it and its preference for extracting foreign resources rather than trading for them had created a plague of suffering around the world, and the United States was following suit. Du Bois's phrase "ownership of the world" captures both this colonial competition and the heedless and obtuse behavior displayed daily by white Americans, whether they were refusing to share an Atlanta sidewalk or to make space in their academic institutions. White people could not see their own degradation, a tragedy that Du Bois treated here almost as an afterthought, but he doubtless hoped his writing would motivate them to change. Yet he recognized that white folk, who had crowned themselves as the great intellects of humanity, were conspiring to remain ignorant of the crimes that comprised their behavior.

IGNORANCE ON TWO LEVELS

Only someone who is pathologically obtuse about the rights and interests of other humans will act as if any territory they stumble upon is theirs to do with as they will. People who assume that they may treat others as their personal resources or commit violence against them without consequence are even worse. Yet this had been the white modus operandi since the development of human rights as a western idea.[24] White comportment, on both individual and national levels, is reliably, with regard to nonwhite people, contrary to the moral imperatives of classical moral theories. However, as Du Bois demonstrated (and Charles Mills has discussed at length), most white people do not appear to understand that these vaunted principles, explained and celebrated in many thousands of pages, apply to their interactions with people of color.[25] In *Darkwater*, Du Bois discussed two manifestations of white ignorance: first, ignorance of the humanity of people of color and thus of white people's moral duties toward nonwhite people; second, ignorance about whites' long history of moral crimes.

White supremacy, as Du Bois pointed out, is a fantasy. Yet through rapaciousness and misplaced self-confidence, white people have built vast material empires on it. They have seemed unable to recognize that their victories are always rigged because they have both defined the contests and appointed themselves to be judges. Whites have had the resources, the power, and the resolve to ensure that challenges to their supremacy are treated as violations of the natural order. But the extent of white brutality hints at a deep fear—that they are mistaken, that they must obliterate the evidence of Black humanity whenever they glimpse it because they cannot contemplate the possibility that they are wrong about the relative moral worth of whites and people of color. Du Bois suspected that whites have always known that their supremacy is a sham. In "The Souls of White Folk," he wrote, "I know their thoughts and they know that I know."[26] As a consequence, he and others could not help but feel *Schadenfreude* at the destruction wrought in Europe during World War I, though it was a pale shadow of the damage that Europeans had done on other continents.[27]

The white world's inability to recognize and redress the suffering of people of color is a recurring theme in *Darkwater*. In one essay, "The Hands of Ethiopia," Du Bois quoted a "great Englishman" who argued that publicizing the suffering of sub-Saharan Africans was unlikely to motivate the white world to stop exploiting them and their resources: "There does not exist any real international conscience to which you can appeal."[28] In this regard, Du Bois laid the groundwork for Charles Mills's *The Racial Contract*, which tracks the epistemic and moral shortcomings of European and American white supremacist culture vis-à-vis the injuries done to people of color, especially during the period of European expansion. Mills explains that the European conception of Black and other people of color as "savage" or "animal" implied that only whites were rational and free and thus moral agents.[29] He uses the term *untermenschen* to capture the subhumanity of this view.[30]

Du Bois's analysis of the white relation to wealth and real estate illustrates this dynamic. In the essay "Of Work and Wealth," he explained that the "stage for tragedy" was set when white folk presumed that they were entitled to anything their money could buy and everything they could wring from the forced labor of poor or enslaved people of color: "the armored might of the modern world urged by the bloody needs of the world['s] wants, fevered today by a fabulous vision of gain and needing only hands, hands, hands!" Unwilling to endanger profit by paying the laborers a living wage, somehow released even from the awareness that labor must be paid for, the white world exhibited a strange and entitled forgetfulness.[31] Thus, in the aftermath of the Civil War, "black slavery arose again in America as an inexplicable anachronism, a willful crime," with sharecropping, tenant farming, and convict leasing offering the perverse benefits of compelled labor and the ability to deny that one was a slaveholder.[32]

This moral bankruptcy was thrown into relief when white laborers began publicly challenging Black workers' brutal exploitation, not because of its injustice but because they feared it would undercut their own employment. Writing of the 1917 riots in East St. Louis, Illinois, Du Bois described white workers' fear that Black workers would take "the bread and cake from their mouths."[33] As he would explain at length in *Black Reconstruction* (1935), such fear was underwritten by epistemic opacity. The white workers would have been better off joining causes with the Black workers to demand higher wages. Instead, their fear resulted in the murder of roughly 150 African Americans who had committed the moral crime of working to feed their families. Despite the race hatred embedded among white laborers, Du Bois believed the murders would not have occurred without the tensions over employment and wages. The extent of the violence was explicable only in light of the epistemic distance—the Veil—between the rioters and their targets. Labor violence between white groups certainly occurred, but the heedless bloodshed of the East St. Louis riots was a direct result of white supremacist practices.

Throughout *Darkwater*, Du Bois allowed both fictional and real white voices to reveal their epistemic shortcomings. In the essay "Of Beauty and Death," for instance, he inserted a brief imaginary conversation with a "white friend"—a tactic he would reprise in *Dusk of Dawn* twenty years later. The fictional conversation allowed him to explore the ignorance that white people, even those acquainted with Black persons, so often display about the work of whiteness in the United States. The imagined interlocutor is a "pale and positive" woman who is incapable of believing the reported experience of a person of color—a situation that is familiar to many. Du Bois as speaker shares various daily trials: the "intentional failure" of his milk delivery; taking a forty-block walk to a café that will serve him lunch—only to find that it no longer serves lunch; denial of employment premised on customer racism; denial of employment in the fields of science, art, and literature due to doubts about Black abilities. The fictional white woman picks at details, offers alternate explanations, always missing the point that the number and regularity of such events is unimaginable and should not be borne by anyone. She tests every report and tries to catch him in a lie. When this fails, she reiterates a familiar refrain: he is "overly sensitive."[34] "Haven't you the courage to rise above a—almost a craven fear?" she asks, when he admits that he is not disrespected at every moment of every day but is apprehensive that it may happen at any moment.

As Du Bois demonstrated, whites do not listen, instead choosing to insist that Black individuals are untrustworthy and even cowardly. Of course, no one wants to believe that injustice is rife, that people live in fear of anticipated injury. Yet the "pale and positive" white woman's challenges go beyond reasonable doubt. Because she is sure that he is wrong before he even begins to offer evidence, she fails to offer the basic respect that she owes him. She imagines facing each of these obstacles as accidents of circumstance instead of absorbing the pattern and seeing the intention behind the words. Moreover, she denies the evidence of her own senses that there are racist actions and policies in the United States in 1920. This resistance is a primary mechanism for upholding whites' ignorance, and on some level they are satisfied with it, even grateful; pale, positive Americans do not wish to live in a society as mean and petty as the one Du Bois described. Yet this epistemic opacity means that people of color cannot receive even the satisfaction of white sympathy, let alone support. White epistemic failure is a maddening feature of white supremacy that stunts Black life and separates white Americans from the truth of their own existence.

"Of Beauty and Death" is the penultimate essay in *Darkwater*, and it concludes with a few painful, powerful paragraphs sketching the mechanism of white supremacy that segregates Black Americans' life experience from whites'. After a rhapsodic celebration of New York City and its inhabitants, Du Bois suddenly changed tone:

> And then—the Veil. It drops as drops the night on southern seas—vast, sudden, unanswering. There is Hate behind it, and Cruelty and Tears. As one peers through its intricate, unfathomable pattern of ancient, old, old design, one sees blood and guilt and misunderstanding. And yet it hangs there, this Veil, between Then and Now, between Pale and Colored and Black and White—between You and Me. Surely it is a thought-thing, tenuous, intangible; yet just as surely is it true and terrible and not in our little day may you and I lift it.[35]

His yearning for a new humanity, one not rent by the Veil, is tangible. Yet neither Du Bois nor the reader can vanquish "this vast hanging darkness."

Because of the Veil, "the Doer never sees the Deed and the Victim knows not the Victor and Each hates All in wild and bitter Ignorance."[36] The Veil is "a mere thought-thing," yet its vastness and the reluctance of white people to acknowledge it means that tearing it down will require an extraordinary effort. White folk cannot see, because they do not want to, that normal human foibles do not account for the suffering beyond the Veil.

Du Bois's most extended and best-known engagement with white ignorance appears in "The Souls of White Folk."[37] Unusually, the piece opens with Du Bois the speaker in an elevated position, above "the loud complaining of the human sea."[38] From this place of discernment, he reveals that he is both intrigued by and "clairvoyant" about white folk: "I see in and through them. I view them from unusual points of vantage."[39] As in Du Bois's discussions of double consciousness, the essay highlights Black Americans' insight into the nature and tendencies of whites—and the devastating ignorance of whites:

> I see these souls undressed and from the back and side. I see the working of their entrails. I know their thoughts and they know that I know. This knowledge makes them now embarrassed, now furious. They deny my right to live and be and call me misbirth! ... And yet as they preach and strut and shout and threaten, crouching as they clutch at rags of facts and fancies to hide their nakedness, they go twisting, flying by my tired eyes and I see them ever stripped,—ugly, human.[40]

In this powerful passage, Du Bois allowed himself a rare opportunity: he taunted white readers with his awareness of their pathetic inner lives, regardless of the avalanche of pseudo-scientific bunkum, the reams of legislation, and the etiquette of white superiority; regardless even of their vast power to do harm. In his discussions of double consciousness in *Souls*, he emphasized the oppressive force of the dominant white worldview on Black Americans. Here, however, he described the souls of white folk as naked, crouching, and miserable—all because of their own choices. The color line creates a powerful asymmetry: Black folk know (and know that they know) more about whites than whites know about them. Yet the essay also suggests that white folk know how well Du Bois the speaker understands them.[41] If the white people he was describing had been truly and completely ignorant, the author might have continued to offer them evidence of Black humanity. Instead, he moved toward revealing white ignorance as an artifice, a masquerade. The speaker declares that whites do not know Black folk, and they do not know themselves. Nonetheless, they *do* know, and they are scrambling every day to prevent that knowledge from becoming apparent, where they would have to acknowledge it, and acknowledge that their supremacy is not simply unearned, but a great and horrific crime. This connection leads us to Du Bois's introduction here of perhaps the most destructive element of whiteness: its attachment to innocence.

A RESILIENT, IF COUNTERFEIT, INNOCENCE

Du Bois's claim—that white Americans are aware that Black Americans know who they are—may seem to conflict with his conviction regarding white epistemic shortcomings. But the repressed awareness attributed to whites is psychologically complex: they are not entirely conscious that their claimed superiority is unfounded and that they have not fooled anyone. This makes sense if we consider the violence that white supremacists use to defend their superior position, as if they know on some level that their claimed supremacy is a sham. More vexing still, that violence itself casts doubt on their claims of superiority. Even denying the humanity of the targets gets them only so far: historically, the desire to torture and murder nonhumans, let alone revel in it, has not been treated as a virtue.

In this light, whites' presumption that they are innocent, regardless of the harm they inflict, is galling. Whiteness, as James Baldwin and others have noted, is about nothing so much as innocence.[42] White folk may insist, for example, that they have always dealt honorably with people of color; but as Du Bois's writings demonstrate, what they are actually feeling is that they *must* have done so because innocence is crucial to their understanding of white racial identity. Du Bois's "pale and positive" interlocutor not only refuses to believe that his accounts accurately represent his experiences, but also does not suspect that she bears any responsibility for them—not to mention her comportment during their conversation, when she assumes she has the standing to challenge him.

"The Souls of White Folk" was the first of Du Bois's writings to look at the impact of whiteness on white folk explicitly and at length. While he did not forsake his earlier tactic of countering racist stereotypes with demonstrations of Black humanity, he also offered white readers a startling observation: that passionate and mistaken belief in one's right to "ownership of the earth forever and ever" is dangerous to both the professed owner and the victims: "After the more comic manifestations and the chilling of generous enthusiasm come subtler, darker deeds. Everything considered, the title to the universe claimed by White Folk is faulty. It ought, at least, to look plausible."[43] Yet it does not look plausible; it cannot be a laudable accomplishment that whites have convinced themselves that every great soul, thought, and deed has been white. The lordly personality generated by this belief system is no more than a bit of foolish comedy. Yet, as Du Bois noted, "comedy verges to tragedy," for whites who are inconvenienced by "ingratitude" will react swiftly, believing that "Negroes are impudent, that the South is right, and that Japan wants to fight America."[44]

When comedy verges into tragedy, and the fool manages to harm millions, the targets of tragedy are entitled to rage. "The Riddle of the Sphinx," a poem that follows "The Souls of White Folk" in *Darkwater* (and echoes questions that Du Bois had already posed in *John Brown*), demonstrates some of this anger. Here, Du Bois offered a rare window into his fury at the counterfeit innocence of those self-defined white civilizers and the damage they have done to the world of color—especially to Black women:

Crying and sighing and crying again as a voice in the midnight cries,—
... the burden of white men bore her back and the white world stifled her sighs.

The white world's vermin and filth:
>   All the dirt of London,
>   All the scum of New York;
>   Valiant spoilers of women
>   And conquerers [sic] of unarmed men;
>   . . . .
>   Bearing the white man's burden
>   Of liquor and lust and lies!

. . . .
>   I hate them, Oh!
>   I hate them well,
>   I hate them Christ!
>   As I hate hell!
>   If I were God,
>   I'd sound their knell
>   This day.[45]

Du Bois's wrath was warranted, and it was precisely aimed. However, more than one white reader, including Oswald Garrison Villard, thought his sentiments were too angry, too bitter.[46] Given whites' attachment to their innocence, they find it difficult to be the target of nonwhites' negative emotions. White Americans have not recognized African Americans' right to express anger at them: they presume that they are the only appropriate judges of their own wrongdoings, and they stereotype angry Black people as overly hostile or clownish. This refusal to face anger shows up in other situations of asymmetrical power or legitimacy. For instance, children's anger is not often taken seriously when directed toward an adult, especially a parent. Women have long been evaluated as hysterical when angry, and their anger is often not taken seriously; instead, men attempt to pacify angry women. Even so, various theorists have noted that white women have a difficult time accepting the anger of women of color.[47]

In "The Souls of White Folk," Du Bois noted that white folk who are challenged may come to hate their challengers. Moreover, their insistence on supremacy leads them to react personally to behaviors that in fact have nothing to do with them personally:

> Down through the green waters, on the bottom of the world, where men move to and fro, I have seen a man—an educated gentleman—grow livid with anger because a little, silent, black woman was sitting by herself in a Pullman car. He was a white man. I have seen a great, grown man curse a little child, who had wandered into the wrong waiting-room, searching for its mother.... In Central Park I have seen the upper lip of a quiet, peaceful man curl back in a tigerish snarl of rage because black folk rode by in a motor car. He was a white man.[48]

These examples, easy to imagine and even tame when compared with many instances of white supremacy, ingeniously illustrate the twisted impact of this ideology on its devotees. Why would anyone be bothered by a quiet woman, a little child, a passing motor car? Yet most white readers will immediately recognize this anger, rising from a resentment of those who are out of their proper place. Some might even agree that these interlopers are legitimate irritants. In the early twenty-first century, speaking Spanish or wearing sagging pants or a hooded sweatshirt might be the innocent acts that trigger a snarled lip. As Du Bois made clear, the expectations of white supremacy are not simply irrational but ludicrous.

Having made this point, he turned his focus to the more violent exercise of such emotions:

> We have seen, you and I, city after city drunk and furious with ungovernable lust of blood; made with murder, destroying, killing, and cursing; torturing human victims because somebody accused of crime happened to be of the same color as the mob's innocent victims and because that color was not white! We have seen,—Merciful God! in these wild days and in the name of Civilization, Justice, and Motherhood,—what have we not seen, right here in America, of orgy, cruelty, barbarism, and murder done to men and women of Negro descent.[49]

Rather than simply mourning the victims and condemning the perpetrators, Du Bois tried to understand the perpetrators. How had white supremacy transformed otherwise normal white citizens into murderers and worse? How did they nevertheless manage to perceive themselves as above reproach? How were they acquitted by a legal system that accepts white people's fear of African Americans as reasonable? White supremacy tells white folk that if people of color are going to exist, they had better be of use and keep their place. An unspoken "or else" lurks menacingly in the background. White people know, whether or not they admit it, that the system of white supremacy has been a catastrophe for people of color. But in *Darkwater*, Du Bois began to demonstrate how white folk, too, have been damaged. Provocatively, he admitted, "There surged in me a vast pity" for people so enthralled by "a phantasy."[50] Clearly, Du Bois would never have argued that pity should preempt accountability, yet his reaction is still compelling. Imagine possessing such a twisted moral sense that one revels in causing suffering to one's neighbors! Imagine the contortions necessary to believe that any such tragedy is richly deserved! This is how misguided American whites have been. In *Darkwater*, Du Bois noted that Americans were criticizing Turkish atrocities in Armenia without imagining they might be criticized themselves for their atrocities toward African Americans: "A true and worthy ideal frees and uplifts a people; a false ideal imprisons and lowers."[51] For Du Bois, the lowering of human beings was always a tragedy.

It is easy to see how white readers such as Villard might have interpreted Du Bois's analysis as motivated by anger, hatred, or bitterness. Those who never consciously doubt their superiority—or, worse, cannot allow themselves to do so—have a difficult time accepting that they are the proper objects of pity. Du Bois's analysis here thus demonstrates real courage: written as if he viewed their folly from above, yet advantaged by his perspective from below. From that double vantage, he not only saw the weakness of his oppressors but also recognized it as a tragedy. His rage is accompanied by the ability to recognize the humanity in his oppressor: "Neither Roman nor Arab, Greek nor Egyptian, Persian nor Mongol ever took himself and his own perfectness with such disconcerting seriousness as the modern white man," he wrote, more pitying than bitter.[52]

"THE COMET" AND FAITH IN HUMANITY

"The Comet," a short story, is the last piece of prose in *Darkwater*. It portrays the artificiality of whites' claim to supremacy, hypothesizing that, under the right apocalyptic circumstances, a white woman might cast aside her racism and relate to a Black man as a human—not just as equal but as necessary. In this story, Jim Davis is literally the last man on Earth, after the population of Manhattan is annihilated by poisonous gases when the planet passes through the tail of a comet. He is a Black man who works as a messenger at a bank, and he survives the catastrophe because he has been sent deep into the vaults on a trivial, burdensome errand. Julia, who is white and wealthy, is similarly spared, having been shut away in a darkroom developing photographs. They find each other after spending several frantic hours searching the city for families, friends, or anyone else who might have survived. As they join together to continue the search, they begin to see in each other a partner who may help them survive tragedy. The two cross both racial and class lines: Jim is poor, Julia a socialite. With their gender roles mostly intact, she begins to depend on him for nearly everything.[53]

The imagined partnership never comes to fruition, however, for the catastrophe turns out to be a local event. Eventually, Julia's father and her fiancé turn up, as does Jim's wife; they are all reunited on a skyscraper rooftop at the end of the story. The gases have only killed the people of Manhattan. The rest of the world has survived, and both families have been saved by coincidence. Yet the fantasy becomes a near-nightmare when Julia's fiancé realizes that she has spent several hours alone in the company of a Black man. He charges at Jim, calling him "n—" and accusing him of rape. This prompts the small but growing crowd to threaten a lynching. Julia belatedly steps in, reassuring all that Jim has been a gentleman. At this point her father hands Jim some cash, transforming Jim and Julia's experience together from an inspiring episode in which two human beings saved one another at the end of the world into a tawdry tale of a rich man compensating his inferior for having protected his property (beloved, yes, but property nevertheless). I read more entitlement in this payment than gratitude, a reminder of who owns whom. In the final sentences, Jim rejoins his wife. Their infant child has died, but at least they have each other, and there is joy in their reunion.

Early in the story, when Julia and Jim first meet, she behaves imperiously toward him; but as time goes on, he begins to act protectively toward her—and she allows this. At one point, he literally takes the wheel of her car. The implication is that the artificial hierarchy of race has been destroyed along with the races, and their class differences have faded as well.[54] He cossets her, bringing her food and wrapping her up in a shawl, "touching her reverently, yet tenderly."[55] We can forgive Du Bois for believing, like most of his fellow Americans then and now, that men are natural protectors of women, especially during an apocalypse. Indeed, Julia refreshingly does not go to pieces when faced with the end of humanity but becomes more creative and resourceful. Only after they begin to face a possible future together do Julia and Jim revert to something like standard gender roles.

In "The Hands of Ethiopia," Du Bois had proposed that neither argument nor fact will move white people to question whether Black folk are subhuman: "Only faith in humanity will lead the world to rise above its present color prejudice."[56] The relationship that develops between Jim and Julia suggests this kind of faith. The post-apocalyptic context removes all solid ground of race- and class-based expectations from beneath them. Moreover, in the absence of other people, neither character is subject to the social expectations and judgments of the "measuring tape of the other world."[57] For Du Bois, an honest relationship between a Black man and a white woman requires the absence of a recognizable social context as well as a common project that outruns white supremacy. This allows Jim and Julia to see each other as human, gain faith in the other's humanity, and be inspired to begin anew.

In the end, however, both must return to a world structured by the demands of race, gender, and class. After Julia returns to her father and fiancé, she fades back into that life without a word of thanks or parting, as if her friendship with Jim must dissipate before witnesses. Her humanity has been submerged in her white womanhood. Jim, having discovered his wife, is apparently unbothered by this abrupt withdrawal. Nevertheless, though we are led to believe that Julia will accept his return to subhuman status, we have learned that a white person may see the humanity in a Black person if they are isolated and believe that their isolation is permanent.[58] Through this thought experiment, Du Bois illustrated the extent to which white supremacy is propped up by group expectations and systems. It seems likely that any flesh-and-blood Julia would be more immured in white supremacy in her interactions with Jim, but in the brief time period of the story she quickly comes to the revelation that "he was no longer a thing apart, a creature below, a strange outcast of another clime and blood, but her Brother Humanity incarnate, Son of God and great All-Father of the race to be."[59] "The Comet" is speculative fiction; as an experiment, the story powerfully demonstrates the social and cooperative nature of white supremacy.[60] Only in other-worldly circumstances can whites be emancipated from it, for the destruction of Julia's family, social set, and race are what allow her to see Jim's humanity.

CONCLUSION

> Are we not coming more and more, day by day, to making the statement "I am white" the only fundamental tenet of our practical morality?
> —W. E. B. Du Bois, "The Souls of White Folk"

Du Bois is not often considered a militant, but one theme in *Darkwater* echoes his declaration that "John Brown was right!" Now and then, and never with apparent pleasure, the book predicts that whites' failure to relinquish the social and material advantages of supremacy will lead to a violent uprising by people of color. In "The Souls of White Folk," Du Bois spoke to the state of race relations in the United States after World War I. People of color, he wrote, recognized the war as "wild and awful" and shameful, but *"it is nothing to compare with that fight for freedom which black and brown and yellow men must and will make unless their oppression and humiliation and insult at the hands of the White World cease. The Dark World is going to submit to its present treatment as long as it must and not one moment longer."*[61]

In the aftermath of the war, Du Bois and other progressive thinkers interpreted it as a struggle among the world's rich and white to maintain the upper hand in their exploitation of the other, especially in Africa and Asia. In "The Hands of Ethiopia," he asked white readers to put themselves into the position of "a Japanese or [Chinese], an East Indian or a Negro," with education and knowledge. In such a position, what would they want for the future? Indubitably, "freedom from insult, from segregation, from poverty, from physical slavery."[62] If his readers believed that Europe and America were going to continue their current policies toward this person of color, "then there is but one thing for the trained man of darker blood to do and that is definitely and as openly as possible to organize his world for war against Europe."[63]

This prediction of physical violence marked a notable break with Du Bois's earlier writings. No doubt his work on the biography of John Brown as well as the horror of the war and the bloody riots of 1919 made violence seem like a conceivable response to the outrages of whiteness. Marable suggests that *Darkwater* was meant to help white Americans understand and appreciate "what it means to be black," and this might require losing patience with white humanity.[64] In addition to showing whites the ludicrous figure they cut in the world, Du Bois reminded them that violence is a game that nearly anyone can play—and that the majority of the world's population is not white. To the best of my knowledge, he did not make this reminder a regular part of his efforts to reach white folk, but it does reappear in the work of many of those who followed him.

Darkwater may have been the last volume in which Du Bois was perfectly frank with a white audience. Its essays, stories, and poetry range from rage to wonder. Tragedy and farce rub shoulders, and Du Bois was as protective of Black womanhood as he was perplexed by the failure of whites to relinquish their delusions of superiority. He admitted, in "Of Work and Wealth," that he did not trust white people, though he told his students the opposite. (They did not believe him.)[65] He revealed that, at his public lectures on sociological issues, whites would still approach him to ask where they might find good "colored help." Apparently, these upper-class whites had sat through a public lecture and seen only a well-behaved "Negro."[66]

The "Negro problem," Du Bois insisted, was an American social and political system, one that had not advanced in its treatment of African Americans since 1903, when he had published *Souls*. By focusing on the epistemic and moral failings of whiteness, he attempted to show white America its missteps and failures of leadership, to poke holes in its conviction of innocence. But his honesty got him only so far. White critics of *Darkwater* found it inferior to *Souls*, precisely because of its explicit diagnosis of white shortcomings and its expression of the full range of human emotions. In his remaining years, Du Bois continued to present whiteness as a harmful and damaging phenomenon, writing in various genres, from academic history to fiction. But he apparently gave up hope that white America might respond to direct critique.

CHAPTER 5

Black Reconstruction

The true significance of slavery in the United States to the whole social development of America, lay in the ultimate relation of slaves to democracy.

—W. E. B. Du Bois, *Black Reconstruction*.

THE ANALYSIS OF white supremacy in Du Bois's 1935 monograph, *Black Reconstruction*, has received considerable scholarly attention. For instance, in *The Wages of Whiteness*, labor historian David Roediger highlighted its considerations on the power of white supremacy to split the potential alliance between white and Black workers after the Civil War, emphasizing that white labor sacrificed its economic interests to maintain race loyalty.[1] Indeed, after *The Souls of Black Folk*, *Black Reconstruction* is likely Du Bois's best-known book, and it is widely regarded as a classic in revisionist American history, presenting persuasive evidence that Reconstruction was not a misbegotten failure. Du Bois's arguments in *Black Reconstruction* became a springboard for the modern consensus that Reconstruction failed because the federal government did not effectively back it. However, fewer scholars have focused on Du Bois's extended point: that the government lacked the social and political will to overcome white supremacy and fully integrate formerly enslaved Americans into the nation.[2]

In his introduction to the Oxford edition of *Black Reconstruction*, David Levering Lewis recalls Du Bois's claim in *The Gift of Black Folk* that, "dramatically, the Negro is the central thread of American history." Lewis calls this both an overstatement and an essential truth, for the part played by Black Americans "continued to be written as separate, unequal, and irrelevant."[3] I disagree that the claim is an overstatement—certainly not if we consider their histories in Texas, Oklahoma, Kansas, and even beyond, where the concept of *free state* was driven by the central controversy of slavery and a desire to code new members of the Union as white.[4] American social and political history has long circled around the question of white identity, given its foundation in Indigenous dispossession and the nagging problem of millions of formerly enslaved people and their descendants. As Du Bois knew, the defense of whiteness, whether conscious or not, was a top priority for American political actors at every major moment in our history. *Black Reconstruction* delves deeply into one of those long moments, when, in the aftermath of slavery, white supremacy became a many-headed hydra, oppressing and excluding Black Americans while preventing whites from recognizing the requirements of their own humanity.

That very fact that *Black Reconstruction* is seen as revisionist history reflects the white supremacy of those who codified the view that Reconstruction was a disaster, a farce of major proportions, wrecked by scheming northern white swindlers (known as carpetbaggers), their southern partners in graft (the scalawags), and their ignorant but willing minions—recently freed Blacks whose appetite for citizenship was overwhelmed by their taste for luxury. Having lived through the period (during his childhood in the North), Du Bois was eager to revise this view of Reconstruction, in part to rescue the reputation of African Americans but also to illustrate his new convictions involving Marxian economic analysis, which he had been studying on his own. While some of his particular claims have been debunked by more recent research, his larger arguments about the agency of African Americans during and after the Civil War and about the role of white supremacy in defeating Reconstruction still stand.

Reconstruction was not rotten at its core, and the legalized segregation of Jim Crow was not simply a natural sequel to slavery. Rather, white Americans chose to defeat Reconstruction, often violently and resentfully; they decided that the United States would not rebuild itself as an integrated and racially just nation. For Black communities in the South, of course, the cost of whites' choice was tremendous. As Senator Charles Sumner bluntly noted, once federal troops were removed in 1877, "the old overseers [were] in power again."[5] In their quest to disenfranchise the Black population, white southerners erupted in a storm of violence, driving out elected officials from Arkansas to North Carolina and rewriting state constitutions. Their efforts were so intentional that they christened the movement Redemption.[6] It is a mark of the perversity of white supremacy that whites of every class, from menial laborers to statesmen, were united against the threat of racial equality, regardless of the ramifications of this stance to their social, political, and economic futures.

Du Bois published *Black Reconstruction* early during his second sojourn at Atlanta University. Its scope required him to rely on specific evidentiary support and to take a different tone from the one he had used in *Darkwater*. With this book, Du Bois was picking up the gauntlet thrown down by Claude G. Bowers's *American Negro Slavery* (1930). In response to that book (and to the work of William A. Dunning, infamous for his anti-Black interpretation of Reconstruction), Anna Julia Cooper, the Black feminist and educator, implored him to write the history of Reconstruction.[7] Though the resulting book differs from his early work, its analysis of white actors in the Reconstruction era and of the white historians who had profoundly misconstrued the period reveals the impact of the irrevocable license of whiteness on world-historical events. The book's excoriation of inept and hate-filled Andrew Johnson and its more measured examination of Abraham Lincoln illustrate the catastrophe of heedless comportment and white epistemic opacity at the highest levels of government. Du Bois showed that, by prioritizing white reconciliation over justice for the formerly enslaved, America reinforced the fallacy of white innocence, even among Confederate leaders, and intensified the overall impact of whiteness on racial justice.

THE TRAGEDY OF RECONSTRUCTION

The end of slavery should have meant bringing 4 million previously enslaved people into full citizenship. Imagine what might have been possible had the resources previously devoted to the war effort been made available to the Freedmen's Bureau. Those 4 million people, refugees from a brutal regime, might have received basic necessities and the resources necessary to build good human lives. Instead, white leadership prioritized white reconciliation over reparation and plunged Black citizens into a long nightmare of racial terror that has changed its outlines but has never ended. The ideology of white supremacy that had rationalized slavery flourished as whites scrambled to regain the social and political power that postwar constitutional amendments had endangered.[8] While it is tempting to argue that this ideology had become so normalized that the outcome was inevitable, most Black Americans and many whites had been fighting this belief system for decades, even centuries. Resources existed to support a robust Reconstruction led by a multiracial coalition of brilliant minds—what Du Bois called "abolition-democracy." Instead, "because of the attitude of [some] men's minds" and their political and economic power to act on those beliefs, whiteness prevailed.[9]

Reconstruction—that is, a set of federally supported programs for the compensation and peaceful assimilation of the formerly enslaved—was a rational response to the situation. Du Bois wrote:

> These [formerly enslaved people] wanted freedom; they wanted education; they wanted protection. They had been of great help to the Union armies and that help had been given under great stress. Black soldiers had been outlawed, and in many cases ruthlessly murdered by the enemy who refused to regard them as soldiers or as human.... Yet after the war they were still not free; they were still practically slaves, and how was their freedom to be made a fact? It could be done in only one way. They must have the protection of law; and back of law must stand physical force. They must have land; they must have education.[10]

However, even though "the sheer logic of facts" demanded the existence of a "program for the freedom and uplift of the Negro," other logics were at play.[11] The law supported former slaves and Black soldiers only temporarily, and force backed up that law inconsistently. By 1877, the South had regained control over the lives of the formerly enslaved. "The bitterness of [the] campaign against the Reconstruction governments was almost inconceivable," Du Bois wrote.[12] It was comprehensible only in the context of the South's ongoing sense of having been wronged and given the assumption that all white Americans, regardless of wartime behavior, were more desirable, more valuable, than any Black ones. The federal government was clearly not averse to this judgment, eventually restoring all confiscated lands to the former traitors.

Consequently, white leaders who had refused to reckon with the humanity of enslaved people now scrambled to subjugate the emancipated. A series of infamous laws known as the Black Codes were enacted in former Confederate states in 1865 and 1866, putting freed people at the mercy of whites who saw them as subhuman.[13] These laws were interpreted by judges who had been trained in and remained loyal to a legal system that had recently held that "Negroes" were not only not citizens of the United States but also "had no rights which a white man was bound to respect."[14] As Du Bois had made clear in his earlier works, while the abolition of slavery was the end of one moral catastrophe, white Americans worked swiftly and brutally to enact another.

In simple economic terms, white laborers would have benefited had they allied themselves with the emancipated and shared the fight for decent wages. Du Bois was the first historian to recognize that their refusal to do so required explanation. The fear that African Americans would gain "civil and political rights, education and land" prompted white laborers to overcome their former alienation from the plantocracy, joining forces across class boundaries to prevent those gains: "The Poor White South deserted its economic class and itself," choosing instead "racial bribery."[15] As Du Bois explained, white workers were seduced by the "American idea," which encouraged them to envision themselves as "future exploiters."[16] Thus, maintaining the basic labor and economic conditions of the antebellum South—especially the tremendous social and economic gap between Black and white laborers—had great appeal.

Abolition-democrats, in contrast, saw the Union victory as an opportunity to enact their conviction that "the reduction of a human being to real estate was a crime against humanity."[17] According to Du Bois, these radicals openly challenged the social and political elevation of whites by proposing legislation designed to mandate racial equality:

> Only one forward step President Lincoln insisted upon and that was the real continued freedom of the emancipated slave; but the abolition-democracy went beyond this because it was convinced that here was no logical stopping place; and it looked forward to civil and political rights, education and land, as the only complete guarantee of freedom, in the face of a dominant South which hoped from the first, to abolish slavery only in name.[18]

Tragically, however, white supremacy prevailed, and at a terrible cost.[19]

The federal government's primary goal was to unite the (white) nation by reconciling with southern whites. Thus, the Johnson and Grant administrations failed to seriously consider the humanity of the formerly enslaved or the logic of the abolition-democrats. Over time, nearly the entire machinery of government supported the oppression of Black Americans. The Supreme Court, in the so-called Civil Rights Cases of 1883, undid much of the work that the abolition-democrats had done in passing postwar amendments and federal civil rights legislation.[20] Moreover, by codifying servitude for convicted felons, the Thirteenth Amendment allowed slavery to continue through the simple expedient of anti-Black criminal legislation.[21] By 1900, every new state constitution in the former Confederacy had disenfranchised African Americans, despite the Fifteenth Amendment's apparent prohibition of such policies.

THE ARROGANT, IRREVOCABLE LICENSE OF WHITENESS

Andrew Johnson was, without doubt, one of the few men whom Du Bois wholeheartedly disliked. He often used Johnson as a model of heedless comportment. The president's hostility to postwar civil rights legislation was profound, and he completely lacked the subtlety one might expect from the holder of the nation's highest office. Johnson so alienated Congress that he barely survived members' exasperated efforts to remove him from that office.[22]

Black Reconstruction describes Johnson's 1866 meeting with Frederick and Lewis Douglass and other esteemed Black leaders in which the president refused to support the freedmen's right to vote, arguing that it would effectively deny democracy to white voters who preferred not to enfranchise Black Americans. As Frederick Douglass reported, the president apparently failed to note the irony of this position: that any number of decisions had been made and enforced against Black Americans who had lacked the franchise since the birth of the nation. It is a measure of the epistemic opacity demanded by whiteness that he could not see how offensive and obtuse his comments were.[23]

Andrew Johnson's hostility to racial equality has been well documented, but Abraham Lincoln's case is more complex. Du Bois found himself imagining how the early days of the war might have gone if Lincoln had treated the enslaved as human beings who were falsely imprisoned, if he had arranged help for escapees and allowed them to serve in the Union army. Instead, he prioritized the welfare of the Union over the welfare of the enslaved—assuming that these could not be harmonized—and assiduously ordered his generals not to allow them to escape into Union lines. Pacifying the powerful instead of rescuing the marginalized is a common political reaction; here, it suggests that Lincoln perceived slavery as a tolerable institution and saw its victims as disposable. Early in the war, when he'd had hopes of a short conflict, he had instructed the Union army to diligently return fugitive Black people to plantations and ordered General McDowell and General Frémont to return any who had escaped under cover of military action.[24]

Lincoln's approach to compensation after the war is another sign of his moral and epistemic shortcomings. Du Bois wrote that, as the larger slaveholding capitals (including New Orleans and Vicksburg) fell to the Union, the question of compensating slaveholders for "lost property" was brought before legislators and, in more than one case, passed. Meanwhile, the enslaved never received payment for years of unpaid labor and every imaginable physical and emotional injury. This, for Du Bois, demonstrated a tremendous lacuna in Lincoln's thinking: "Lincoln was impressed by the loss of capital invested in slaves, but curiously never seemed seriously to consider the correlative loss of wage and opportunity of slave workers, the tangible results of whose exploitation had gone into the planters' pockets for two centuries."[25] Lincoln's incapacity extended to the hypothetical question of the settlement of former slaves after the war: "He simply could not envisage free Negroes in the United States. What would become of them? What would they do?"[26]

For Du Bois, Lincoln's puzzlement reflected not his postwar political burden but his inability as a white man to conceive of emancipated Black people *as* people: autonomous agents able to work and learn and make valuable contributions to their communities and their nation. If they had been white people emerging from terrible trauma, he would have recognized that they needed what all people in such a situation would need: time to recover, seek assistance, rebuild their families, and find work. Lincoln's political conundrum was a function of racial identity, his own, and that of the formerly enslaved. Had it been otherwise, he would have known that he had a moral duty toward these future citizens.

Instead, the president turned his attention to the New York City draft riots of 1863, triggered by desperate white men who were too poor to buy their way out of conscription and were convinced that they were being sacrificed for the questionable cause of Black emancipation.[27] Notably, instead of seeing the liberation of the enslaved as the rescue of fellow workers, they believed that fighting for such freedom was a shameful cause. The draft riots highlight the failure of white Union leadership to conceive that it would serve their cause to encourage whites to see the enslaved as fully human and their freedom as worth fighting for. Rather, this work was left to private philanthropists who identified as abolitionists, a failure of imagination that prolonged the war and provided fertile ground for the lost-cause narrative after Appomattox.

Writing of white South Carolinians after the war, Du Bois noted that, although they were well qualified to "help and advise in the reconstruction of the state, [they] refused even when there was no legal barrier. The attitude of most whites was childish."[28] Committed to the failure of the Reconstruction government, they obstructed all attempts to integrate white and Black labor and refused to support efforts to create a political system that would respect the rights of all its citizens. Instead, they complained repeatedly and volubly about the scoundrels, rascals, and thieves who were attempting to create a more democratic state government. As Du Bois pointed out, it is unlikely that every member of the Reconstruction government was dishonest or worse. Still, because most white South Carolinians were focused on defeating Reconstruction, they were willing to destroy reputations and effective government. Du Bois's book offers compelling evidence that white South Carolina did not want reform or care about stealing and corruption. What it feared most, even more than bad government by African Americans, was good government by African Americans.[29] In this way, white citizens prioritized a blinkered view of their own interests over anyone else's well-being. We expect such egoism from an infant but not from an adult.

During the 1868 Arkansas constitutional convention, William Murphy, who had been previously enslaved, directed trenchant remarks to

> the men that have been our masters, men whom we have brought to the very condition they are now in, and have not only fed them, but have clothed them, have tied their shoes, and finally have fought until they are obliged to surrender. . . . Now that they have surrendered, they say we have no rights. Has not the man who has conquered upon the battlefield gained any rights? Have we gained none by the sacrifice of our brethren?[30]

Murphy's logic was unassailable; he and his comrades had run up against white Americans' assumption that they owned the Earth. They were immune to change or doubt: even after losing a war, even after being subjected to occupation, even after constitutional amendments plainly stated that their preferred way of life was illegal, southern whites comported themselves as unvanquished, morally superior, and ultimately untouchable. The license that they had arrogated to themselves could not be revoked.

According to Du Bois, the nation's postwar failure to ensure that emancipated African Americans would become full citizens continued to reverberate in 1935, when he was writing *Black Reconstruction*. Jim Crow laws were rampant, and the United States maintained a two-tier system of citizenship. Surely Lincoln, had he lived, would have been a better advocate for the rights of new citizens than subsequent presidents were, but could he have maintained this goal in the face of southern white redemption policies? Certainly, he was apt to prioritize the health of the nation over the rights of Black Americans—as if the health of Union were not itself threatened by the systemic oppression of some 4 million of its members. We can speculate about what might have been, but the fact is that "all the hatred that the whites after the Civil War had for each other gradually concentrated itself on [Black Americans]."[31] White supremacy had badly compromised whites' basic human capacities.

Du Bois pointed out that the defeat of Reconstruction required more than just the North's willingness to forfeit much of the victor's spoils: "The wide distortion of facts which became prevalent in the white South during and after Reconstruction as a measure of self-defense has never been wholly crushed since."[32] He documented several examples of epistemic opacity, though few reach the level of President Andrew Johnson's inability to imagine Black Americans as intelligent, even as he was meeting with Frederick Douglass and his associates. But one particularly complex situation was the inability of white laborers to understand that collaborating with Black laborers would support their material interests. Instead, they chose to receive what Du Bois called a "public and psychological wage" from clinging to their white racial identity.

In the note titled "To the Reader" that opens the book, Du Bois wrote:

> It would only be fair to the reader to say frankly in advance that the attitude of any person toward this story will be distinctly influenced by his theories of the Negro race. If . . . he regards the Negro as a distinctly inferior creation, who can never successfully take part in modern civilization and whose emancipation and enfranchisement were gestures against nature, then he will need something more than the sort of facts that I have set down. But this latter person, I am not trying to convince.[33]

Typically, including an author's note that blames readers for a book's failure to convince might be seen as tremendous cheek. Here, however, Du Bois's remarks offered white readers an extraordinary opportunity to reflect on their ability to read as if they believed in the average ordinary humanity of Black Americans. From the very beginning of the book, he was arguing that "nothing so bad could be said about [the enslaved] that it did not easily appear as true to slaveholders."[34] Could white readers really exempt themselves from this misperception?

Later in the book, Du Bois specifically attributed the failure of Reconstruction to "the color problem," which made "logical argument almost impossible."[35] He explained, "It was the American Blindspot that made the experiment all the more difficult, and to the South incomprehensible. For several generations the South had been taught to look upon the Negro as a thing apart. He was different from other human beings. The system of slave labor, under which he was employed, was radically different from all other systems of labor."[36] Because this attitude served a number of white workers' own interests, they accepted these beliefs. These 5 million non-elite white people were not the registered owners of other human beings, but their willingness to oversee and police the enslaved, to throw in their lot with slaveholders, made them the allies of the masters. As Du Bois had suggested in *John Brown*, white Americans who lived easily in a land stained by slavery had to deny the full humanity of the slaves and the awfulness of slavery. This is why the epistemology of the slaveholder became the epistemology of most American whites.

Roediger has explored Du Bois's innovative analysis of white southern workers' devotion to their racial identity over their class interests.[37] After the war, they supported segregation to the detriment of their own wages, and their inability to imagine solidarity with Black workers prevented them from negotiating effectively with their employers. This problem became part of the legacy of organized labor, which discriminated more or less openly against nonwhite workers well into the twentieth century.[38] However, the profound epistemic, social, and moral impact of this largely unacknowledged white supremacy went well beyond the failures of white labor, as devastating as they were. As Du Bois wrote, "for the average planter born after 1840 it was impossible not to believe that all valid laws in psychology, economics, and politics stopped with the Negro race."[39] This claim was not hyperbole but an accurate description of slaveholders' epistemology, despite daily contact with enslaved people and exposure to irrefutable evidence that they were capable and intelligent, that they deeply loved friends and family (and even, sometimes, those who held them in bondage). Slaveholders could not integrate this evidence into their worldview because doing so would have destroyed their social and moral frames. How could they have lived with the knowledge that they and their ancestors had perpetrated such a crime? How could they see themselves and their neighbors as moral monsters?

Slaveholders were convinced that Black people would not work without force, that slavery was their natural condition. Du Bois argued that this belief was as certain to southerners as the rising and setting of the sun, and the United States never implemented a widespread reeducation program to correct this or any other misperception regarding African-descended people. Instead, when southerners rebuilt after the war, they attempted "to make Negroes slaves in everything but name."[40] This is a shameful and shamefully underreported truth of American history. And yet, Du Bois pointed out, on some level, southern planters did understand the human capacities of enslaved people:

> It is nonsense to say that the South knew nothing about the capabilities of the Negro race. Southerners knew Negroes far better than Northerners. There was not a single Negro slave owner who did not know dozens of Negroes just as capable of learning and efficiency as the mass of poor white people around and about, and some quite as capable as the average slaveholder. They had continually in the course of the history of slavery recognized such men. Here and there teachers and preachers to white folks as well as colored folks had arisen. Artisans and even artists had been recognized. Some of these colored folks were blood relatives of the white slaveholders.[41]

Andrew Johnson, for example, was exposed to ample evidence of the humanity of Black people. He had held title to eight slaves; surely he had regular dealings with them, knew their names and how they related one to another, these people over whom he held absolute power.[42] Southern slaveholders daily acted on their knowledge of enslaved persons' abilities: they assigned slaves complex tasks, consulted their judgment about agriculture and animal husbandry, and gave them primary responsibility for the care of their own children. Understanding what enslaved people valued gave slaveholders more power to manipulate them. Thus, it is difficult to believe that slaveholders fully denied the humanity of enslaved people.

We need a more complex epistemology if we are to make sense of American slaveholders' beliefs and actions, given that they could grow up under the care of enslaved women, make friends with children who were enslaved, and then, as adults, torture, mutilate, and murder Black individuals and families. My use of *epistemic opacity* is no more than a signpost for a deep and persistent problem that allows such apparently contradictory beliefs and profoundly immoral behavior. White folks' resilient sense of innocence in their behavior toward Black people only highlights the complexity of the knowledge practices demanded by whiteness. Most white Americans did not perceive slaveholders' actions against the enslaved as crimes against humanity. Du Bois argued, "It is easy for men to discount and misunderstand the suffering or harm done [to] others. Once accustomed to poverty, to the sight of toil and degradation, it easily seems normal and natural; once it is hidden beneath a different color of skin, a different stature or a different habit of action and speech, . . . all consciousness of inflicting ill disappears."[43]

As I have discussed, white Americans had an existential interest in remaining deluded about the moral wrongs of slavery. Du Bois is explicit about this matter: for southerners, the legal right to own the mind and body of another person had "disastrous effects" on their moral sense.[44] Especially egregious was southerners' inclination to believe so strongly in their own honor—the conviction of being inherently correct—that they were able to equate the suffering of the enslaved as morally equivalent to the suffering of livestock. This notion of honor, for Du Bois, was a "vast and awful thing, requiring wide and insistent defense."[45] Having worked so hard for so long to hold onto this worldview, white southerners made every effort after the war to maintain white supremacy in thought, deed, and legislation.

The Union accepted General Robert E. Lee's surrender on generous terms: he and all of his troops kept their horses; Lee was allowed to keep his weapons. This is often chalked up, perhaps rightly, to Lincoln's and Lee's shared desire to bind up the wounds of the nation. Yet it excluded African Americans from membership in the nation—people who had been wounded for centuries by enslavement, people whose wounds were never bound. Meanwhile, Lee was not shamed or tarnished by defeat. His memory continues to be honored throughout the South, along with that of other white heroes, because of the irrevocable license he took in his actions toward people of color.[46] This ongoing celebration of Confederate officers, soldiers, and political leaders demands an explanation that extends beyond the needs of the nation. Often, governments and judiciaries hold that wrongdoers should acknowledge their wrongdoing and offer recompense before being restored to full membership in a community. How was it possible for white folk to imagine the aftermath of such a war without including punishment for treason or a program of reparations for those freed from bondage? Yet as Du Bois made clear, an honest confrontation with these issues was inconceivable. In a context in which recently freed Black people were seen as the problem, white southerners became welcome co-workers in the rebuilding of the nation.

Before and during the war, skin-deep differences were used to bolster claims that the enslaved were inherently unlike whites, and institutional resources were devoted to defending the primacy of such differences. One might have expected that a nation newly committed to the ideal of racial equality would employ similar resources to dismantle this racist narrative. Yet the United States never explicitly undertook the difficult task of undoing the presumption of subhumanity that was attached to Black Americans. While they and other people of color have fought for centuries to teach their children appropriate levels of self-respect to combat the history of white supremacy, most white Americans have not taken on the responsibility to actively undo the impact of white supremacy on their own children. As the theorist Christina Sharpe has written, "the ongoing state-sanctioned legal and extralegal murders of Black people are normative and, for this so-called democracy, necessary; it is the ground we walk on."[47] Most white Americans simply deny the impact of white supremacy on all sectors of society, even as they benefit from its operation and are regularly reminded of statistical data proving it.[48] In other words, whites not only deny their material interests to maintain white supremacy but also compromise their ability to perceive this fact accurately.[49]

The bitterness of the white South and the collaboration of the white North in denying the political and moral crimes of the Confederacy are further evidence that whiteness involves an inherent and resilient sense of innocence. As Du Bois pointed out, the so-called Bargain of 1876, which ended the dispute over that year's presidential election, meant that the federal government would cease "to sustain the right to vote of half of the laboring population of the South, and [leave] capital as represented by the old planter class, the new Northern capitalist, and the capitalist that began to rise out of the poor whites, with a control of labor greater than in any modern industrial state in civilized lands."[50] Politicians commonly make unsavory deals; but the reality that one group of white people relinquished all claims to retribution against another group of white people who were, barely ten years prior, attempting to kill their sons in warfare demonstrates that any lingering enmity had since been overwhelmed by white solidarity. It is no surprise that Black access to the ballot box was another casualty of this process. Moreover, southern whites maintained an attachment to their idealized lost cause—one that, despite being premised upon the ownership of other human beings, did not seem to implicate them morally. This unlikely state of affairs, Du Bois argued, came about because the nation was convinced, a priori, of the moral worth of those former combatants. There was only one quality that differentiated white southerners who had fought against the Union from Black southerners who had fought in support of the Union. Their racial identity constituted their qualification to be part of the reconciled nation. That we are not more conversant with this irony is an effect of the phenomenon itself.

CONCLUSION

My rise does not involve your fall.
—W. E. B. Du Bois, *Black Reconstruction*

As Du Bois made clear, Reconstruction was guaranteed to fail. Its flaw was not a lack of material resources; the nation was wealthy enough to provide for the newly freed citizens, had those resources been rationally distributed. Rather, loyalty to whiteness forced the nation to renege on every promise made to distribute land to the emancipated millions, and that land was instead returned to those white folk who had taken up arms against their own government. Reconstruction's death was not the failure of a difficult project but an intentional killing. White Americans could not discard their long-held assumptions about Black folk or their view of themselves as superior to nonwhite people.

Du Bois noted, with palpable grief and anger, that the white majority, impressed by the Black soldiers' heroism in war and African Americans' successes during the "crusade of the New England schoolmarm,"[51] seemed briefly to perceive them as having full human status. The passage of the postwar amendments suggests that African Americans were expected to join the civic community as equals. In fact, if they had not been granted the vote in 1867, they may never have become part of the American democracy: "There has never been a time since when race propaganda in America offered the slightest chance for colored people to receive American citizenship."[52] Yet this brief period before the white United States moved "back toward slavery" had to be erased from white historical memory.[53] Many white Americans have no idea that a generation of Black Americans exercised the franchise during Reconstruction; that many became federal and state legislators, local representatives, sheriffs, and other municipal officers. Rather, white Americans tend to imagine the post–Civil War United States as an unchecked descent from Emancipation into Jim Crow. This error minimizes the impact of white supremacy in our history.

White epistemic and moral capacities were so diminished that this period of Black political and economic flourishing was almost immediately reinterpreted as an era of corruption and chaos. The record of white Americans in the century after the Civil War is rife with failure: notably, the failure to question the persistence of white supremacy and the failure to notice that it was not inevitable. I suspect that few have wondered why the Voting Rights Act of 1965 was necessary, given that the Fifteenth Amendment already prohibited abridging the right to vote based on color. The answer lies in the fact that the United States abandoned Reconstruction and the Supreme Court refused to uphold the human and civil rights encoded in the postwar amendments. "Even the right to vote," the historian Carol Anderson writes, "despite the Fifteenth Amendment, was not federally protected." In two cases heard in 1874 and 1875, Chief Justice Morrison Waite managed to find that the Constitution did not confer the right to vote on anyone; the states were still the source of that right.[54]

Northerners, according to Du Bois, gave up on Reconstruction after only ten years because they could not believe in the equal humanity of Black Americans. They could not or did not want to live in a world in which Black folk advanced politically, received college degrees, succeeded in the professions, married into white families, and produced "mulatto descendants."[55] It is devastating to consider that the North preferred to fall back on the mythology of Black inferiority than to share breathing space and family connections with people of African descent. Despite countless examples of Black humanity and excellence, white northerners chose their own ignorance and the side of moral wrong:

> For a brief period—for the seven mystic years that stretched between Johnson's "Swing Round the Circle" to the Panic of 1873, the majority

of thinking Americans of the North believed in the equal manhood of Negroes....

[W]hile after long years the American world recovered in most matters, it has never yet quite understood why it could ever have thought that black men were altogether human.[56]

Black Reconstruction was not Du Bois's first engagement with the historical question of how supporting the institution of slavery affected whites' conception of themselves or of people of color. However, by the time he wrote it, he had broadened his conception of the mechanisms that supported white supremacy beyond the moral deception emphasized in *Suppression of the African Slave-Trade*. The entanglement of economic and psychological pressures on working-class white folk moved them to support parasitic institutions—white supremacy and slavery—that often worked against their interests. For both Roediger and Du Bois, the white working class's attachment to racial supremacy "undermined not just working class unity but the very *vision* of many white workers."[57] Succumbing to the myth of white supremacy not only supported white workers' material exploitation but damaged their critical faculties.

Today, white Americans are regularly exposed to information about significant racial disparities in the criminal justice system and other key U.S. institutions, yet they apparently believe that these institutions are fair enough, for now. This state of affairs is perfectly captured in James Baldwin's observation that white people are "basically confused, bewildered, pathologically fearful beings, in need of a pitying love . . . from the very [B]lacks who have suffered so grievously because of them."[58] Confusion, fear, and the need for pity are not desirable states: white ignorance is clearly harmful to whites. Unfortunately, that harm, now as ever, is not limited to white people. If there is to be a change, white folk must show a greater willingness to read the insightful, if unflattering, portraits of whiteness found in the work of thinkers such as Du Bois and those who now carry that work on. Perhaps the first step is to recognize that "ownership of the Earth, forever and ever," is an inexcusable presumption we must commit to unmake.[59]

CHAPTER 6

Dusk of Dawn and the Triumph of Unreason

> All white folk are not scoundrels and murderers. They are, even as I am, painfully human.
>
> —W. E. B. Du Bois, *The Dusk of Dawn*

Dusk of Dawn: An Essay toward an Autobiography of a Race Concept was published in 1940, when Du Bois was seventy-two years old. Like *Souls* and *Darkwater*, it is composed of a series of essays weaving his analysis of the American race problem into *recollections* of his life experiences, although the throughline of the pieces is more explicit than in the earlier volumes. *Dusk* differs from its predecessors in containing neither fiction nor poetry. As the subtitle suggests, Du Bois was convinced that his life story could provide insight into the role of racial identity in the United States. Thus, *Dusk* expands on the biographical elements of the two earlier collections, offering a multilayered study of the workings of white supremacy and its twisted influence on the lives of people of color. In the "Apology" that prefaces the work, he wrote that he was trying to record "that subtle sense of coming day which one feels of early mornings even when mist and murk hang low."[1] *The Souls of Black Folk* and *Darkwater*, he said, had been written in tears and blood, but this third volume was "set down no less determinedly but yet with wider hope in some more benign fluid."[2] Whether because of the perspective offered by age, or his perception of new and hopeful signs on the horizon, he worked in this volume to untangle the race concept—in particular, the workings of whiteness—with unprecedented depth and generosity.

In my estimation, *Dusk* contains Du Bois's most powerful written observations and his richest analysis of the diabolical impact of white supremacy. In passages ranging from the sardonic to the heartbreaking, he set forth fictional exchanges between himself and white Americans that illustrate every element of his conception of white irrevocable license. In addition to "Apology," which serves as a foreword, the book contains nine chapters. Generally speaking, the first four and the last two are organized autobiographically, and the three middle ones—"The Race Concept," "The White World," and "The Colored World Within"—focus on race. Draft titles of chapters 6 and 7 revealed more bitterness: "White Dilemma" and "The Inferior Culture."[3] I suspect that the titles he eventually settled on reflect expanded discussions and exhibit a bit of tact. While Du Bois's anger is not as explicit as it was in *Darkwater*, the second half of *Dusk of Dawn* pulls no punches regarding what must be done to achieve racial justice.

In the opening "Apology," Du Bois explained he had come to believe that tackling the issue of race would never be a simple task. His reading of Sigmund Freud had shown him that white supremacy's hold on white people (and indeed, the hierarchy of value implicit in the race concept) was not merely a matter of greed, ignorance, and poor character.[4] Rather, understanding this problem requires "the charting, by means of intelligent reason, of a path not simply through the resistances of physical force, but through the vaster and far more intricate jungle of ideas conditioned on unconscious and subconscious reflexes of living things; on blind unreason and often irresistible urges of sensitive matter."[5] Du Bois demonstrated in *Darkwater* and *Black Reconstruction* that such reflexes are powerfully constitutive of white Americans' identity as white, sometimes conditioning their ways of being in the world so firmly that even the barest questioning of the regime of white supremacy looks like an existential threat.

Du Bois understood that white supremacy is not the outgrowth of greed and callousness, nor is it perpetrated by demons and monsters. Instead, it flows from the actions and beliefs of deeply flawed human beings, and this recognition is a core element of *Dusk*. The book's tone suggests both world-weariness and new hope. It also displays his growing familiarity with the world beyond the United States. By the time of the book's publication, he had traveled to Africa as a special ambassador to Liberia and taken two trips through Europe and Asia.[6] In these essays, he often relied on understated humor to reveal his anger at white Americans and their tightly held ignorance, occasionally recalling the styles of Mark Twain and Sinclair Lewis. Like them, Du Bois used his amusement as a cover. In no sense had he become patient with the international regime of white supremacy or with individual white people and their defective, catastrophic worldview.

THE EVOLUTION OF AN IDEA

Dusk's first chapter, "The Plot," summarizes Du Bois's life experience: "In the folds of this European civilization I was born and shall die, imprisoned, conditioned, depressed, exalted and inspired." *Souls* and *Darkwater* had offered relatively rosy depictions of his early life in Great Barrington, Massachusetts; thus, the words "imprisoned" and "conditioned" are surprising amidst the more positive adjectives. Every phase of his life was influenced by the demands of whiteness—from his mother's financial struggles, to his education at Fisk, to his struggle to find an appropriate academic position. As one of civilization's "rejected parts,"[7] Du Bois was constrained by a world-historical problem that had originally arisen from nothing more than visible differences between human groups. He described the taxonomy of human subgroups that flourished as a result of Atlantic slavery, first as an identifying scheme, then as a justificatory one. By the end of the nineteenth century, "color had become an abiding and unchangeable fact chiefly because a mass of self-conscious instincts and unconscious prejudices had arranged themselves rank on rank in its defense."[8] In this short passage, Du Bois captured the idea of race as myth, a social construction made elemental because it served white profit and white self-conception. The "instincts and unconscious prejudices" that multiplied around racial oppression were a bulwark against racial justice; they determined that Black American children would be excluded, as Du Bois was, from the benefits of life in a democracy. Every fundamental American institution arranged itself to distribute resources and opportunities "along the color line," creating the very conditions that whites then used to defend it.[9] White supremacy was visible the world over, even as white philosophers celebrated the inherent value and equality of all men.

According to Du Bois, he was a child when he began to plan for the uplift of his people: he believed that a solid education would allow them to become valuable partners in the project of civilization. Yet he came to realize, after World War I, that the problem could not be solved by such a rational solution. Whites were unable to absorb the obvious evidence of Black ability, even as they witnessed the crushing effects of white racism on the Black community. He noted in "The Plot" that white supremacy continues to withstand all empirical evidence: "Not science alone could settle this matter, but force must come to its aid. The black world must fight for freedom."[10] In earlier works, especially in *Darkwater*, Du Bois had predicted the violent uprising of people of color—who then and now constitute a global majority. I believe, however, that this was the first time he recommended such a solution for white supremacy. He went on: "I saw defending this bar not simply ignorance and ill will . . . but also certain more powerful motives less open to reason or appeal." He was referring to economic motives but also "unconscious acts and irrational reactions, unpierced by reason, whose current form depended on the long history of relation and contact between thought and idea." Clearly, Du Bois was continuing to struggle to explain how white Americans could remain wedded to such spurious ideas. Thus, "not sudden assault but long siege was indicated; . . . with the education of growing generations and propaganda."[11]

In chapter 4, "Science and Empire," Du Bois recounted his professional career, emphasizing his early conviction that social science, if properly undertaken, could prove to the white world that shortcomings in the Black community were the result of constraints arising from white racist beliefs and policies. To illustrate his early ideas, he included a lengthy quotation from *The Philadelphia Negro* that summarizes his former reliance on the power of data. The passage also offers a powerful challenge to white ignorance: "If we would solve a problem we must study it, and there is but one coward on earth, and that is the coward that dare not know."[12] Taunting the white community was an odd move for a newly minted African American academic at the end of the nineteenth century, yet it demonstrated Du Bois's early faith in direct communication with other academics and his presumption that white readers might actually have good intentions. It also revealed Du Bois's early conviction that white ignorance was the key obstacle to Black Americans' advancement and his growing suspicion that a deep fear lay behind whites' reluctance to cure their ignorance.

Chapter 4 contains Du Bois's extended meditation on his long struggle over the power of science alone to overcome white supremacy, which had been brewing long before he expressed it publicly in *Darkwater*. The crucial moment followed the death of Sam Hose, the Georgia grocer who, in

1899, reportedly killed his landlord's wife under complicated circumstances. That complexity was, of course, ignored by the white mob that demanded his lynching. While walking to the office of the *Atlanta Constitution* to meet with its editor, Joel Chandler Harris, and plead for the publication of an anti-lynching editorial, Du Bois learned that Hose had already been lynched just outside of Atlanta and that his knuckles were currently on display in a grocery store on the very street where Du Bois was walking.

Du Bois remained at Atlanta University until 1910, and during his tenure there he continued teaching the data-driven techniques of social science. But even as he continued that work, his attitudes were changing. Hose's murder and mutilation had pushed him to recognize that evidence alone could not change whites' deeply pathological relationship to white supremacy or stop their limitless brutality. Sam Hose had been burned, hanged, and dismembered. It should come as no surprise, even to a white audience, that Du Bois's proximity to the event and his inability to prevent or even effectively condemn it would eventually drive him away from the role of a careful social scientist toward a career as an activist and propagandist.[13]

Nonetheless, the work that Du Bois and his students did between 1897 and 1910 was groundbreaking sociology. As Aldon Morris writes, "no comparable research programs existed that produced empirical research on African Americans."[14] The white world, however, was indifferent. Du Bois recounted in this chapter the months of meticulous work his team did on a study of agriculture in Lowndes County, Alabama, for which the U.S. Labor Commission paid $2,000. Then, after submitting the report, Du Bois received word that the commission had declined to publish it. He wrote to Washington to ask for the report's return and was told that it had been destroyed.[15] On the day he received this blow, the 1906 Atlanta riot began, a race-inflected rampage that burned out city blocks and left many Black Atlantans homeless. Du Bois later recalled that he spent a night on his front porch with a shotgun across his knees, ready to defend his family against the rioters.[16] By 1910, he had become convinced that European imperial aspirations in Africa and Asia were being echoed in American labor and political relations: "the expulsion of black men from American democracy, their subjection to caste control and wage slavery."[17]

After chapter 4, Du Bois paused his autobiographical narrative and devoted the next three chapters explicitly to race—although he never strayed too far from his personal experience. In "The Concept of Race," he offered his most explicit explanation of the metaphysics of race since his 1897 speech "The Conservation of Races." He began by recounting how race was presented in his formal education. In primary and high school, the subject was mentioned in geography classes, where people of color were typified "by their most uncivilized and bizarre representatives" and whites, predictably, by "some kindly and distinguished-looking philanthropist."[18] The intended inference was that people of color were morally and intellectually inferior. As Du Bois wrote with some satisfaction, this was an impossible conclusion in his own classroom because his schoolwork was clearly superior to that of his white schoolmates. At Fisk University, Du Bois entered an atmosphere in which race problems were openly discussed and racial equality stoutly defended. At Harvard, however, he "began to face scientific race dogma."[19] The top minds at the most prestigious universities in the country were working assiduously and without shame to document white superiority in both academic and popular journals—a sobering reminder of the power of white supremacist ideology. In both the United States and Germany, scholars used their examinations of regional history and culture (neither of which, they reported, could be found on the African continent) to reinforce white supremacy.[20] Without fail, these great white thinkers allowed self-serving pseudoscience to overwhelm their critical faculties, creating a legacy that haunts our racial thinking even now.[21]

By 1940, Du Bois had thoroughly rejected these racist judgments. He had always felt a strong family connection to Africa, though these feelings were, for the most part, not explicable in rational terms. He spoke affectingly of such feelings after his first trip to Liberia in 1923, when he discovered the virtues of African family life (though he admitted that he personally preferred to live in New York City).[22] In *Dusk*, he emphasized the catastrophic effects of the slave trade, which tore millions from their villages. From the perspective of their families, these loved ones had disappeared forever. Du Bois acknowledged that he and others were fighting an almost hopeless battle in their attempt to convince white Europeans and Americans to really study Africa and its peoples, The cost of the slave trade to the Africans who remained, to those who endured the Middle Passage, and to those who were pressed into slave labor was unspeakable.

Uncharacteristically, Du Bois admitted in this chapter that the strain of "rising above" racist bigotry during his early adulthood "began to have serious repercussions upon [his] inner life."[23] He wrote, "It is difficult to let others see the full psychological meaning of caste segregation.[24] *Difficult* soon became an obvious understatement—not only because he wished to avoid revealing his struggle but because the white world would not recognize that Black Americans *were* struggling. He felt, he said, as if he were trapped in a dark cave on the side of an "impending mountain," watching others passing by, going about their activities in the daylight outside. Any attempt to communicate was ineffective: the barrier was too thick. Others were trapped inside the cave with him, and all the world would have benefited from their talents and wisdom, but they, too, could not make themselves heard.

Such a situation is nothing like Plato's cave: in this case, the truth is held by those within, and they are dying, often literally, to escape the cave and come into the sunlight.[25] Du Bois wrote, "It gradually penetrates the minds of the prisoners that the people passing do not hear; that some thick sheet of invisible but horribly tangible plate glass is between them and the world."[26] Perhaps because describing this struggle was so difficult and revealing, he switched from first to third person within one paragraph. No longer was Du Bois describing his own experience, using the analogy of being in this cave. "The people within," some other people, are the ones who are trapped:

> [They] get excited; they talk louder; they gesticulate. Some of the passing world stop in curiosity; these gesticulations seem so pointless; they laugh and pass on. They still either do not hear at all, or hear but dimly, and even what they hear, they do not understand. Then the people within may become hysterical. They may scream and hurl themselves against the barriers. . . . They may even, here and there, break through in blood and disfigurement, and find themselves faced by a horrified, implacable, and quite overwhelming mob of people frightened for their own very existence.[27]

Joel Olson argues that this cave allegory is "a pessimistic revisiting of the Veil, which has solidified from a hazy curtain to a thick plate of soundproof glass."[28] Over the course of a long career, Du Bois had honed his capacity to express the agitation, even hysteria, of Black Americans who are frantic to be understood, to be released from captivity, not only for their own sake but for the good of the community. He himself had spent seventy-two years bashing against this glass, and that experience resulted in a passage as powerful as any work of fiction.

The detour from autobiographical material continues with chapter 6, "The White World." Du Bois returned here to a more impersonal mode, despite inserting himself into dialogue with two fictional white associates, the better to demonstrate the disordered nature of white thinking. The focus on the concept and impact of the notion of race and its lived identities concludes with chapter 7, "The Colored World Within." In a set of vignettes and corresponding analysis, Du Bois now focused on the diversity of the African American population and the friction caused by consciousness of the weight of white judgment. He showed that both professional and working-class Black Americans feel the reputational damage of white supremacy but that the Black elite is also frustrated when white people associate them with "those kinds of Negroes."[29] It appears to be easier for the better-off class to blame white race prejudice on the failures of poor Black people than to point to the true enemy: the enormous structure of white supremacy. Doubtless that is because the failings of disreputable Black folk seem within reach, reparable in a way that white supremacy is not.[30]

The final two chapters of *Dusk of Dawn* return to an account of Du Bois's life from the turn of the century to World War II. In it, he surveyed antilynching campaigns and the difficulty of working in interracial groups, where white people "take charge of the committee, guide it and use the colored membership as their helpers."[31] This familiar phenomenon is a particularly succinct example of arrogant license, especially of heedless comportment. The final chapter, "Revolution," recounts Du Bois's surmise that the peasant uprising in the Russian Revolution could be a blueprint for fighting white supremacy and the oppression of American capital. Apparently, he was contacted more than once by those who were eager to initiate a similar revolution in the United States, but he remained adamant that Black Americans would suffer most in any attempt at violent overthrow. Moreover, "after what I had seen of the effects of war, I could never regard violence as an effective, much less necessary, step to reform the American state."[32] Nonetheless, he gleaned a lesson from Russia: that faith in the masses is a key element in any work to overthrow an oppressive group.

Du Bois then outlined his disagreement with the leadership of the NAACP in the 1930s, citing his conviction that only economic organization—a consumers' movement—would ensure that Black Americans could earn decent livings:

> I did not believe that a further prolongation of looking for salvation from the whites was feasible. So far as they were ignorant of the results of race prejudice, we had taught them; but so far as their race prejudice

was built and increasingly built on the basis of the income which they enjoyed and their anti-Negro bias consciously or unconsciously formulated in order to protect their wealth and power, in so far our whole program must be changed.[33]

Here, he looked beyond the economic motivation for white supremacy, appealing to Freudian psychology to explain why the fight for racial justice has been so prolonged: "We were facing age-long complexes sunk now largely to unconscious habit and irrational urge, which demanded on our part not only the patience to wait, but the power to entrench ourselves for a long siege against the strongholds of color caste."[34] Such long and deeply held habits entangled themselves almost inextricably with whites' sense of well-being. Thus, he noted, those fighting white supremacy must create some measure of self-sufficiency. Waiting for white folk to relinquish their hold on wealth and civil rights would be fatal.

Du Bois ended *Dusk of Dawn* by reassuring readers of his ultimate gratitude for the beauty of the world and for the opportunity to do work that was both interesting and important and to which he was suited. The final chapter includes a version of his "Basic American Negro Creed," which he had recently tried and failed to publish via Alain Locke and the Adult Education Association.[35] In it, he articulated that the race consciousness of Black Americans and their communal work toward economic self-sufficiency is a strategy not simply for racial justice but for "a united humanity and the abolition of all racial distinction."[36] He did not suggest what such a world would look like but emphasized that it is neither inevitable nor reachable through assimilation with white Americans. Even in this relatively late work, he retained his early belief that humanity would eventually no longer need racial difference.

Dusk of Dawn has prompted more philosophical writing than has most of the rest of Du Bois's oeuvre, primarily due to his explicit attention to the metaphysics of race. As Eric Porter notes, Anthony Appiah's initial foray on this topic—the claim that, in *Dusk,* Du Bois had not succeeded in breaking free of his old-fashioned biological essentialism—was responsible for a flood of subsequent arguments against his uncharitable reading.[37] In my opinion, Du Bois's conception of the metaphysics of racial identity was primarily pragmatic, aimed at supporting the sense common among many African Americans that Black racial identity is deeply meaningful while also undercutting viewpoints that might support white supremacy. In this context, Du Bois's work to articulate an African American identity is richly valuable.

HEEDLESS COMPORTMENT

In *Dusk of Dawn,* Du Bois eloquently portrayed the behavior of white Americans, in all of its disastrous boorishness, while reminding himself and his readers that white people are nonetheless human. He also took great care to reveal what it means to be on the other side of the color line, most powerfully in the cave allegory I have just discussed. As he wrote:

> The entombed find themselves not simply trying to make the outer world understand their essential and common humanity but even more, as they become inured to their experience, they have to keep reminding themselves that the great and oppressing world outside is also real and human and in its essence honest. All of my life I have had continually to haul my soul back and say, "All white folk are not scoundrels nor murderers. They are, even as I am, painfully human."[38]

Whites are human, perhaps, but their inability to recognize the "essential and common humanity" of people of color imperils their human capacities. When the "entombed" become desperate enough to "break through in blood and disfigurement," the white witnesses are horrified by the blood and injuries.[39] Yet instead of attending to the wounded and listening to their testimonies, the frightened witnesses flee.

The chapter titled "The White World" includes a conversation between Du Bois and a composite character he called Roger Van Dieman. When Van Dieman suggests that the two have lunch, Du Bois the speaker reminds him that in many of the restaurants in the "Roaring Forties"—that is, in midtown Manhattan between 40th and 49th streets—a Black person is not permitted to dine.[40] Van Dieman awkwardly points out that this policy does not prove that Du Bois or Black folk are superior to whites, although the reader should perceive that something is wrong with the refusal to serve a man with a Harvard doctorate, a three-piece suit, and a comfortable salary. Nor does Van Dieman's own response reflect well on him. When Du Bois offers a polite reminder that the world is not friendly to him, Van Dieman plows over this, becoming defensive, even combative.

Van Dieman should give up the game immediately, perhaps noting that such practices are, at best, irrational in that they keep capitalists from making money. Unfortunately, he is committed to defending whiteness. No doubt he has a code of etiquette that, in other circumstances, would cause him distress if he could not invite an associate to lunch. In this case, however, he not only shows no distress, but he also pretends not to notice the insult to Du Bois. Instead, he behaves like that famous bull loosed in a china shop, creating chaos to ensure that Du Bois receives no apology. The two do manage to lunch together: he follows Du Bois to Second Avenue, "where Labor lives and food is bad."[41] Yet his heedless comportment demonstrates that he cannot have an authentic relationship with Du Bois, though they may be able to enjoy each other's company from time to time.

Over lunch, Van Dieman remains defensive, pointing out that the modern industrial state far outstrips any achievement of African- or Asian-descended peoples. Of course, all that he demonstrates is his ignorance about Africa and Asia and the extractive, exploitative tendencies of the modern industrial state. While Du Bois the speaker acknowledges the accomplishments of white civilization, he also notes the extreme drawbacks of "this vast Frankenstein monster," which not only chains white labor and management to great industrial machines but also "kills men to make cloth, prostitutes women to rear buildings and eats little children."[42] Because the white world only sees the wealth and the growth, Van Dieman does not recognize how getting and spending harm those who benefit least from the industrial state. And so we lumber on, behaving as if this monster were not our own responsibility, our own problem to solve.

In another scene, Du Bois again introduced a white friend, this one "represent[ing] the way in which my environing white group distorts and frustrates itself even as it strives toward Justice and all because of me. In other words, because of the Negro problem. The average reasonable, conscientious, and fairly intelligent white American faces a continuing paradox."[43] This man understands the formal teachings of Christ but doubts that anyone can live up to that ideal and declares that he personally does not want to. Luckily, his white pastor has assured him that the Christian virtues are aspirational and that his behavior as a gentleman is certainly Christian enough, even if, in order to preserve this lifestyle and defend it from enemies, he must spend a good deal on tools of violence and be prepared for war. This may not be the lesson of the gospels; but as the white friend understands it, authority and discipline are all that can safeguard the world: "Critics may sneer at this and call it caste or fascism, but a country and a world governed by gentlemen for gentlemen is after all the only one worth living in."[44]

In Du Bois's portrayal, this man is obtuse about the contradiction between his commitments and his actions. He may understand the abstract requirements of universal brotherhood, but his quotidian focus is on maintaining his own wealth and the hold of whiteness on the world. Not for nothing had Du Bois initially considered titling this chapter "White Dilemma," whose first drafts centered on this character.[45] In a trenchant and hilarious vignette, the so-called friend (who is "free, white, and twenty-one") lays out a diagram of the codes required of him as a Christian, a gentleman, an American, and a white man.[46] In doing so, he discovers that peace, good will, the Golden Rule, liberty, and poverty—all central to Christian ideals—cannot be reconciled with war, hate, suspicion, exploitation, and empire—all central to the defense of whiteness.

The white friend is certain that his needs are actually needed; that he cannot do without them. As it happens, these needs of his also cause tremendous harm to others, so he feels caught in a tragic dilemma. As Du Bois made clear, however, he is deluded. White people face no such dilemma because those elements that always seem to defeat virtue—wealth, servants, empire—are "necessary" in only the warped worldview of white supremacy. This ideology is, as Du Bois pointed out, held in place by many psychological mechanisms, not least of which is self-love. Whiteness is a jumble of self-delusion, ignorance, and heedless comportment, and Du Bois was not the first writer of color to portray this with derision. Nevertheless, *Dusk of Dawn* is noteworthy for the breadth and depth with which its author addressed the problem.

EPISTEMIC OPACITY

Whiteness commits its adherents to apparently irreconcilable ideals. To "solve" their cognitive dissonance, white people have long emphasized myth over fact, warping white epistemic mechanisms to minimize doubts. This triumph of unreason has required all manner of cognitive contortions; and as Du Bois matured, he came to understand that such robust epistemic dysfunction required a new strategy to upend white supremacy. Rather than providing clear evidence of Black humanity, the most crucial "scientific task of the twentieth century" would be studying "the role of chance and unreason in human action, which does not yield to argument but changes slowly and with difficulty after long study and careful development."[47] However, given the failure of most white Americans to recognize the rigidity of white supremacy, the psychological mechanisms of whiteness have only recently become objects of scholarship.[48]

By way of his metaphor of the cave, Du Bois reconceived the barrier preventing white Americans from accurately perceiving African Americans. Yet even when the prisoners in the cave manage to crash through the "thick sheet of invisible but horribly tangible plate glass"[49] and speak to the white people outside, their words are ineffective: the watchers are both horrified and terrified by the newcomers. This sequence offers a profound vision of white epistemic opacity. Their commitment to whiteness and years of careful training in not hearing what people of color have to say makes them everything from doubtful of to utterly obtuse to reports about racist experiences and hate crimes. When frustration or injury moves the victims of racism to "breakthroughs" that exhibit desperation or anger, the white onlookers may well be "horrified, implacable," sometimes even transformed into an "overwhelming mob . . . frightened for . . . [its] very existence."[50]

Who, in such a situation, would be able to calmly soldier on, offering charts and graphs and lyrical poetry to explain their situation, even as efforts are misunderstood or ignored? This is the question that *Dusk* seems to ask. White readers must commit to listen openly and honestly to such testimony and to then take the next step: consider who has built this cave and blocked it up with thick plate glass. The truth is that the cave is their own construction; and in order to see "the full psychological meaning of caste segregation," white readers will have to break through this Veil, this glass—the myriad social and psychological mechanisms that protect their stubborn ignorance.[51]

In a later passage, Du Bois explained the exhausting work of being Black in a white-dominated nation:

> I could not stir, I could not act, I could not live, without taking into careful daily account the reaction of my white environing world. How I traveled and where, what work I did, what income I received, where I ate, where I slept, with whom I talked, where I sought recreation, where I studied, what I wrote and what I could get published—all this depended and depended primarily upon an overwhelming mass of my fellow citizens in the United States, from whose society I was largely excluded.[52]

This explanation amounts to an extended illustration of double consciousness, which Du Bois had not explicitly mentioned since *The Souls of Black Folk* in 1903. Calm and precise, it serves as both a memoir and a prediction of how whites will continue to receive him: "This surrounding group, in alliance and agreement with the white European world, was settled and determined upon the fact that I was and must be a thing apart."[53]

The dialogue with the fictional Van Dieman, which I discussed previously in the chapter as an illustration of heedless comportment, also portrays the disaster of white epistemic opacity. Du Bois ironically described the man as "quite companionable," when he is not obsessed with his own race consciousness. However, on this subject, he is "impossible"—that is, incorrigible, immoveable, unreasonable. Van Dieman wants Du Bois the speaker to admit that Black people are inferior to whites; Du Bois demurs, arguing that they are "much superior." Eventually, the two settle down to a discussion in which they attempt to determine which race is superior, based on the four qualities that Du Bois suggests are central to human excellence: beauty and health of body, mental clearness and creative genius, spiritual goodness and receptivity, and social adaptability and constructiveness.

After the two agree that beauty is too subjective to judge, they set out to determine which race has shown greater mental powers. Du Bois is aware that most white Americans will automatically presume that whites are superior across all categories; like Van Dieman, they don't know enough about Black people to make any other judgment. In his attempt to break through this opacity, he offers grandiose but supportable claims, beginning with an absolute denial of white intelligence: "I know no attribute in which the white race has more conspicuously failed. This is white and European civilization; and as a system of culture it is idiotic, addle-brained, unreasoning, topsy-turvy, without precision; and its genius chiefly runs to marvelous contrivances for enslaving the many, and enriching the few, and murdering both."[54]

We know that Du Bois was a lifelong lover of European art and culture. His caricature of white genius was no doubt intended to startle white readers, yet it was not merely a rhetorical move. The contradictions of European culture, which developed a philosophical commitment to universal human rights and fundamental equality alongside the depravities of the Atlantic slave trade, are often explained away in familiar terms: human beings are greedy; they are irrational; they learned to dehumanize in order to exploit. While these points are not false, none seems to get to the heart of the matter. Du Bois was asking readers to think harder: should we appreciate anything about a people whose greatest achievements depend on barbarity? Stately marble mansions, mahogany furniture, chocolate-filled pastries, coffee sprinkled with nutmeg—all were made possible by colonial plunder, impressed labor, and brutality. The genius behind this beauty is tainted by its association with unspeakable crimes.

Any measure of creative genius, Du Bois next insisted, involves bias or is impossible of comparison. For instance, how can we objectively compare the importance of one group's discovery of iron welding to another's innovations in textile weaving, of one group's development of printing to another's thriving village democracy? While admitting that well-being is more widely diffused among whites than among other races, Du Bois the speaker points out to Van Dieman that this is due to colonial brutality and rapine rather than to a superior culture.[55] Their argument comes to a draw over the question of which group excels in "native human endowment."[56] Van Dieman, frustrated, challenges Du Bois to predict whether a randomly chosen group of ten white or ten Black men would be better able to "carry on and preserve American civilization." Although Du Bois agrees that whites would be more likely to succeed at the job, he also suggests that this goal has dubious value and is an unfair task to assign to people who have been assiduously denied access to relevant institutions.

Dusk asserts that "the greatest and most immediate threat of white culture, perhaps least sensed, is its fear of the Truth, its childish belief in the efficacy of lies as a method of human uplift."[57] Whites know little but believe they know all that is necessary and refuse to learn what does not cohere with their presumptions. Van Dieman, struggling to grasp the enormity of white ignorance and its attendant moral failure, accuses Du Bois of believing that white people are "about the meanest and lowest on earth." He suggests that Du Bois should leave the United States if he thinks white folk are so awful. But in an echo of his comments in "The Souls of White Folk," Du Bois reminds Van Dieman that there is nowhere to go: "[white people] have annexed the earth and hold it by transient but real power."[58] Moreover, Du Bois points out that his own heritage is entangled with whiteness. His ancestors "starved and fought" for the United States, and some of them were white. He goes so far as to insist that racial identity is a historical fiction, that every white person has mixed blood, just as every

Black one does—in both biology and culture. When Van Dieman responds by challenging Du Bois to prove that there is any real meaning to Blackness, Du Bois famously replies that the definition of Blackness is apparent and sanctioned by law; the Black man is one who "must ride 'Jim Crow' in Georgia."[59]

In the following passage, still in the chapter "The White World," Du Bois's central insight anticipates a key axiom of various academic and activist movements of the late twentieth century, including feminist theory and critical race studies:

> The first point of attack is undoubtedly the economic. The progress of the white world must cease to rest upon the poverty and the ignorance of its own proletariat and of the colored world.... To attack and better all this calls for more than appeal and argument.... the quickest way to bring the reason of the world face to face with this major problem of human progress is to listen to the complaint of those human beings today who are suffering most from white attitudes, from white habits, from conscious and unconscious wrongs which white folks are today inflicting on their victims. The colored world therefore must be seen as existing not simply for itself but as a group whose insistent cry may yet become the warning which awakens the world to its truer self and its wider destiny.[60]

White Americans who come to accept the existence and intolerability of racism are often flummoxed about what they can do in response. The quoted passage suggests their first and perhaps best choice: they should attend to the testimony of those who suffer most from white supremacy. Whiteness has traditionally ruled such testimony inadmissible and false before it has even been expressed. As Du Bois illustrated via his fictional dialogues, a white interlocutor may appear to listen but only in order to reject claims that challenge the white worldview. Whites do not come by such epistemic opacity voluntarily. However, once aware of it, they can recognize it and work against it. Du Bois's portrayal of these white acquaintances as pitiable or laughable may provide the motivation to do so.

In the chapter "The Colored World Within," Du Bois offered insight into how the epistemic shortcomings of whiteness insidiously affect African Americans. It opens with a conversation among a group of middle-class (that is, elite) Black Americans who are condemning the bad behavior of poor and working-class "Negroes." They are unable to escape residential or school segregation, and blame their lack of comfort and convenience on the poor people around them—people who lack jobs and, apparently, any interest in improving their position. Distancing himself from the views of this group, Du Bois diagnosed its basic problem: the inability, even among Black folk, to believe in "essential Negro possibilities."[61] African Americans cannot, he pointed out, escape the impact of white supremacy. One of the more successful members of the group admits that there is an occasional "exception" among lower-caste Black folk, "but he cannot ordinarily believe that the mass of Negro people have possibilities equal to whites."[62] The conversation articulates the power of white supremacy and the ignorance it requires of all those who want to flourish in a world owned by whites. Those who wish to live with any equanimity in a society riven with racial inequity must take on board the worldview that makes it work. Those who manage to accumulate wealth must explain to themselves why they do not share it widely: because those who lack wealth do not, for any number of reasons, deserve it.

Here, Du Bois laid the groundwork for Charles Mills's later expansion on the phenomenon first hypothesized in Du Bois's conception of double consciousness. "White ignorance" does not only afflict those racialized as white.[63] All of us who have been socialized in the Anglo-European worldview tend to assume the generalized "truth" of white supremacy. Black people and other people of color may prove the rule by excelling along conventional cultural paths, but the rule remains. This worldview masks the humanity of people of color and the exploitative tendencies of a socioeconomic system descended from slavery, and those who recognize this are constantly challenged to maintain their clarity of vision against the onslaught of messages insisting that our society is basically fair. Racism, according to this claim, is the anomaly, the occasional setback. The fundamental truth is justice and equal opportunity; after all, is this not required by law? As Du Bois made clear, African Americans may take this perspective in order to understand the dominant white supremacist worldview and thereby avoid conflict. Here, he showed that they may also take white supremacist beliefs on board because they help make sense of a world that might otherwise be too painful to contemplate.

THE RESILIENCE OF WHITE INNOCENCE

In *Black Reconstruction*, Du Bois pointedly noted how whites from Andrew Johnson to Abraham Lincoln found it virtually impossible to conceive of

Black talent or even humanity. He revisited this topic in *Dusk of Dawn*, using an episode from his own life. Du Bois had long hoped, and even expected, to go to college, given his standing among his fellow high school students. White benefactors in Great Barrington conspired to help him obtain his goal. Because his high school's curriculum had not prepared him adequately for admission to his first choice, Harvard, these kind New Englanders gave him a scholarship to Fisk University in Memphis, Tennessee, where he could begin as a sophomore. Du Bois wrote that he was perfectly happy with this plan, seeing it as an adventure and simply a slight delay on his way to Harvard. But his family "said frankly that it was a shame to send [him] South" rather than find him work or schooling in his own state: "The educated young white folk of Great Barrington became clerks in stores, bookkeepers and teachers, while a few went into professions. Great Barrington was not able to conceive of me in such [a] local position. It was not so much that they were opposed to it, but it did not occur to them as a possibility."[64]

Du Bois's autobiographical writings reveal little evidence that the white citizens of Great Barrington saw him as anything other than a delightful, virtuous, and accomplished child. He did, in *The Souls of Black Folk*, mention the "tall newcomer" who had rejected his calling card in primary school, an anecdote that set the stage for his famous discussion of double consciousness. Nonetheless, he made it clear that he was able to thrive as a youngster, despite his mother's struggles and his family's poverty. Even so, the well-meaning white people of Great Barrington could not conceive of him as an adult member of their community, not because he lacked ability but because his exceptional ability made him unemployable in any of the positions that the town reserved for Black Americans.[65] Thus, Du Bois's own experience with white folk who seemed to know him well and were even fond of him offers telling insight not only into whites' epistemic opacity but into their perceptions of themselves as unerringly good.

Du Bois was surprisingly sanguine about this apparent failure of perception. Beggars cannot be choosers, and no doubt the young man was aware of his relative good fortune. Nevertheless, it must have been difficult to maintain his sense of being a bright child of whom town leaders were both fond and proud. To the best of my knowledge, the description of his situation in *Dusk* was the first time he described his hometown benefactors as anything other than generous. There is no doubt that Du Bois was happy at

Fisk; he did not wish he'd become a teacher or a bookkeeper in Great Barrington. Yet his discussion here occupies the minor key, as he once characterized the tone of *The Souls of Black Folk*: it acknowledges that the white people who had made his satisfying life possible—in all of their toddling, well-meaning, ignorant innocence—did not conceive of him as a favorite son but as a mascot.

Of all of Du Bois's books, *Dusk of Dawn* best demonstrates the role of white innocence in the perpetuation of white supremacy. The imaginary Van Dieman directly complains, as so many "good" white people do, that people of color should stop talking about race so much, making it clear that he has no conception of how offensive and potentially enraging this is. Du Bois the speaker does not seem to doubt his interlocutor's conscious conviction of the legitimacy of this plaint and is gracious enough to attempt to correct his perceptions. Yet *Dusk* makes clear that "the greatest and most immediate danger of white culture, perhaps least sensed, is its fear of the Truth, its childish belief in the efficacy of lies as a method of human uplift."[66] For Du Bois, this fear reveals the full figure of white supremacy. Like children, white supremacists insist on the version of reality that they desire. But why do they fear having to accept and live with truths that do not portray the world and its details in the manner they have always insisted on? Because they cannot bear a world in which they are not the center, not the favorite child, a world in which the long, long accounting of their misdeeds will be widely revealed. They fear a world that will no longer tolerate those misdeeds, one that refuses to attend to their fabulous stories about the nature of humanity. White folk fear the truth because they cannot abide giving up their sense of innocence. As Du Bois noted, national and world powers have long made use of lies to hold on to power, but this lie of whiteness is unique in the absolute need of the liar to believe the lie: "We deliberately and continuously deceive not simply others, but ourselves as to the truth about them, us, and the world."[67]

In the metaphor of the cave, white witnesses are horrified when the imprisoned people emerge; they fear "for their own very existence." Although Du Bois did not explain the source of this fear, I suspect it arises from more than the bloody and bedraggled appearance of the escapees. If the witnesses listen to the testimony of these newcomers, they will learn about a world that is very different from the one they believe themselves to occupy. They will also learn something distressing about themselves. They will find out that their daily lives have taken place alongside an almost unimaginable crime; that they have been insensible to evidence of this crime, despite its clarity; that they have helped to build the barrier that has separated them from these sufferers.

This knowledge will require white folk to change their conception of themselves. Not only are they not innocent, but they are not even commonly virtuous people with ordinary joys and sorrows. As they take in the available evidence, they will find that they, their families, and others very much like them have built their lives upon the suffering and death of others. They will learn that they have bricked themselves off from the suffering, day by day, to avoid knowing about their own crimes. This epiphany will be unbearable, especially for those who for centuries have insisted that they represent the highest forms of human genius, of human achievement, and of human virtue. Their understanding of the self and of the world will, at the moment of comprehension, be undermined and overturned.[68]

CONCLUSION

Eric Porter reads *Dusk of Dawn* as "a generalized critique of modernity and the racial knowledge supporting it."[69] The psychological and social complexity of Du Bois's account undermines both the scientific community's contemporary conclusion that racial categories are not supported by biology and thus are mere illusions and the pseudoscientific account of race developed over the preceding centuries that has given whites license to treat the world and its peoples—those who are visually distinct from Europeans—as resources to consume and discard. Du Bois, of course, had his own reasons for rejecting this conclusion. He understood race as embedded throughout the social and political strata of American history and everyday practice. His move in this book toward excavating the shared psychological and political depths of the problem of race for whites and for people of color reveals how these shared psychoses have solidified white political and economic advantage. *Dusk of Dawn* is a journey through the world made by race and racism, and it illustrates the architecture shaped by these beliefs at a time when some scholars were arguing that it should be abandoned.[70]

Du Bois's attitude toward liberalism seemed to change even within the pages of *Dusk*. He certainly saw liberalism as antagonistic to racism and explicit white supremacy, yet he noted that most white liberals were comfortable with segregation and workplace tyranny: "The democracy which [African Americans] ha[ve] been asking for in political life must sooner or later replace the tyranny which now dominate[s] industrial life."[71] Real progress in uplifting Black folk was stymied by the fact that "the whole set of the white world in America, in Europe and in the world was too determinedly against racial equality."[72] The success of individual people of color, as Du Bois's own life and others had proven repeatedly, would not change the presumption against Black competence or intelligence. Mass action would be necessary, not only to build up Black institutions but to demonstrate their promise, to show the white world what they were missing: "So long as we were fighting a color line, we must strive by color organization."[73]

As Porter notes, while Du Bois continued to believe in the promise of social science and political theory, his particular situation as both a subject and an object of social studies of racial difference and exclusion permitted him to see that these professional fields lacked the tools to adequately capture the workings of white supremacy in both everyday life and epochal political shifts. The "American Blindspot," as Du Bois called it in *Black Reconstruction*, prevented engaged social scientists and theorists from authentic scientific accuracy.[74] Du Bois, Porter asserts, perceived these disciplines as needing "enrichment to understand the centrality of race to social and political life and the exclusionary place of race in their own epistemologies."[75] Given the historic whiteness of nearly all academic disciplines, the need for such enrichment is hard to overstate.

Du Bois's claim that science could not yet report whether the myriad subtle differences of race really "mean anything" was not, writes Porter, "a retreat into the biological" but a commentary on the incapacity of a white-dominated field (as the sciences, both natural and social, still are) to say anything meaningful regarding the lived experience or social salience of race.[76] The exclusions and deprivations of white supremacy have run amok in American institutions, and they hamper the adequate production and interpretation of data on the key questions. As the dialogue with Van Dieman also demonstrates, they make a mockery of white commitment to objectivity.

CHAPTER 7

The Postwar Collapse of Whiteness

In *Dusk of Dawn*, published on the eve of U.S. entry into World War II, Du Bois had demonstrated some small hope that the days of white supremacy were numbered. Change was in the air; and in the war's aftermath, the global instantiation of the color line (which, as Nahum Dmitri Chandler insists, had been part of Du Bois's itinerary from his earliest works), was brought to the fore.[1] Although ultimately that line remained resilient, circumstances seemed to offer a chance for the deconstruction and amelioration of the components of white supremacy. As the so-called democratic nations negotiated the disposition of territories whose fates were now in the hands of major powers, they had the opportunity to confront their own legacies as empires. The destruction in Europe allowed Du Bois to hope that the bearers and defenders of whiteness might finally begin to question their long-held assumptions. Within the ruins of the battle-weary continent, he saw the scant but real possibility that white people on both sides of the Atlantic might reconsider the status of the Africans and Asians who had been exploited for centuries, in part because of their obvious competence in politics and war on both sides of that world divide. In 1944, he was heartened as powerbrokers made tentative moves toward international cooperation during conferences in Bretton Woods, New Hampshire, and Dumbarton Oaks, in Washington, D.C. He also saw reason for hope, and concern, in the developing United Nations.[2]

Sensing the possibility of a newly open-minded audience, Du Bois scrambled to write and publish two books within little more than two years: *Color and Democracy: Colonies and Peace*, released by Harcourt, Brace in 1945; and *The World and Africa*, released by Viking Press in 1947. In *Color and Democracy*, he unveiled the complex racial dynamic of postwar negotiations. In *The World and Africa*, he urged the white world to educate itself about the contributions of African peoples to human culture. In both works, he pressed world leaders to fulfill the promise of their victory against Hitler's genocidal racism by finally ending colonial exploitation and racist exclusions. Du Bois hoped that the effective participation of Asians and Africans, both in battle and in talks following the war, would force the white world to recognize their efficacy and thus their full humanity. Tentatively, he touched on the horror of the atomic bombs dropped on civilians in Japan. Noting President Truman's heedless celebration of that brutal power, he implied that even the arrogance of whiteness might shudder at such destruction.

From the perspective of the twenty-first century, it is tempting to see Du Bois's optimism as not simply anodyne but foolish. Yet a visionary change agent must be able to recognize opportunities for upheaval, even if they never come to fruition. The work done in such intervals can build a foundation for future success. As is all too obvious today, racial justice will never arrive nicely packaged as jubilee; it requires layers and layers of change, with small advances disguised as failures and failures disguised as victories. Du Bois may have hoped for jubilee, but he knew he could not wait passively for it; he could not remain silent, even if the moment was not at hand. One of Du Bois's great talents was the ability to keep looking ahead, moving forward, even when times were bleak.

The two books he wrote immediately after the war continued to hold a mirror up to whiteness. But while Du Bois's conception of whiteness can still usefully be encapsulated by my formulation of it as arrogant, irrevocable license, his discussion now expanded in two directions. First, he believed that white Europe in 1945 was on the verge of collapse. Not only had Hitler's defeat suggested the hollowness of white supremacy, but the cost of the war to the European and Japanese governments had been devastating. London, Dresden, and Tokyo were shattered, and the moral costs of the atomic destruction of Hiroshima and Nagasaki seemed to be incalculable.[3] Second, Du Bois hoped that international acceptance of China as an Allied power as well as the skillful and courageous performance of Black soldiers from around the world would finally cast fatal doubt on the ideology of white superiority.[4] To him, the causes of the war were plainly linked to white colonial scrambles for territory that, by rights, belonged to no European nation.[5] Since the American Revolution, whites had been killing one another in their millions. Now, he hoped, they might finally be able to settle their differences nonviolently, not only with each other but with the people who were most entitled to the resources of their lands.

The passage of time revealed, however, that the leaders of Western Europe and the United States were not significantly shaken (or perhaps not in the necessary manner) by Europe's material deprivation or by the millions of war deaths. In the aftermath of catastrophe, their sense of moral authority remained unshaken.[6] Perhaps understandably, defeating Hitler's Third Reich gave the United States the conviction of being on the side of the angels, yet this sense of moral superiority should not have survived the recognition that the Nazis learned much from U.S. eugenicists and the architects of Jim Crow. Nevertheless, leaders of white nations did not hesitate to draw up plans for fresh colonial arrangements without consulting the residents of those regions, even as they constructed a war crimes tribunal to punish Hitler's regime agents who had taken the American ideology of racial superiority to extremes.[7] They remained impervious to evidence that they were startlingly unqualified, in the absence of massive new conduits for democratic input and deliberation, to construct just and fair political boundaries across the globe or to evaluate the moral culpability of the prime movers of genocide. Du Bois, however, made it clear that such tendencies would eventually come back to haunt Europe, the United States, and other white powers, given their extreme numerical disadvantage in the regions they were colonizing and the spread of affordable, accessible global communication.

This chapter is called "The Postwar Collapse of Whiteness," echoing the title of the first chapter of *The World and Africa*, "The Collapse of Europe." Of course, Europe did not collapse, and neither has whiteness. But the signs and portents, Du Bois believed, pointed in that direction, and he hoped that white folk would not only learn to see them but also learn to understand that this collapse would not be a tragedy for anyone, not even for white people.

COLOR AND DEMOCRACY: COLONIES AND PEACE

Du Bois conceived and produced *Color and Democracy: Colonies and Peace* more quickly than any other volume in his oeuvre. In November 1944, he wrote to Harcourt to inquire whether it would be interested in a work covering this "field of study," and the finished book appeared in May 1945. Its main point was summarized in the catalog copy and on the dust jacket: "A ringing challenge to post-war peace plans from the point of view of the colored races."[8] The speed at which Du Bois produced the volume reflected his urgency and the long years he had devoted to the tangled problems of global white supremacy, wealth inequality, and democracy. Though the strange, indefensible era of colonialism should have ended long before the mid-twentieth century, the presumptive license of whiteness was driving it well into the present era. The obstacles posed to democracy by white supremacy and chronic poverty (driven by exploitation), even in the United States, were staggering. Thus, in Du Bois's view, the global situation would require an unprecedented intervention. He hoped that *Color and Democracy* would do that work.

Yet white world leaders remained unaware that colonialism was a moral catastrophe. They perceived entire swaths of Africa and Asia as uncivilized, as the Americas had once been, and thus properly appropriated for the benefit of white people in Europe and the United States—who would, in return, bring civilizing benefits such as roads and radio. Of course, those roads primarily benefited foreign business interests and were built at the cost of thousands of local lives, but the moral calculus of the white supremacist has always been faulty. Even if the inhabitants of those lands had been as benighted as Europeans were claiming, there was no plausible justification for undermining local autonomy and destroying cultures and thousands of individual lives.

"Henceforth," as Du Bois wrote in the preface, "the majority of the inhabitants of earth, who happen for the most part to be colored, must be regarded as having the right and the capacity to share in human progress and to become copartners in that democracy which alone can ensure peace among men, by the abolition of poverty, the education of the masses, protection from disease, and the scientific treatment of crime."[9] His argument was simple: colonialism and other forms of racialized oppression are fatal to democracy—a principle held in nearly divine esteem by most Americans.

The anti-democratic comportment of colonization is the essence of whiteness. Whites enter the scene at great cost to those who have been making their lives and communities together; they are unaware of the social and economic networks that have supported local lifeways for years or centuries. They stomp about and make pronouncements, backing up their demands with threats and violence. Forests that sustain communities are leveled, laborers are torn from their usual work and conscripted into extractive projects, and bonus inducements are exchanged for obedience when this seems to be required for efficiency. Christianity may be implemented if it encourages compliance with the new regime. Du Bois pointed out, however, that the internal logic of colonialism flows from the fact that "the colonial peoples are of colored skin.... [I]t proves to most white folk the logic of the modern colonial system: Colonies are filled with peoples who never were abreast with civilization and never can be."[10] Meanwhile, the colonizers overlook the fact that these territories have long been home to complex civilizations well suited to local conditions.

The epistemological failure here is obvious: the inability to perceive as fully human those whose skin is dark and the inability to recognize as civilization forms of human social life that do not resemble one's own. But even if Du Bois had doubts about the ability of rational argument to sway the white rulers of the world, he had good reason to think that appeals to democratic values would move hearts and minds. The notion was a clarion bell among Americans, and President Roosevelt's 1941 "four freedoms" speech about the democratic ideal was popular enough to inspire a set of Norman Rockwell's most famous paintings.[11] In an attempt to trade on this popularity while breaking through the epistemic Veil, Du Bois argued in the preface to *Color and Democracy* that failing to end colonial exploitation would maintain the stressors that had led to two world wars and give people of color justified grounds for unrest in these lands. His combination of exhortation and veiled threat was not a new strategy, but it was neither foolish nor unfounded in a historical context that should have shaken white supremacists.

Color and Democracy argues by analogy that the arrogant, irrevocable license of American whites also exists among Europeans. Chapter 2 announces that "colonies are the slums of the world" and places responsibility for these slums on those who control the flow of jobs, goods, and services.[12] Like a slum within a nation, a colony is a font of cheap or free labor—except that, in a colony, those who benefit are geographically more distant from those who are exploited and do not nominally answer to the same sovereign. This creates an even more opaque version of white epistemic incapacity, as those who benefit from exploitation and its attendant violence and misery are not simply encouraged to disregard these byproducts: there are real and often complex obstacles to their discovery.[13] Whether the white beneficiaries of such colonial patterns are based in Boston, London, or the urban centers of Mumbai, the flow of people and goods comes to seem quite natural, obscuring the impact of white comportment from whites themselves. Etiquette and a distaste for discomfort prevent any real reflection on any evidence that does appear.

Du Bois urged the United States and Western Europe to recognize that competition for colonial resources had been the primary driver of two world wars and much intervening instability.[14] As on the domestic front, acting with such license harms both actor and target, although in different ways. Indeed, it is both expensive and exhausting to maintain a colonial stance against human beings who would prefer to live otherwise while also having to delude oneself into remaining ignorant of one's part in this monstrous regime. For Du Bois, the case was overwhelmingly clear. The meetings among world leaders at Dumbarton Oaks should have been devoted to dissolving the colonial project and requiring wealthier countries to compensate and trade fairly with the colonized nations. Leaders should have begun by recognizing the political sovereignty of peoples in those resource-rich regions who, due to colonial theft and extortion, lacked access to cash, technology, and global commercial connections. But to Du Bois's horror, the accords merely protected existing colonial relations with military might. He wrote, "We ... who are filled with conflicting hope and doubt must ask ourselves how far a peace resting on force will ensure the defense and rebirth of civilization, and what the real relation can be between military power on the one hand and wealth, contentment, and progress on the other. Ultimate and lasting peace will rest on consent and agreement, not on armies."[15] The prospects for peace were not good, and the brutality of colonial exploitation would eventually result in rebellion.[16]

As a member of the NAACP's delegation to the founding United Nations conference, Du Bois had pressed the gathered powerbrokers to address the injustice of colonial domination in the organization's founding documents, but to no avail.[17] He wrote repeatedly during this period, including in *Democracy and Color*, that the proposed structure of the United Nations—created by white-dominated United States, Britain, and Russia—was clearly devoted not just to the maintenance of the status quo but to the dominance of white leadership. China, a western ally during World War II, was offered a seat on the Security Council, but excluded from the meaningful core of discussions at Dumbarton Oaks and invited to participate only at the end of a six-week review of the drafted agreements, a wrap-up process that lasted a total of six days. China's attempt to present a declaration of racial equality as part of the Dumbarton accords was tolerated, but action on the antiracism proposals was put off and finally suppressed.[18]

China's treatment at Dumbarton Oaks and its role in the United Nations, Du Bois argued, could be attributed to the country's internal turmoil. Without aid from the West, the Chinese government was doomed; thus, its ability to function independently in any of the contemporary or future proceedings was in grave doubt.[19] Yet, he pointed out, rather than support their former ally, white victors in the war simply sidelined China and went about their postwar designs for leading the entire globe. It is telling that the flourishing of a wartime ally was not a priority for the United States, preoccupied with the nascent Cold War and less than concerned about the fate even of millions of people of color thousands of miles away. As Du Bois argued in *Color and Democracy*, these powerful, white-dominated nations lacked the moral authority to consult honestly and humbly with less powerful political entities, particularly those whose futures were at stake.

Du Bois's concerns about the undemocratic structure of the United Nations were manifold. He noted that the General Assembly, which includes a larger cross-section of nations than the Security Council does, had the power to appoint an Economic and Social Council to deal with matters such as economic cooperation, public health, and human rights. Negotiations on the status of colonies and their inhabitants could have been held under its aegis, and it could have fielded "questions relating to the unfree peoples, to the minorities, and to the depressed social classes" around the world. With such problems addressed in free and open discussions among all affected nations, one might have hoped for real progress. However, even on paper the Economic and Social Council would have had no power to act; it could have made recommendations only to the white- and western-dominated Security Council and to any states indicated as relevant. "All too often," Du Bois predicted, "... proposals and complaints may simply beat the air in vain."[20]

It may seem reasonable that the most powerful, capable, and victorious nations should lead postwar negotiations regarding control of surrendered territories and the structure of the United Nations. But as Du Bois pointed out, these nations failed to notice—because they did not have to—that their own morally abhorrent behavior had triggered the conflicts that had repeatedly erupted during the lives of all those at the table. This was heedless comportment on a grand scale, supported by epistemic opacity at the cultural level. Convinced that they stood on the moral high ground, the United States, France, and England did not hold themselves accountable for their many shortcomings, thus exuding a kind of national innocence, a masquerade of immense proportions. One does not have to pretend that other nations are moral beacons before demanding that one's own nation exhibit greater integrity and justice. Certainly Du Bois never did.

The western nations' transparently domineering response, at a moment ripe with other possibilities, evokes the metaphor of a greedy child in summer who wants to possess all of the peaches yet fails to notice that, in scurrying away with an armful, they have dropped and ruined more than half of the fruit. The nations had an alternative: they could have stopped to negotiate in good faith and on fair terms with previously colonized and enslaved peoples, working to build a future acceptable to all. Instead, an interplay of epistemic failure, blithe confidence, and insupportable self-promotion led to large-scale tragedy.

Some have criticized Du Bois for suggesting that the Mandates Commission, a relic from the aftermath of the First World War, might in 1945 manage the colonies' transition to independence after the Second. They insist that he should have pushed for immediate self-determination, arguing that his appeal to the Mandates Commission was, as Gerald Horne notes, "overly cautious."[21] In any case, however, the Dumbarton Oaks negotiations did not consider the matter, preferring to make the formerly Axis-controlled colonies "integral parts of present empires."[22] Du Bois was horrified to learn that the drafted foundational documents represented a step backward from the Mandates Commission. The colonized people subject to the Allied nations would simply be at the mercy of the colonizers, with no external oversight.[23]

In a strange echo of *The Souls of Black Folk*, Du Bois reminded readers of *Color and Democracy* that he was at home in both European-American high culture and radical progressivism. Recalling "the thrilling melody of Lohengrin's swan above his disaster," he begged what is best in humanity to overcome destruction and chaos.[24] This is the same tune that the protagonist of "The Coming of John" hums as he turns to face a lynch mob, "that high and striving chord of human unity above the discord of hate, hurt, and pain."[25] One might take this reference as a touch of optimism, with Du Bois once again reaching for hope at a time of bleakness. But it may also be read as a cynical nod to the white audience that still can choose the better path, given the right prompting. Du Bois may have been whistling past the graveyard.

The chapter titled "Democracy and Color" offers a précis of Du Bois's thoughts about the impact on democracy of white supremacy and the concentration of wealth. It walks readers through an argument that stretches back to some of his earliest essays, one that crystallized during his studies of Marxian theory in the 1930s as he prepared to write *Black Reconstruction*. Notably, in an unpublished work from 1937 (which was also prompted by his 1936 travels through Europe, Russia, and China), he argued that no nation or international body is a successful democracy so long as its population is riven by a color line or extreme inequality of wealth or both.[26] His point became ever more urgent as he watched organized wealth, domestic racism, and colonial exploitation drive national policy and wartime strategy in Britain, France, and the United States.[27]

"None of the democracies fighting for democracy today is really democratic," Du Bois proclaimed.[28] His analysis of Hitler's use of antisemitism to unite "real" Germans behind a ruthless policy of dispossession at home and aggression abroad emphasized the parallels between the race science in Germany, the United States, and elsewhere: "Britain points to miscegenation with colored races to prove democracy impossible in South America."[29] The "greatest modern democracy," he fumed, stands on white supremacy and industry's desire to smother democracy within its jurisdiction. The suppression of African American voters in the South was one obvious facet of this injustice. In his book, Du Bois included data from the 1944 presidential and congressional elections to prove that southern white voters had an extraordinary advantage due to the way in which congressional representatives were apportioned: "In Mississippi 172,000 voters have the same power in the Senate as 6,000,000 voters in New York."[30] This scheme, like the Electoral College, perpetuated "eighteenth-century American Tory hatred and fear of democracy" and translated into southern control of powerful Senate committees and other policy drivers in the former Confederacy.[31]

Democracy in any form may be an imperfect mechanism, leading to an imbalance of power over government policies. We don't have sufficient examples of different forms of democracy to draw solid conclusions in this regard. What Du Bois noted, however, is that inequalities will always favor the white and wealthy in the United States and other powerful nations until the current order receives real, objective, fair-minded scrutiny. He concluded that "democracy has failed because so many fear it."[32] In other words, real democracy would deprive them of their dominion over the world's resources, including human labor and intelligence. According to any dispassionate appraisal, a world in which whites and people of color suffer at the same rate—and in which people of color suffer much less than they do now—would not be worse than the one we have. The power of white supremacy is that it allows whites to both avoid that world and subjectively believe that it would be an objectively worse one. Whites take themselves to be the only truly *human* human beings. They cannot imagine living in a world characterized by chaos and misfortune at unpredictable and unendurable levels; more tragically, they cannot perceive that this world, this reality, already exists for millions, perhaps the majority of people of color, due to their vulnerability to white supremacy.

For my purposes, a crucial accomplishment of *Color and Democracy* is its illustration of how arrogant white license functions as a tendency of nations. A structural injustice such as white supremacy depends on a complex set of psychological, sociological, economic, and other elements that combine to keep a clearly false and damaging ideology in place. While the book was not the first in which Du Bois addressed the damage done by white supremacy on a large scale, it shows the global reach of the behavioral, epistemological, and moral elements that comprise whiteness.

THE WORLD AND AFRICA

As Du Bois watched the promise of postwar negotiations dim, he quickly began work on his next book, which he hoped would reveal Africa's historical greatness to a world still unwilling to believe in it. *The World and Africa* would be his third and best attempt to upend white assumptions that Africa and Africans were little more than useful resources. Like *Black Reconstruction*, it is an urgent reinterpretation of generally ignored facts. Du Bois's goal was to communicate the history of the "dark continent," which had, since the beginning of the modern era, been denied any history at all.[33] In the shadow of a devastated Europe, he strove to present an accurate accounting of African nations and their cultures—to show that they stood alongside the ancient civilizations of Greece and Rome; to prove that the gifts, human and geographical, that had fueled those impressive states still existed and were the rightful assets of Africans themselves. Like *Color and Democracy,* the book emphasizes that powerful white nations lack the moral authority or even competence to rebuild the world. In addition, it demonstrates that nations and peoples traditionally seen only as resources or as burdens on progress must be valued as necessary partners in humanity.

In *The World and Africa,* Du Bois demonstrated that Africans were entitled to chart their own courses in the mid-twentieth century and provided evidence that they had long traditions of local democratic leadership and education. Throughout his life, Du Bois had focused on disclosing the breadth and depth of Black humanity to the white world, but his present urgency was prompted by the postwar talks. The newly formed United Nations, the ongoing scramble for influence and resources in Latin America, Africa, and Asia, and discussions about aid to Western Europe had created a context in which new ideas—or long neglected ones—might gain traction.

He titled the first chapter "The Collapse of Europe," in part to emphasize that the continent's postwar chaos was linked to a long history of moral decay, which had begun with the colonial project, especially the extraction of African people's labor and African natural resources for the use of Europeans. Both world wars, Du Bois argued, were the result of avarice and industrial plunder that had been characteristic of European (and, later, American) whites in the era of colonialism. They had put their humanity at risk by ignoring the moral claims of African people to local resources and to recognition as moral equals. The end of whiteness would be, for Du Bois, the imminent result of whites' own actions. Only by "reaching across the color line and abolishing race discrimination," and by providing meaningful work to all, could humans survive the devastation brought about by the current global excrescence of white supremacy.[34]

Du Bois emphasized that "the habit, long fostered, for forgetting and detracting from the thought and acts of the people of Africa, is not only a direct cause of our present plight, but will continue to cause trouble until we face the facts."[35] He had long been making similar arguments. In 1935's *Black Reconstruction,* he explicitly asserted that the book's demonstration of white supremacy's harm to white labor and other white interests would make sense only to those who already believed that African Americans were humans. In 1947, he knew how few white readers shared such a belief. *The World and Africa* was explicitly written to convince them that history could "easily prove"[36] that Black Africans were fully human.

Du Bois's interest in international peace was not new. According to the scholar Joy James, as early as 1920, he had declared that the end of white supremacy was a necessary condition for "the attainment of international peace and justice."[37] Yet as he had made clear in *Dusk of Dawn*, he also knew that whites would defend white supremacy as if their lives depended upon it, for to relinquish its presumptions would be to admit centuries of moral depravity. The situation was grim: international peace required precisely what white people could not bear to give up. Nevertheless, in the postwar context, with the vulnerability of white supremacy in evidence, he hoped that some white people might be receptive to revolutionary ideas, such as the proof of Black human brilliance he aimed to demonstrate in *The World and Africa*. He also knew that Black folk themselves needed every available reason to maintain the belief in their own humanity.

The World and Africa may offer Du Bois's most direct warning that the continued existence of white humanity depends on whites' ability to recognize Black humanity. He laid aside the subtlety of earlier texts and spoke directly:

> We hereby warn the world that no longer can Africa be regarded as pawn, slave or property of Europeans, Americans or any other people.
> Africa is for the Africans: its Land and Labor; its natural wealth and resources; its mountains, lakes and rivers; its cultures and its Soul.
> Hereafter it will no longer be ruled by Might nor by Power; by invading armies nor police, but by the Spirit of all its Gods and the Wisdom of its Prophets.[38]

While this declaration is aspirational, it is also uncompromising. The white world must finally and fully understand that, despite the claims of G. W. F. Hegel and other supposed authorities, Africa has a history as long and rich as any other continent populated by human cultures.

The World and Africa is thus a record of Du Bois's growing conviction that global white supremacy and its partner in crime, global capitalism, were unsustainable. In my view, he perceived the seeds of their destruction within the epistemology of white supremacy. In addition to the crimes of enslavement, he pointed out the alienation and exploitation of people and resources during the Industrial Revolution, which, he argued, were a consequence of the increased availability of goods made possible by slavery.[39] He had long held that the scramble for African and Arabian colonies in the nineteenth century had led to the First World War and had laid the ground for the Second.[40] An overreliance on the promise of capital rather than on the creativity of labor grew out of the "idea . . . in European minds that no matter what the cost in cruelty, lying, and blood, the triumph of Europe was to the glory of God and the untrammeled power of the only people on earth who deserved to rule."[41] The daily life of white folk in Europe and the United States became increasingly dependent on products obtained through colonial exploitation; even the white working class demanded tea, coffee, sugar, and imported oils. The domination of African and Asian nations for the sake of western markets seemed to be predestined—except from the perspective of the exploited. Yet the imbalance between capital and labor, greed and extraction was "hollow and fatal . . . as the next few years quickly showed."[42]

Many activists today insist that the global nature of production and profit management create a deep disconnect between the labor of the colonized and the benefit of the consumer. Du Bois agreed:

> Because of the stretch in time and space between the deed and the result, between the work and the product, it is not only usually impossible for the worker to know the consumer, or the investor, the source of his profit, but also it is often made impossible by law to inquire into the facts. Moral judgment of the industrial process is therefore difficult, and the crime is more a matter of ignorance rather than of deliberate murder and theft; but ignorance is a colossal crime in itself. . . . [It is] an indication of a collapsing civilization.[43]

To illustrate, he drew on an effective image: a young, white, British woman at a piano keyboard, the mahogany brutally extracted through exploitation, the ivory keys made possible by the murder of elephants, both dependent on the absolute degradation of a human culture and political system with its basis in democracy. The young woman is perhaps picking out a Mozart melody while contemplating where to take a summer vacation, blissfully ignorant of the pain and misery that underwrites her life.

In what sense did Du Bois mean that this civilization was on the brink of collapse? He wrote of "our present nervous breakdown, nameless fear, and often despair," which had arisen, in his view, from having to face, despite decades of confidence in the near-perfection of European and American cultures, that these nations were nearing breakdown.[44] Seemingly poised on the brink of "perfect accomplishment," these nations, which had grown out of the Industrial Revolution and had ushered in the prosperity of modernity and the flourishing of democracy, were now mired in the aftermath of the Great Depression, world wars, and genocide.[45] Whatever one's political stance or nationality, the news coming out of Germany and the sudden reversal of the former Allies' relationship with the Soviet Union were evidence of deep rifts in the human character. Western Europe, long perceived by white folks as the source of human culture, was now almost inconceivably in need of charitable aid.

The perfection of human culture, then, could not rise from the ashes of World War II. The fear and despair that Du Bois had identified were signals of a spiritual and moral collapse. Even though the Nazis had lost the war, Du Bois found little to celebrate, unless Europe and the rest of the white world could use its current vulnerability as an opportunity to take its rightful moral place in the world. As Mahmood Mamdani points out in his introduction to *The World and Africa*, Du Bois's project was not primarily to produce an accurate history of the "new nation-states of Africa." Rather, he "wanted to outline a world history that would provincialize Europe."[46] Such a strategy makes perfect sense against an ideology that held whiteness to be the summit of humanity and the center of civilization.

The World and Africa takes aim at the presumed naturalness of claims to white racial superiority by exploring the relatively recent idea that people can be sorted by skin color into useful categories that indicate human worth or ability. Having long accepted the consensus of the anthropological community that culture rather than race determines many group-based similarities, Du Bois wrote that "the separation of human beings by color seemed to have had less importance among the Egyptians than the separation by cultural status."[47] To support his arguments against the relevance of racial category to group-based human abilities and the concentration of human ability in whites, he focused on the wide range of African cultural achievement. In each chapter, he emphasized the people's artistic, scientific, and political activities to demonstrate both their humanity and their potential contributions in the larger human community. He also made it plain that democracy was not a theory or a practice that white folk had brought to Africa. Instead, to complicate the existing discourse on the postwar political stage, he showed that the capacity of African peoples for self-determination was their own particular inheritance. As white leaders made plans and doled out opportunities for participation in the United Nations, the North Atlantic Treaty Organization, and other multinational political, military, and economic projects, Du Bois asked them to step back and allow people of color to participate in their own destinies. Given his belief in the precarious hold of whiteness on global power, he may even have hoped to save white people from their own folly.

CONCLUSION

The World and Africa was Du Bois's final attempt to overcome the global presumption that Africans had no history, and, unlike the others, it appeared at a unique historical moment.[48] None of his attempts were complete histories of the Black people of the world, for their archeology, sociology, and historical research were incomplete. He would never have had time to steep himself in the archives of African nations, especially not as he approached eighty years of age. He was also aware that the white world, still steeped in prejudice and mistaking "personal desire for scientific proof," was not ready for a magisterial, scholarly work on the history of Africa and its diasporic peoples.[49] Instead, he wrote the book he was able to write, one he hoped would be useful to a Black diaspora who needed the reminder that they, too, were descended from genius.

Still, *The World and Africa* appeared at a curious, faltering moment in the history of white people. The upheavals of the first thirty years of the century, not least the Great Depression, suggested that capitalism was in real trouble economically. In Du Bois's view, it was in even greater peril morally. Thousands of white people had made or lost fortunes gambling on undertakings that relied on the brutal overwork and death of millions of Black people—the twentieth century's replay of the triangle trade.

In the foreword to *The World and Africa*, Du Bois described the burden of attempting, again, to present evidence of the indispensability of Africa and Africans to the flourishing of humanity and the anxiety of possessing so little time and expertise. But he recognized the urgency of the moment and his own position as grand old man of African American letters, and this moved him to take on the responsibility. His lifelong project—to hold up a mirror to white faces, to show them their own shortcomings, to ask the question that he himself so often faced: "What is it like to be a problem?"—obliged him to make the effort.

When Du Bois declared that the Holocaust was a moral calamity that had outstripped all previous programs of extractive violence and murder, he did not mean that it differed in kind from earlier atrocities.[50] In fact, "there was no Nazi atrocity—concentration camps, wholesale maiming and murder, defilement of women or ghastly blasphemy of childhood—which the Christian civilization of Europe had not long been practicing against colored folk in all parts of the world in the name of and for the defense of a Superior Race born to rule the world."[51] The Nazi achievement was to use bureaucratic means to make wholesale slaughter bloodless and efficient, removing it from the day-to-day lives of those in its midst. Employing a dehumanizing ideology, not against "exotic" forms of life on continents far from home but against neighbors and partners: this was the Third Reich's ghastly achievement. For Du Bois, the crucial explanandum was not how the Nazis were able to dehumanize local Jewish citizens but why the white world was able to see the Holocaust as a crime while tolerating the wrongs of colonialism and Jim Crow. In *The World and Africa* and *Color and Democracy*, he showed that white global leaders were working from a false belief in their own competence and moral aptitude. Du Bois hoped that this moment of white collapse and global reconsideration might allow for a new evaluation of white license, but he was profoundly disappointed.

In terms of wealth and power, white supremacy seems alive and well today. However, like Du Bois, we can never know what moments will mark a resurgence or a dying gasp. He understood that white supremacy would not go gently. Yet while the American prosperity of the 1950s might be used as a data point to counter his thesis, it was accompanied by the rise of the civil rights movement and by independence movements in African and Asian colonies. The birth pains of a post-whiteness Earth will be mighty, the upheavals will last a long time, but we cannot say that Du Bois was wrong.

CHAPTER 8

The Promise of the Black Flame

IN THE POSTSCRIPT to the first volume of *The Black Flame* trilogy, *The Ordeal of Mansart* (1957), Du Bois (as was his wont) spoke directly to the reader. He explained that he would have preferred to present and discuss the events in these books in a scholarly manner, but he was nearly ninety at this time and had few material resources. Thus, he turned to historical fiction—as he had in *The Quest of the Silver Fleece* (1911) and *Dark Princess* (1927)—to portray the material and ideological currents that had been flowing through the United States since the Civil War. With "much truth and no falsehood," he relied on his usual romanticism and his penchant for dotting fictional narratives with real people and histories to demonstrate the power of capital and white supremacy to shape the course of human life at every level, from individual opportunities to international affairs.[1] The second and third books in the trilogy, *Mansart Builds a School* (1959) and *Worlds of Color* (1961), are remarkable for the breadth of their scope in this regard. Though the books are uneven, their powerful account of interconnected racist and colonial repressions across half a century has led Gayatri Spivak to dub them "Du Bois's best novels."[2]

The trilogy's protagonist is Manuel Mansart, born during his father's lynching in Charleston, South Carolina, in 1877 and raised by his mother and grandmother to help lead the Black community. Mansart is drawn to higher education and through most of the narrative he serves as the president of a fictional Black land-grant college in Georgia. Mirroring Du Bois, he marries young and has children, is a fair-to-middling father, and meets the love of his life when he is much older, marrying this firebrand only after his first wife dies. Though various other fictional characters contribute to the books' moral, political, and sociological heft, the heart of the narrative is Mansart's lifelong work to understand the oppression of people of color and to support their struggle to lead decent lives within the stranglehold of white supremacy.

Most scholars hold that, by midcentury, Du Bois's political commitments became increasingly radical and his critical faculties less nuanced. He developed a growing affinity with socialism and even communism, though he sometimes parted from those ideologies around issues of race consciousness. (At least some communists were eagerly fighting white supremacist tendencies in the United States and Europe.)[3] Still, as Eric Porter argues, there was a point "after 1952 where his criticism [became] significantly less nuanced," especially vis-à-vis "communist states and leaders."[4]

The general assumption that Du Bois's work after *Dusk of Dawn* was compromised by political errors and age means that his later works are more often caricatured than studied. Yet Spivak notes the complexity of his thought in the trilogy, especially regarding the parallels between antiracist movements in the United States and anticolonialism elsewhere: "His efforts at making these connections were in sustained evolution, and found literary expression in the Black Flame trilogy."[5] I agree. These fascinating novels reveal midcentury moral and political dilemmas for Americans seeking justice and are especially intriguing on the subject of Du Bois's conception of whiteness, which continues to appear as arrogant, irrevocable license.

Generations of two fictional white families, the Breckenridges and the Scroggses, appear throughout the trilogy, although never with as much depth as they do in the first book. Du Bois used their interactions with each other and their impact on Mansart to explore how the psychological and moral contortions required by white supremacy may have deep implications for white Americans' own humanity. The two white families, vastly different in class and culture, are tragically alike in that all members are willing to shred their integrity, their intelligence, and much of their talent to maintain the relational structure of white supremacy. The narrative offers white readers tremendous insight into the damage that can be done by and to white folk who desperately strive to maintain the comfort of the familiar. *The Black Flame* trilogy may have literary and historical shortcomings, yet these sprawling books are unjustly ignored, especially insofar as they give white readers an unusual opportunity to study how white individuals and institutions construct their own narrative and material advantages to the detriment of people of color.[6]

During the 1920s and 1930s, Du Bois was able to travel, study, and make contacts that allowed him to investigate the global effects of white supremacy, and he repeatedly objected to material analyses that lacked the perspective of workers of color. In his view, white supremacy allows for the super-exploitation of people of color, who are compelled to do work that white laborers see as undignified or wretched. According to Henry Louis Gates Jr., both Du Bois and Frederick Douglass came to see the "status of the American Negro as part and parcel of a larger problem of international economic determination."[7] Yet as I have argued throughout this book, white Americans have more at stake than material advantage in their desperate attachment to white supremacy. Recognizing and making restitution for the wrongs of racism require a new way of understanding the world and our place in it, especially the moral status of ourselves and of those we have been taught to admire.

Like Gates, I believe Du Bois recognized that white supremacy is buttressed by global economic interests, and he clearly perceived that this goal lay behind the Atlantic slave trade. However, he never reduced the motivations of white supremacy to specific troublesome instances of material exploitation. The psychology, epistemology, and social practices of white supremacy, conscious and otherwise, had built a culture with ramifications far beyond simple economics. As the social and economic hierarchy reinforced the psychological and epistemic elements of whiteness, human interaction and self-perception became entangled in this racial regime, which now runs like a mineral substrate through all aspects of daily life. Racial oppression was not the first system of oppression in human history, but for white folk it has radically affected their sense of self and world order.

These themes recur throughout *The Black Flame* trilogy. Notably, the novels allow us to see, from the perspective of white characters, how law and custom work to obscure evidence of Black humanity. White epistemic failures to absorb such evidence are brought into sharp relief, and white characters end up much the worse for these errors. Readers cannot overlook the moral costs to white persons of a white supremacist system. In vignettes that combine comedy with tragedy, pillars of white society make ridiculous efforts to remain upright and morally innocent under the terms of an archaic hierarchy—whether by insisting that a Black member of the legislature be met at the side door rather than front door, by repeatedly attempting to hold their children to the conflicting and confounding expectations of white supremacy, or by denying themselves the talent and expertise of gifted employees of color.

For Du Bois, the post–Civil War era was key. He was convinced that slavery had been abolished primarily through the efforts of the enslaved, who, by refusing to work to support the plantocracy, traveling North to support the Union, and taking up arms against the Confederacy, had helped to ensure northern victory and trigger the postwar Reconstruction legislation that had recognized Black civic and political equality. Now African Americans faced the problem of overcoming white patterns of thought, feeling, and behavior that had been nurtured over centuries. Thus, although the trilogy can be seen as a narrative of failure—white failure to take up the challenge of recognizing Black humanity and dismantling white supremacy during and after Reconstruction—it is not a narrative of despair. Rather, it offers realistic portraits of characters who strive, on both sides of the color line, to build lives of good work and loving connection, despite hostile circumstances.

OVERVIEW OF THE TRILOGY

In *The Black Flame*, Du Bois's characters interact with a broad array of historical personages, from Booker T. Washington to Cecil Rhodes. World events repeatedly come up in discussions or are simply reported by the narrator, often in a fairly flat-footed manner. The novels explore the economics of the post-Reconstruction South, not only in terms of funding for a segregated educational system but via the political maneuverings of wealthy whites in the plantocracy, industry, and finance. Du Bois made it clear that, for abolition-democrats, including many of the emancipated, Reconstruction was a time of great hope, and his richly detailed characters help explicate the interests and motivations—conscious and otherwise—that drove events during that era.[8] Broadly speaking, the trilogy considers these historical currents via the interactions of four families: the Scroggses, the Breckinridges, the Du Bignons, and the Mansarts. By following three generations of white and Black American families, he explicates events in the United States and abroad from the end of the nineteenth century through the middle of the twentieth.

The trilogy opens in 1876, in the domestic parlor of Colonel Breckinridge and his wife Clarice.[9] Although their wealth has somewhat diminished since the Civil War, they still own a fine mansion on the waterfront in Charleston and still belong to high society there. The colonel is in demand this morning: two visiting men, Tom Mansart and Sam Scroggs, are making political appeals disguised as social calls. The vignette illustrates the tension within the postwar plantocracy, fated to lose its traditional power unless it joins forces with white labor or the formerly enslaved. Breckinridge is seen by others as "quality," as a man of integrity, yet he is befuddled and very unwilling to come to terms with a more perfect democracy. Clarice is equally confused about what the new era demands, especially about good etiquette. Together, lacking any real moral center, they ultimately fail to make solid connections with either group and, in their thoughtlessness, cause Tom Mansart's death.

Manuel Mansart, Tom's son, is the trilogy's protagonist, and Du Bois painted a vivid picture of the shifting, uncertain social, political, and economic environment into which the character is born. As the trilogy opens, the African American community in Charleston, across town from the Breckinridges' neighborhood, is cautiously optimistic, strategizing about how to realize the promise of postwar legislation as the faded and bewildered white population struggles to grasp the ramifications of abolition. During this time of uncertainty, Tom Mansart is serving in the South Carolina state legislature, where he was elected as a reform candidate.[10] As the situation devolves into tragedy, the book dramatizes on a human scale the dynamic Du Bois documented in *Black Reconstruction*: the fate of the formerly enslaved after the withdrawal of federal oversight, when poor and wealthy whites scrambled to obtain or preserve power without ever considering the possibility of an alliance with freedpeople.

Manuel Mansart, who is born at the very moment and place of his father's murder, grows up with a commitment to the uplift of his people. Through his eyes we see the founding of the Niagara Movement and the NAACP. He mourns Red Summer and celebrates the Harlem Renaissance. He advances from managing the Black schools in Atlanta to becoming president of the Georgia State Colored A&M College at Macon: in this fictional world, he is the first Black president of a Black college. There he meets Jean Du Bignon, a light-skinned descendant of a storied New Orleans Creole family, who comes to work for him as an administrative assistant, despite holding a PhD in sociology from the University of Chicago.[11] Du Bignon is relieved to be working and living among Black folk. Nevertheless, she is "not unconscious of the fact that these her people would not automatically or easily accept her, veiled as she was in a hated color of skin. . . . Acceptance would come ... for race was not color; it was inborn oneness of spirit and aim and wish; and this made this school her home; her very own."[12]

As Mansart and Du Bignon collaborate to make the college a center of learning and aspiration, Du Bignon works to educate him about world events and ideas that will allow him to lead more effectively. Meanwhile, the novels portray decades of American history via the experiences of Mansart, his children, and his students, including, as Du Bois wrote, "the worst experience through which the freed Negro had ever gone"—the terrible racial violence of 1919, which erupted in at least twenty-five African American massacres in New York City, Arkansas, Washington, D.C., and elsewhere around the United States.[13] Mansart's adult son Douglass is in Chicago on business when whites there start attacking Black Americans, and the violence continues for a week. After riding a Jim Crow car back to Atlanta, he vows to become rich enough to escape the power of white violence.[14] While his children are not all so lucky, Douglass does make good on this vow.

The character of Du Bignon is fascinating for many reasons, and her perspective on whiteness is particularly acute. She claims at one point that she wants to live with and come to know "colored people" because "they explain the whites," a stance that upends the centuries-long tradition of presuming that whiteness is a norm that needs no explanation.[15] For Du Bois as much as Du Bignon, observing Black lives and documenting the shapes into which they have been forced by white supremacy is a way to reveal the shape of whiteness. That is, Black experience constitutes a reflection of white pathology around race because it is the outcome of that pathology.[16] The segregation of education, religion, and public institutions and the violence that destroys black individuals and communities are demanded and sustained by white desires. Despite all evidence to the contrary, the majority of white people have long behaved as if they cannot work, live, or be educated or entertained alongside African Americans; the persistence of this racial injustice reflects the pathology of the white psyche in U.S. culture. Through Du Bignon's narrative, as well as through the experiences of other Black characters in the trilogy, we witness the depth of the white need to control Black Americans and the brutality that results when whites feel that their control is at risk. In the end, Du Bignon's confidence that she can solve the problem of whiteness through study gradually erodes into hopelessness—perhaps a reflection of Du Bois's own experience of the United States.

Like Du Bois himself, Mansart is influenced by a smart and committed woman to move leftward politically—although he never goes as far as Du Bois did. Yet Du Bignon eventually convinces him that the Black community should be working with white labor rather than looking for support among the "honorable" white upper class. The varied experiences of Mansart's children also teach him about politics. While the oldest, Douglass, becomes a wealthy businessman in Chicago, Revels, the second son, works diligently to enter the white-dominated legal community in New York and becomes a respected lawyer. For much of the trilogy, however, Mansart's daughter Sojourner remains a puzzle, repeatedly described as unattractive, shy, almost invisible: "There seemed no place for her in the world."[17] But she, too, finally comes into her own, discovering a love of African music and embarking on a successful and complicated marriage to an AME pastor, Roosevelt Wilson.

Yet there are tragedies among the children as well. Bruce, the youngest son and his mother's favorite, wanders into some petty scrapes that are exacerbated by the white supremacist legal system. After attempting to flee jail, he is caught and eventually executed. Du Bois's writing makes it clear that he saw the violence of the carceral system as a key component of white supremacy. Even Revels, who eventually becomes a judge, faces discrimination so extreme that he barely survives professionally.

Alongside the travails of Du Bignon and Mansart's family, the trilogy offers glimpses into the world of Sam Scroggs, the white labor leader who had competed with Tom Mansart for Colonel Breckinridge's attention in 1876. Two generations of Scroggses are betrayed, in ways, by the promises of wealthy whites and by their own conviction that they deserve better than to join forces with Black labor. Meanwhile, the Breckenridges' children also fail to thrive, primarily because their parents are more concerned with status than with their own family. The parents' assumption that good breeding will produce happy, virtuous children results in both heartache and further cruelty toward vulnerable Black families. As the trilogy moves into the twentieth century, it reveals that new wealth does not lead to happiness any more than old money did. On both sides of the color line, the characters who lead rewarding lives are those who work toward justice and progress for all.

As Mansart reaches middle age, Du Bignon advises him to travel and study the world, to gain knowledge that will make him more impressive to white politicians and philanthropists and make him more effective as a leader. He visits England, France, and Asia, paralleling Du Bois's own travels during the 1920s and 1930s. There, Mansart witnesses both white wealth and white poverty. He is haunted by a scene in a pub in the London slums, where a "drunken

Madonna" is enjoying a night out with her baby in her arms. But the child's crying disturbs the crowd, and a barman threatens to toss her out if she cannot quiet the baby. She does so by giving the child a gin-soaked handkerchief to chew on. From this incident Mansart learns that there are white people in other twentieth-century "civilized" nations who suffer as much as Black folk do in the United States. He considers the scene in the pub, with "the usual number of beer-sodden men cradling head on arms in despairing attempt to get away from it all."[18] They may not be getting their arms cut off for failing to work fast enough on a Belgian colonial plantation, but a life spent toiling for others for minimal pay, where the only respite involves drinking to oblivion or addicting infants to gin, is not a good life.

As the trilogy progresses, some of Mansart's grandchildren begin to flee America for African cooperatives or seek out other ways to step outside of a world controlled by whiteness. Among them is Adelbert, Douglass's son, who concludes that the key characteristic of white folk is their "wealthy, loud, swaggering."[19] He believes that his own father, who shares these characteristics, has become virtually white, and he wants none of it. There are hints that Mansart, too, like Du Bois, has come to see greed and the desire to exploit labor as the heart of oppression. Still, when socialists attempt to claim that all laborers are in the same situation, one of Mansart's students pointedly observes that "most eligible American Negroes still can't vote; we still ride 'Jim Crow' cars; we are still, in most cities, refused accommodations by hotels, motels, restaurants; we still have difficulty getting a decent place to live; we're still refused better paid jobs and a chance for promotion."[20] White supremacy and capitalism work hand in hand to divide the laboring classes and kill talented Black children.

After Mansart's wife Susan, long-suffering and nearly silent, dies, he considers retiring in order to marry Du Bignon and share a life of travel and study with her.[21] But then the two fall victim to red-baiting. Like Du Bois, Du Bignon is indicted as a foreign agent and is then acquitted in a trial that differs from Du Bois's only in its drama. After she and Mansart finally marry and try to begin a modest life together, they are hounded by government informers who cause trouble by reporting the wide-ranging conversations hosted at their home. When Mansart is diagnosed with stomach cancer, the couple moves in with Revels. Mansart dies, surrounded by family, understanding that he has played some role in the ongoing struggle for justice.

CHAPTER 8

WHITE LICENSE

The opening scene of the trilogy almost deserves a diorama. On a fall morning in 1876, the occupants of the Breckinridge manor await two very different supplicants: one who is poor, white, and hateful; another who is poor, Black, and hopeful. Sam Scroggs wants the landed gentry to back white workers who are fighting Black laborers' quest for political power and economic parity. Meanwhile, Thomas Mansart, once enslaved and now a Black member of the South Carolina legislature, hopes to persuade the colonel that the gentlefolk should ally politically with the freed people, with whom they supposedly share a sense of honor. Members of the Black community have dispatched Mansart to invite Breckinridge to a meeting that evening, where they hope to show him how they can benefit the old guard. Colonel Breckinridge is not happy to see either man.

Though Mansart arrives earlier, he is sent around to the side entrance, as is traditional, so Scroggs gets the first audience with Breckinridge. As it happens, the white political establishment has no intention of diluting its power in favor of either side, but it does need votes from at least one of these groups in order to maintain control of the state capitol. Thus, Breckinridge has been told to promise that the elites will support white labor. Scroggs will accept this guarantee only from the colonel, as the poor whites trust no one else. Meanwhile, the Black community also views the colonel as a man of quality who will keep his word.

Breckinridge promises Scroggs that white laborers will be hired for good and important work at decent wages and that Black labor will be relegated to menial jobs at low pay. Then, at his wife's insistence, he meets briefly with Mansart. The colonel is honest enough to acknowledge that Black folk can defend their interests against the racism of poor whites only if they have the vote. In his befuddled virtue, he is moved by Mansart's straightforward request for help in safeguarding the Black community's interests and agrees to meet with the Black activists to give them counsel. When he realizes that his promises conflict and that he cannot serve both camps, he visits his club—a gathering of political power and wealth—to ask for advice.

The ensuing conversation is predictably quarrelsome as most of the club members do not possess even Breckinridge's minimal scruples. That meeting takes so long that Breckinridge misses his appointment with the Black community. But his wife, Clarice, worried about his honor, has attended in his stead, determined to assure participants that her husband means to keep his word. Meanwhile, the poor white workers have learned about the Black community's gathering and are alarmed anew at the idea of Black organization. In an all-too-plausible confluence of events, Mansart struggles to bring Mrs. Breckinridge safely home (and away from their meeting, where the presence of a lone white woman would spell disaster for the Black attendees) just as the whites decide that the Black activists have taken her hostage. The ensuing violence is devastating to the Black community, and Tom dies in a hail of bullets at his front door. Miranda, Tom's wife, gives birth to their son Manuel literally in the blood of his father.

These encounters and their tragic dénouement reveal a crucial element of white comportment. Notably, Breckinridge insists that Mansart use the side door because he is aware that Scroggs is "lurking" and will witness their exchange.[22] This illustrates the extent to which white comportment is a performance for other white people. Even though postwar circumstances have encouraged the colonel to alter his approach to Mansart, he still needs to be seen as truly white, especially before a witness of lower status. Thus, he comports himself with the arrogance to which he feels entitled. This comportment overlooks Mansart's evident humanity as well as his perfect manners, both of which, were Mansart white, Breckinridge's moral code would require him to respect.

Scroggs despises rich white folk only slightly less than he despises those who were formerly enslaved, yet he and his fellow workers are willing to throw their votes to the incumbent governor, Wade Hampton, and the traditional ruling class if white laborers are guaranteed decent wages and, more importantly, the promise that Black citizens will not receive either the vote or equal opportunity in employment. For, as Du Bois wrote:

> [Scroggs] hated Negroes with a deep, blind hatred. They typified to him all of his unavailing struggle to be a man. They took the food out of his mouth, they made it impossible for his children to be educated; they sneered at him and his scrawny, ill-clad wife and dirty cabin. For all he had suffered at the hands of the rich white world, he was going to take it out on these Negroes, and this man Breckinridge and Wade Hampton were going to make compact with him and keep it, or "By God!"[23]

Yet Scroggs is not a one-dimensional villain. His malice toward people of color is not justified, but it is explicable. He has absorbed the message that the world owes him a certain standard of living, yet he remains trapped in a different, lower status. Via Scroggs, Du Bois was able to reveal the narrow social, political, and economic structures that have driven poor white laborers to aim their greatest hatred at the only people who are even less favored by those structures.

Eventually, we learn that Sam Scroggs has also been killed in the riot that killed Tom Mansart.[24] His young son, Abe, then becomes "the main support of the large family."[25] Abe comes of age in the early 1890s, and he is drawn into the political snares of Tom Watson, a populist leader, and Ben Tillman, a white supremacist whose political message focuses dehumanizing Black Americans. But his hatred of the Black community can be traced to one awful event in his childhood. After her husband's death, his widowed mother struggles to feed her ten children, so poor that she has to live among Black neighbors. One day, those neighbors slaughter a fat hog as food for the winter. In a careful interchange, Mrs. Scroggs asks one of them, Nancy, to sell her a bit of meat for her children's dinner, as the stores are closed. The widow promises to pay for the meat soon, but everyone knows there is no money. Nancy refuses, knowing that she has her own children to feed, but Mrs. Scroggs lays claim to some offal within her reach and gathers it up. Even such poor stuff is a loss to Nancy, but her children turn the theft to their advantage, taunting the Scroggs family as "crackers stealin' hog-guts!"[26] The complexity of this ugly moment is exquisite. Nancy knows that any attempt to stop Mrs. Scroggs's theft will fail, not least because the police and courts will take the widow's side. Meanwhile, Mrs. Scroggs tries desperately to maintain the pretense that she will pay for these chitterlings, and Abe is cut to the bone by the mockery of the Black children who witness his mother's shame.

With this history in his past, Abe joins the Klan after leaving school at age fourteen and takes an active role in a horrific lynching that haunts him thereafter. To live with his brutality, he convinces himself

> that he was doing God's appointed work in helping restrain or exterminate black criminals. His attitude toward black folk now changed. He had disliked them before but now he despised them because they were not really human. He learned something of this in school, more of it in the newspapers, and read one or two frightening books. Manifestly it was his duty to make it impossible for this vermin to live like other men.[27]

This exploration of hatred illustrates the connection between white comportment and the epistemic opacity and sense of innocence demanded by white supremacy. Abe has judged poor Black families as lazy or otherwise responsible for their own hardship. He refuses to see the similarity between his mother and Nancy; he must convince himself that these struggling families are not the same. Yet both women deserve better; neither should be forced to face her children's hunger. Abe will not blame his family's deprivation on his father's shiftlessness or on inequalities in the economic system. Instead, he sees his mother's humiliation before her Black neighbors as not just a violation of the proper order but as the fault of those Black folk. The consistent presumption that whites are the center of the moral and economic universe plays out in a dramatic and terrible way.

It is not surprising that white license plays out in both individual careers and, as Du Bois might have put it, the destiny of races. We see this clearly in the genocidal campaign against Indigenous Americans and the enslavement of Africans, which were followed by every manner of insult toward these patient (in two senses) groups. When people of color made the rational decision to try to control their own destinies, white supremacists viewed such efforts as presumptuous and worthy of punishment; and white Americans of all classes believed they were entitled to mete out punishment to people of color. *The Black Flame* repeatedly portrays instances of this sort of arrogant white comportment. White school leaders, mayors, and governors, who are nominally equally responsible to both their Black and white constituents, repeatedly direct the bulk of their budgets to whites-only facilities and spend a pittance on infrastructure in Black communities. They find African American factotums who are happy to accept small favors in return for remaining silent about graft and injustice. Manuel Mansart treads a fine line in this regard. Somehow he is able to maintain his job as college president, even when he disagrees with his white superiors' decisions. Though the narrative attributes his professional success to talent and to his political and financial skills, his sons are quick to accuse him of Uncle Tomism.

The Black Flame was published in the years after the Supreme Court's decision in *Brown v. Board of Education of Topeka* (and its companion case, *Brown II*, which allowed desegregation to take place "with all deliberate speed"), during early municipal efforts toward desegregation.[28] Du Bois had been shocked that the Court was willing, to any extent, to relinquish white supremacy and gratified by the ruling, despite his disagreement with the NAACP's general aim of integration.[29] He expressed that surprise through the character of Mansart, who is concerned that Black teachers and principals will lose their jobs en masse and that Black children will be forced into white schools where they will be terrorized, abused, and made to doubt their own capacities.[30] Desegregation is, of course, a just outcome, particularly if it results in equality of educational opportunities among all pupils. Yet under white supremacy, funding, mapping, and all other decisions involving public education were historically made by white people in consultation with other whites. Mansart attempts to influence such decisions, especially budgetary inequities, but he has little success in moving his white superiors. Even now, when legally mandated discrimination has been dismantled, whiteness often runs roughshod over the life chances of community members.

Early on, Mansart became aware that white people "had the power, they had the wealth; they owned the earth."[31] His children learn the same lesson. Though they are middle class, well educated, and talented, they struggle to create comfortable adult lives. Du Bois wrote: "The education of the Mansart children had emphasized being unselfish, not lying, nor cheating, nor stealing. Yet much of this moral teaching was nullified by the example of the surrounding white world."[32] That example includes everyone: from their neighbors to the president of the United States. In the Potsdam peace talks, "the war of the worlds was reborn because Truman held the greatest secret of the modern world. It gave him a power which drove him wild. He was sure the United States was master of the universe. At Potsdam he only whispered it but the arrogance with which he conducted himself was unbounded."[33]

The trilogy's second volume portrays the impact of World War I on the African American community, one of Du Bois's lifelong interests. After Mansart's two sons and nephew are drafted, his wife, Susan, declares, "'They're taking my babies to fight for their country; what country? They have no country; they are stuck pigs in a dirty pen!'"[34] Mirroring Du Bois's own hopes, Mansart tries to find a bright side: the army will have to integrate, and the nation will have to treat Black men as citizens.[35] But this is too optimistic. White nations' colonial squabbles destroy not only the people of color in Asia and Africa but also the Black Americans who serve in the war. The three young Mansart men—Manuel and Susan's two sons and their nephew—are betrayed and bewildered by the violence of trench warfare, aerial bombing, and their own nation's ill-treatment of Black troops. The "colored" troops are, of course, not integrated; in one vivid scene, a Black regiment kills their white southern officers from behind during a confrontation with the Germans in which the Allies emerge triumphant.

The nephew dies in battle, and both of Mansart's sons return home deeply disillusioned, although they respond differently to their experiences.

Mansart's career in education also reveals the role of white heedless comportment. As head of Atlanta's Black schools, he knows that white schools serve only 67 percent of the city's students yet receive approximately 89 percent of available funding; in other words, each white school receives roughly eight times the funding of a Black school. Mansart watches as the city's white-dominated school board does everything possible to funnel extra funds to white students. Its members do not seem to be able to endure anything like parity; they refuse to allow even the appearance of propriety. Higher education also suffers. When Mansart becomes a college president, he observes that whites focus first on "how to divert these [otherwise designated] federal funds mainly to the whites. But the silly Negroes protested, as if they had any real right to federal income!"[36]

It may be easy to dismiss white corruption as typical human greed. But when whites who already enjoy relative luxury at home or in school spend precious energy working to deprive already poor schools of their fair share, the extent of white arrogance is obvious.[37] Such people cannot be satisfied until every dime is theirs; they assume they have the right to the whole world and everything in it. It does not naturally occur to them to them that they are stealing from those who have the least. Without shame, they openly divert money to the most advantaged and congratulate themselves in full view of the few Black administrators who work behind the scenes.

In the final book of the trilogy, Mansart begins to see the global consequences of white comportment, ignorance, and innocence. When Jean Du Bignon convinces him to take a world tour, his first stop is the English country estate of Sir John Rivers. Mansart is immensely appreciative of the life of the manor house, the beautiful grounds, and the excellent manners of his hosts. Nevertheless, when asked what strikes him about this life, he replies, "The idleness." When pressed for explanation, he points that Sir John's lifestyle is funded by the work of his grandfather, who "pioneered in the Niger delta," trading in gold, pepper, and tin. Mansart points out that, while the grandfather deserved some reward for his effort, his progeny continue to reap the rewards while doing no work at all. Meanwhile, even if the workers in Niger were compensated fairly for their labor (as we can assume they were not), their descendants do not continue to profit from that labor.

Sir John explains that this apparent difference comes down to the rules of property and thus is not unjust. However, his daughter Sylvia, who is flirting with socialism, reminds him that the rules of property in England are an invention of the wealthy, not a naturally occurring system. Admitting as much, Sir John suggests that this is a brilliant feature of the British system: some people are born to rule, and others are not.[38] Aristocracy, he claims, has led to human advances as no other system has. As a result, those who have more deserve more. Sylvia disagrees, asserting that her family has done nothing but be born into luck. Her family is used to her strange ideas and disregards them as the folly of youth, but Mansart finds her a breath of fresh air, even though her own lifestyle is also supported by this ill-gotten wealth.

While white comportment, ignorance, and innocence are conceptually separate, white people's actions tend to demonstrate various combinations of these traits simultaneously. For instance, the school administrators who run roughshod over the right of Black people to receive a decent, well-funded education demonstrate a comportment that is heedless of anything like justice, among other things. They simultaneously exhibit ignorance of Black students' humanity and merit and the fact of their own mediocrity. Yet they will maintain that they are acting appropriately, that they are innocent of wrongdoing, and they often believe this. Because they hold political power, they will not be held to account, so their half-baked certitudes are sufficient.

In his portrayal of the Breckinridges, Du Bois echoed his repeated comment in *Black Reconstruction* that Black humanity and political equality were "inconceivable" to white southerners with political influence. Even those who had developed intimate relations with enslaved people were so enmeshed in the worldview of white supremacy that they could only conceive of Black people in subhuman roles. Breckinridge's exchange with Tom Mansart is telling in this regard. Even after Mansart clearly explains the advantages to white wealth of a well-educated and well-compensated Black workforce, Breckinridge interprets Mansart's proposal as an ignorant desire for an elevated status that does not suit him and that he cannot fully envision. Ironically, Breckinridge is the one who does not comprehend the truth of Tom's personhood or recognize Mansart and his colleagues as politically interested citizens of Charleston. It requires a good deal of effort to misperceive such plain evidence.

Unlike her husband, Clarice Breckinridge is willing to converse with Tom Mansart, but only out of curiosity. She is confused by his commitment to representing his own people and his insistence on having an immediate answer from the colonel—what could be so urgent? While her comportment is slightly different from her husband's, she is no less affected by the epistemic opacity of whiteness:

> As she crossed the dining room she was thinking: "Of course, I could understand all this so easily if Negroes were folks in the sense that I am; but are they? Could they possibly be? Perhaps, partially—a little; but in just that area of lack they must be restrained, guided. And where there is no real lack nor difference, should they not be free? For who could or would drive or compel them?" She paused for a moment, puzzled; then opened the Colonel's study door.[39]

Elsewhere in his work, Du Bois made it clear that whites' difficulty in recognizing Black humanity has nothing to do with lack of contact. Here we learn that the Breckinridges had held enslaved Black laborers, including house servants, before and during the war. Black men and women had been trusted to raise their daughter and carry out complex tasks. In the postwar years, the real manager of their estate is Sanford, a light-skinned Black man who is the colonel's unacknowledged cousin.[40] The text skillfully captures the epistemic oddness of Colonel Breckinridge's simultaneous knowledge and ignorance: he both knows and does not know that this formerly enslaved man, who is far more gifted at running an estate than the colonel will ever be, is a blood relation and deserves far more than he can legally claim.

Sanford is a rich and intriguing character, though he plays only a small part in the trilogy. After the tragic events that open the novel, Breckinridge moves to his country plantation, which has been falling to ruin. Sanford rescues the property and the colonel's lifestyle. Despite knowing that Sanford is the son of his own uncle, Breckinridge never objected to Sanford's enslavement before Emancipation. Neither has he acted since to recognize the familial relationship. Yet when the colonel's friends and bankers begin hounding him to put a white man in charge of his affairs, he insists that he has been served faithfully and well by Sanford, which the reader knows is true. Even so, the colonel does not reveal that Sanford is a Breckinridge.

Eventually, Sanford's position as manager becomes untenable: he has been challenged too many times by white bankers; and when the Colonel writes a large check for the support of Sanford's daughter and her husband, he is accused of fraud. Breckinridge stands by Sanford, asserting his honor and offering him higher pay, but the manager insists he must leave: "I don't want more pay. I get enough. I want to live like a man—and I don't want to have to kill nobody."[41] In this moment the colonel turns toward Sanford "curiously, as though seeing him for the first time, which was not far from true." He looks the manager in the eye and begs him to remain in service. But Sanford explains:

> John Breckinridge, I'm your first cousin by blood, as you know damned well. I promised my father, your uncle, to look after you as long as you needed me. He said it was my duty as a Breckinridge. I have been honest, hard-working and faithful to my trust as your records will prove. You've treated me like you treated your horses. You took no notice of me as a man and your closest living relative. You pretended to forget my existence because you knew well how close I was to you and how like you I looked. All Charleston knew it and laughed.[42]

Breckinridge reacts to this speech, and to Sanford's departure, as if *he* is the injured one. He cannot imagine what it would be like to be Sanford, an intelligent, feeling human being who has been denied every sort of social recognition. The combination of epistemic opacity and moral failure is stunning but realistic. Du Bois portrayed Breckinridge not as a moral monster but as a weak and ignorant man who suffers from his own shortcomings—though not as much as the others he harms. He knows that his cousin is a better, wiser manager than he would be himself, yet he does not recognize that this fact upends the entire system that has placed Breckinridge where he stands, befuddled amid luxuries.

Du Bois's trilogy repeatedly reminds the reader that white ignorance of Black humanity cannot be accounted for by a lack of contact with African Americans. One example involves the character Henry Grady, a journalist and part owner of the *Atlanta Constitution*, who believes that whites must socially dominate African Americans. According to another character, Sebastian Doyle, a light-skinned Black man, whose political genius can be exercised only on the margins, "Grady knew nothing of Negroes. Brought up beside them, he ha[d] never seen them or realized they are human."[43] This sort of resistance is familiar to readers of *John Brown* and *Black Reconstruction*. Here, however, Du Bois delineated a further sort of ignorance: "Worse than that, [Grady] doesn't even know the mass of whites. He idealizes or fails to see them."[44] This failure even to properly apprehend whiteness complements the white ignorance that cannot absorb evidence of Black humanity.

We see the depth of this opacity in the Breckinridge family's relationship with Aunt Betsy, the mother of Tom Mansart's wife, Miranda. Among the Breckinridges' social clan, Betsy is considered the sagest of the servants.[45] She "seemed to know everything" and had midwifed many of the births in the white community.[46] Yet despite her wisdom and her medical skills, none of the white families see her as entitled to full human dignity. Without a doubt, Betsy would have provided even better service to an employer who had treated her as a knowledgeable professional and compensated her accordingly. Here again, however, whites' need to maintain their sense of superiority undercuts their own interests.

This dynamic parallels Du Bois's research on the public psychological wage that whiteness bestows on white labor, as delineated in *Black Reconstruction* and in a wealth of secondary scholarship. The phenomenon is richly instantiated by the Scroggs family. In one sense, Sam Scroggs wants what he should want, what most Americans want: a good life for his family, including meaningful work and a proper education for his children. But he cannot have this without money, and he believes that money will be out of reach so long as Black labor competes for the same jobs and the same civil status. He overlooks the fact that the plantocracy's stranglehold on wages and opportunity would loosen if white and Black laborers were to join together to demand more. Even more tellingly, he does not recognize that he and his family failed to thrive even when Black workers were still enslaved. It does not occur to Scroggs and his ilk that African American families would like also to survive, to have good clothing and a good education, let alone that they might have the same right to these things as he does. The depth of this mental derangement allows Scroggs to imagine that wealthy whites will pay white workers a living wage even while Black workers and their families are forced to accept lower wages and wretched working conditions. In short, Sam Scroggs and Colonel Breckinridge share a peculiar incapacity. They assume that "men must live as men had lived in the South for centuries; nothing else was conceivable. Therefore slavery must be restored in all but name, with perhaps [the] disappearance of human sale, which after all had nothing to do with the essence of the system. So thought the sons of Southern planters almost to a man."[47]

The ignorance of whites and their false braggadocio, their insistence upon acting as if they own the whole world, reveals the epistemic asymmetry that characterizes white supremacy. White people are not in any way superior to people of color; they carry on the charade, are exhausted by the pretense, and are fearful of discovery. Meanwhile, as Du Bois illustrated, Black folk are fully aware that white supremacy is a sham yet cannot reveal this awareness for fear of injury or death. White characters maintain a stranglehold on their claim to innocence, to supremacy—a grasp that would not be so tight if they were convinced of its truth. Abe Scroggs has seen his mother's unbearable shame witnessed by their Black neighbors; Colonel Breckinridge knows that his Black cousin sees his helplessness. The whole enterprise is a house of cards that routinely disintegrates and is frantically rebuilt as white men and women protect their "dignity" through violence.

Thus, the epistemic shortcomings of whiteness—that they will not see the worth of people of color or their own shortcomings—are linked to comportment. Because whites must maintain their pretense of superiority, they strut, shout, and swagger. These masks may occasionally slip, but they receive frantic adjustment whenever white folk are in danger of being found out—which, given the precarious foundations of whiteness, is almost all the time: "The white always felt a Negro was watching him and acted his assumed part accordingly."[48] Meanwhile, because of the asymmetry of epistemology under white supremacy, they refuse to acknowledge that their charade is doomed to fail: "And Negroes did watch them from behind another veil. This was a veil of amusement or feigned, impudent humility. Through gay laughter ran a vein of cynical contempt and 'schaden-freude': of cutting, jeering mockery. Thus happy, careless guffaws hid bitter hate and even despair with impenetrable good humor."[49]

Still, whatever their similarities, the white characters do not represent a monolithic obstacle. Abe Scroggs, shaped by poverty and shame, resents his own station in life while clinging to the fiction of white supremacy. He kills a Black man during a lynching spree, then quells his guilt by claiming divine purpose, as I have noted.[50] His personal experiences with African Americans, perhaps especially the charity that some had extended to his family, were no match for the lessons in school and church, which told him that whites were the true humans and the children of God. In contrast, Abe's cousin Joe, a labor organizer, is tempted by the prospect of teaming up with Black workers, despite his upbringing as a white supremacist. Joe marries the Breckinridges' granddaughter, who learns to see through the Veil of white supremacy and becomes an ally of Jean Du Bignon in her attempt to organize the union from the left. In this context, Joe Hill and other almost mythical white activists, including John Brown, are invoked as carriers of insight and hope.

Whites' commitment to their moral innocence motivates their epistemic structure, providing cover for much that is abhorrent in white comportment and inspiring many of their most oppressive behaviors. The Breckinridges, for instance, maintain a perverse sense of virtue and the resilient presumption that what they do is always for the best. The colonel is a startling picture of white quality. He is torn by his intention to tell a lie, even though the lie will be to his advantage and will be told to Scroggs, whom he considers to be his inferior. He disagrees strongly with the new legal position of the emancipated but cannot bring himself to support perverting the justice system for the benefit of "money-grabbers" who wish to benefit from convict leasing. He even tells his club colleagues that he will speak the truth to the Black labor group: admit that whites from every class in South Carolina intend to deprive Black folk of the vote and political office. He declares, "I'll do all in my power to stop turning our courts into tools to restore slavery and machinery for manufacturing crime for money-grabbers to fatten on."[51]

Within the bounds of white supremacy, the colonel maintains his stance as a perfect gentleman. But despite this veneer of honor, Breckinridge is repeatedly wrongfooted. He has obviously profited from the enslavement of human beings and has enforced the brutality by which this system was maintained in the antebellum South. Moreover, on the night of Tom Mansart's death, he tarries so long at his club, insisting that he cannot lie to the Black activists, that he never actually gets to the meeting he promised to attend. Neither does he keep either of the fine promises he had made the day before. In the end, Breckinridge's dithering and his wife's gormless behavior result in Mansart's murder. It is Mansart who truly exhibits honor, taking responsibility for Clarice's safety when she comes to the meeting of Black activists and then is trapped there by the white mob. When he attempts to get her to safety, he is killed by people who believe he is attempting to abscond with her.

Revealing the learned delicacy of the female aristocrat, Clarice faints at the sight of Tom's murder and then becomes ill; she does not get to explain that he was innocent until she feels it is too late to do any good. At that point, when she understands her own role in his death, she virtuously faints away again. Afterward she becomes anxious, depressed, unable to function normally. Finally, while her husband is out of town, she commits suicide, unable to live with her guilt and sorrow. At first glance, this act seems to be redemptive: Clarice appears to accept responsibility for her role in the catastrophe. In fact, however, her suicide is the apotheosis of her white guilt rather than any true reckoning with accountability. She does not attempt to publicize her knowledge of the events, does not attempt to clear Mansart's name or provide for his widow and son. Rather, she wallows in her distress until she takes her own life.

The circumstances of Clarice Breckinridge's death are easy to cast as accidental; wealthy white people need only an appearance of propriety to create an acceptable cover for scandal. Yet when the colonel reads his wife's suicide note, he understands that he shares responsibility for Mansart's murder.[52] He is so shaken by this knowledge that he plans his own suicide. Still, like his wife, Breckinridge does not publicize the truth of Tom Mansart's death. His guilt is at best a shadow of true accountability, twisted by his commitment to supremacy. Rather than bearing the weight of Mansart's death and the horror of his family's situation, the Breckinridges see themselves as the center of the tragedy. They plan their suicides to avoid feeling the shame of their errors. Even as Clarice tries to spare her husband by taking responsibility herself, she consigns Mansart to infamy, his wife and child to penury. The public narrative continues to protect the innocence of these pillars of southern white quality.

The trilogy is peopled with white Americans, both fictional and historical, who are aware that racial oppression is an injustice yet never manage to do anything to improve the system that supports it. Joe Scroggs does not quite create a coalition with Black labor; President Franklin Roosevelt, who is generally painted as an excellent man and leader, does not make sure that domestic and agricultural laborers are eligible for Social Security benefits; the children of bankers and politicians critique the system but do not take material steps to end it or join forces with Black activists. All remain satisfied with their own perceived goodness and perspicacity, and many feel that the world's injustices have wronged *them*. President Harry Truman reaches the height of white innocence: convinced of his rightness, he claims to have lost no sleep over his decision to drop atomic bombs on Japanese citizens. According to Du Bois, Truman is so assured in his arrogance that he fails to listen to others whose worldview is more informed than his own. He simply cannot conceive of himself as wrong.

THE HARM TO WHITE PEOPLE

Even as *The Black Fame* painfully demonstrates how catastrophic whiteness is for people of color, it reveals the harm that whites themselves suffer in the grip of white supremacy. Shortly after finishing the trilogy, Du Bois wrote that white folks had been "ruined" by segregation.[53] In his view, artificially separating one group from another had created not only asymmetrical epistemic capacities but any number of unrealistic and ridiculous expectations. Without doubt, the moral impairment and epistemic opacity that arise from perceived supremacy are deeply injurious to whites.

In the trilogy's final volume, Du Bois fictionalized an actual episode that had taken place when he was serving as editor of *The Crisis*. During a business meeting, Oswald Garrison Villard, a white co-founder of the journal and a leader of the NAACP, had declared that, if *The Crisis* were going to print a monthly list of lynching victims, it should also print a monthly list of African American criminals. In the context of the novel, Du Bois wrote, "This aroused the colored editor almost to fury."[54] Consider the moral insensibility that Villard revealed in this so-called attempt at balanced reporting. Perhaps he actually believed that the crimes of Black people were equivalent to the brutality of white violence against Black folk; perhaps he was simply taking a murky stab at fairness. In either case, however, his humanity was degraded. As Du Bois's fictional stand-in, James Burghardt, declares, "Crime is human, but lynching is race discrimination."[55] These words vastly understate Villard's error.

In the trilogy, white supremacy leads to Clarice Breckinridge's suicide and to Colonel Breckinridge's guilt and shame. It influences his incapacity to recognize his business manager's status as his own cousin. They are not the only white characters to self-destruct because of a narrow worldview, expectations of privilege, and social disappointment: politicians, artists, and scholars all find themselves unable to flourish in the rarified air of white wealth, cut off from the satisfaction of real work and genuine human relationships.

Working-class and poor white characters are similarly haunted by white supremacy. After Manuel Mansart becomes a teacher, he moves his family to the small town of Jerusalem, Georgia. Du Bois described the white members of that community: "Fear gripped them, and especially fear of the Negro; especially the black ghost of a past they did not dare forget—why, they could not say. But the Problem was there like a vast, dark hand. They were always conscious of it; their lives were efforts at pretending to escape its grip, but they never could, they never dared."[56] White folk, both good and bad, are afraid to confront a massive, obvious, unspeakable wrong.

CONCLUSION

> [A] majority of the leaders of the Niagara Movement recognized that white cooperation in fighting anti-Negro prejudices was absolutely essential.
> —W. E. B. Du Bois, *Mansart Builds a School*

The Black Flame trilogy was a prodigious accomplishment. Du Bois produced 1,200 typed pages between May 1949 and 1955, beginning when he was eighty-one years old.[57] According to the scholar Brent Edwards, Du Bois had a difficult time finding a publisher for the manuscript, which may have looked like a "sprawling, quixotic indulgence in nostalgia by a very old man."[58] The books are still unjustly neglected, although Herbert Aptheker, Du Bois's literary executor, argues that they are the "most revealing work from Du Bois's pen."[59] Certainly, they do not fit neatly into the genre: single chapters can range from fictional narrative to historical lesson to a political *cri de coeur*.[60] Nonetheless, they offer a unique perspective on the psychosocial, political, and theoretical crises of a long American century.

Du Bois's picture of whiteness had developed complexity since his 1940 publication of *Dusk of Dawn*. His trilogy reveals some sympathy for his befuddled white characters, even his worst villains. They are not shaped by evil but by desperation and smug self-assurance that slides into doubt and then back again. Du Bois did not excuse them from responsibility; rather, he wanted them to show that white supremacy is bigger than everyone in its grasp, whatever color they may be. Many of his white characters are helpless in their own fear and dreadfully contorted by the demands of white supremacy.

CHAPTER 9

Moral Reconstruction

Du Bois's Legacy for a Critical Theory of Whiteness

> How can love of humanity appeal as a motive to nations whose love of luxury is built on the inhuman exploitation of human beings, and who, especially in recent years, have been taught to regard these human beings as inhuman?
> —W. E. B. Du Bois, "The African Roots of War"

Having considered Du Bois's conception of whiteness as demonstrated in his writings over time, I now put his work into conversation with several race theorists of the late twentieth and early twenty-first centuries. My purpose here is to emphasize his foresight as a theorist of whiteness and to flesh out the ways in which white antiracists may usefully turn to his work as they consider how to reduce the harm they cause and begin to repair the centuries of pain and damage caused by whiteness. However, it's important to remember that Du Bois did not and could not have written directly to the problem of whiteness with the aim of uplifting white folk. Even on occasions (as in *Darkwater*) when he may as well have been speaking directly to whites, his points are couched as observations, not as demands for change. My work to extract his observations about white folk and whiteness has created a more programmatic compilation than Du Bois could ever realistically have produced. Had he attempted to offer such an analysis in his lifetime, it would have certainly disappeared into an abyss of forgotten writings. And that would have been the best possible outcome.

In my reading of Du Bois, whiteness always includes a presumption of arrogant, irrevocable license. White individuals and groups (such as white-led nations) comport themselves heedlessly, as if their desires and interests are the only ones that deserve consideration. Their epistemic opacity makes them resistant to evidence of Black humanity and to recognizing the harm that white heedlessness has done to nonwhite people. White exploitation and violence have been historically downplayed, never confronted as behavior that requires apology or reparation. Ongoing white epistemic opacity protects the heart of whiteness, which I see as a resilient commitment to white innocence that compels white people to maintain their ignorance so they can continue to see themselves as morally whole. Of course, in terms of any plausible morality, whites do not have license to act without considering others. The irrevocability of their license is not defensible; but given their position in the racial hierarchy, they usually have sociopolitical power to act as if their whiteness-serving crimes, whether as individuals, groups, or nations, are either excusable as political self-interest or were never wrong. This would be (and sometimes is) quite laughable, if only its consequences were not so dire.

Du Bois's account of whiteness and its operations differs from those developed after the mid-twentieth century in its simple, direct explanation of their power in systems and institutions. The disproportionate number of African Americans in the U.S. criminal justice system, for example, is traceable directly to the white people who control that system and act with the presumed license of whiteness. From his early diagnosis, in *The Philadelphia Negro*, that racism was the cause of Black crime to his depiction of the short, tortured life of Manuel Mansart's son Bruce, Du Bois showed the power of white supremacy to curtail the options of Black Americans and recognized their limited agency.[1] He perceived no mystery or explanatory gap. In his view, state and private systems under the control of whites who act like whites work to the advantage of whites who do not question their right to exploit people of color. Thus, over time, the systems' differential impact on people of color is not only predictable but can be explained by whites' assumptions and objectives. Because white-minded managers of state and private institutions perceive themselves as naturally superior to nonwhite races, and because that belief is protected by their epistemic opacity, these differential outcomes do not puzzle or dismay them.

As Du Bois's writings argue, the arrogant, irrevocable license of whiteness is manifested by individuals identified as white and by states that serve whiteness—the United States being the most obvious institutional carrier of this catastrophe following the Second World War. Presumptions built into social, economic, and political institutions reflect white experience and are thus unfit to serve those whose lives do not run according to white expectations. Du Bois was clear, for example, that the fate of the Freedmen's Bureau was tied to whites' predisposition to tolerate the sufferings of Black Americans, including those of the formerly enslaved. Why expend public funds to ensure that the freed might live flourishing lives? This would not only be a waste of funds but would ultimately inconvenience white capital, which depends on the availability of a large pool of the exploitable. Historically, observers have rarely seen whites' disproportionate advantages and positive outcomes as a mystery or a problem to be solved. White flourishing is the expected outcome of a system founded on white supremacy.

CONTEMPORARY THEORIES OF WHITENESS

By noting distinctions between Du Bois's work and that of more recent theorists, I in no way suggest that his account lacks explanatory power. In fact, I believe his perceptions offer a clarity that more recent discussions sometimes overlook. Nor do I imply that accounts focusing on white supremacy's structural, systemic operation are unnecessary or inaccurate. Such scholarship is particularly useful in contexts in which we take institutional administrators' good will seriously even as we continue to see disproportionate impacts against people of color. For me, work such as Eduardo Bonilla-Silva's "racism without racists" model has been a vital aid in understanding this issue.[2] Du Bois's mature understanding of the complexity of the psychology of whiteness was fully compatible with such accounts.

Charles Mills's *The Racial Contract* (1997) offers a rich, detailed, and history-based theory regarding the triumph of white supremacy in a political system that is nominally committed to universal human equality.[3] For him, white epistemic failure—constructed more or less unconsciously to allow for the exploitation of nonwhite bodies and persons—explains how whites have long engaged in the worst forms of brutality while still seeing themselves as the inventors and carriers of democracy and the philosophy of universal human rights. Mills posits the existence of an unspoken but obvious compact to commit to a metaphysics whereby people of color anywhere on earth are presumed to be subhuman, in contrast to the humanity of whites. This contract makes room for steep inequities despite a modern theoretical social agreement that ostensibly provides equal rights to all human beings. My own thinking and my reading of Du Bois have been deeply influenced by Mills's work, and Mills himself has been powerfully affected by his considerations of Du Bois. Clearly, his conception of white ignorance echoes Du Bois's portrayal of white epistemic opacity as a central element of whiteness.

For Mills, shared presumptions about the subhumanity of nonwhite races affect the moral and epistemological elements of modern political theory. He understands that the racial contract differs from the traditional social contract because its historical bases are actual, not hypothetical. Most liberal political theorists perceive the social contract as a what-if heuristic that allows us to decide what is just and fair on the basis of what reasonable people would agree to under specified conditions. Such theorists suggest, for instance, that most people might agree to live under the authority of a sovereign who enforces laws that apply to all equally and work in everyone's best interests. Yet as Mills and others point out, actual historical regimes have never served the best interests of all of their citizens, nor have they treated all equally. Social contract theory, then, at best suggests how a hypothetical political system could be legitimate. The racial contract, on the other hand, explains how our system in fact works, and why.

In a recent essay, Mills argues that Du Bois was a "Black radical liberal" because he recognized that the material conditions for true democracy do not exist in the United States and never have, due to the depredations of white supremacy. Mills contends that Du Bois's view of whiteness changed over time; in his later works, he held that white supremacy "was not at all a matter of an innocent ignorance, to be remedied by education, but a vested interest in the existing order tied up with one's identity as a white person, and including unconsciously held assumptions about what conferred worth and self-worth upon persons."[4] While I agree with this point, I also see Du Bois's conception of whites' interest in maintaining white supremacy as trading on a model of moral psychology that makes the notion of a vested interest partial at best. It is absolutely fair to say that, after 1930, his conception of the "material foundation of the white-supremacist social order [was] racial exploitation."[5] Nevertheless, until the end of his career Du Bois continued to perceive whites' commitment to their own innocence as a foundational motivation for their attachment to white supremacy.

Still, for Mills, the *liberal* part of Du Bois's Black radical liberalism depended on his insistence that racist exploitation goes well beyond the class exploitation revealed via Marxian analysis. The spoils of this exploitation benefit the white worker and the white capitalist psychologically and materially, as Du Bois famously noted in *Black Reconstruction*.[6] Moreover, cognitive distortions that protect white self-image make it difficult for them to trace the social and political causes of racial inequality. Writing on a passage from *Dusk of Dawn* that I have already argued shows the power of whites' twisted commitment to their own innocence, Mills notes:

> [It] seeks to dramatize through the metaphor of a cave the cognitive plight of blacks trying to communicate with their white overlords. But in a black inversion of Plato's Cave, in which the entombed, deluded, are locked in the world of shadows while the Form of the Sun illuminates the reality above, this is a cave whose black "entombed souls" are the ones illuminated as to the realities of their situation but unable to reach the conscience and awareness of the deluded white world above, indifferent and obtuse to black oppression.[7]

In Mills's view, Du Bois understood that the cognitive opacity of whiteness makes the model of traditional liberalism untenable because the exchange of ideas central to the liberal political ideal becomes impossible to achieve. When the white power structure cannot perceive the depth of racial inequity in the polis, mechanisms to ensure the rights of individuals break down and are insensitive to racial injustice. Du Bois was still a liberal insofar as he was committed to the importance of those individual rights. While my account of Du Bois's model of whiteness does not attend specifically to issues of political rights, it generally coheres with Mills's discussion—although I push further to suggest that the opacity is at least in part motivated by white existential fear. For Mills, Du Bois's long-standing commitment to individual rights justifies his categorization as a liberal, and his convictions regarding global material exploitation are key to his label as a radical. Both he and I would agree that Du Bois's first concern was always to promote racial justice for Africana people, traditionally with attention to individuals.

"The Illumination of Blackness," a piece published just before Mills's untimely death in 2021, focuses on the promise of Blackness and Black philosophy to undo the systemic white supremacy embedded in western philosophy. Without contributions from Black philosophy, Mills suggests, the "costs to the Western psychic economy of admitting the magnitude of the wrong done to the human beings represented as n*****s for hundreds of years in Western consciousness might just be too great for whites to bear."[8] Certainly, this is suggested by whites' defensive and hysterical reactions to the suggestion that they should be held accountable for white supremacy. Du Bois and, I suspect, Charles Mills would have been less concerned about white psychic harm than about the consequences of that pain, given that whites as a group have tended to take out their suffering and anxiety on nonwhite bystanders. Moreover, the alternative to such white reckoning is not easy to imagine. Whites will either change the way they live, or they will be invited off the planet. Perhaps, even for them, working through this pain will be preferable to paying the costs of not doing so.

Linda Martín Alcoff has long engaged with such questions, and she offers a tremendously useful analysis of the complicated legacy and uncertain future of white racial identity, asking "whether this single identity term can even make sense of a grouping so impossibly varied."[9] As I have discussed, Du Bois's fiction and nonfiction demonstrate the functioning of whiteness as deployed by white men and women from various social classes. White license shows up differently among wealthy whites, among working or poor folks, among geographically dispersed white people. Nevertheless, as Du Bois demonstrated in *The Black Flame* trilogy, these diverse actors play their appointed roles in the defense of white license—poor white men at the individual level, wealthy ones at the legislative and policy levels. Similarly, Clarice Breckinridge's white womanhood is performed when she barges into a Black political meeting to serve her husband and, with every good intention, makes Tom Mansart's situation untenable. She knows and somehow does not know that white men are likely to turn murderous in order to defend her against presumed danger—all of them playing their gendered roles in support of white supremacy. They have in common the presumptive license of whiteness to prioritize trivial white preferences in complete disregard of the consequences for Black Americans and other people of color.

For Du Bois, the crux of whiteness is that it is deadly to Black folk, whether through the active violence of men such as Abe Scroggs or through the ignorant actions of women such as Clarice Breckinridge. However, his conception of whiteness leaves room for individual white people to overcome the destructive elements of irrevocable license, as demonstrated by John Brown's commitment and the work of white activists against police violence and other extensions of white supremacy. Alcoff notes that "antiracist activity among white workers, as well as cross-racial alliances around labor, housing, prisons, and police violence, is occurring all over the United States today. . . . Most of the struggles are local, and most are all but ignored by the mainstream press."[10] This is true. Nevertheless, it is also likely that the people of color involved in those struggles regularly deal with their white colleagues' tendency to take up more space than they are strictly entitled to and become defensive when the topic of white supremacy arises.

Du Bois wanted to provide fodder for white readers as well as people of color; he understood white racial identity to be a contingent matter, not "an objective thing, completely outside human agency."[11] As Alcoff points out, white individuals may develop a kind of double consciousness, "see[ing] themselves through both the dominant and the nondominant lens, and recogniz[ing] the latter as a critical corrective truth."[12] Learning to understand what whiteness looks like from the perspectives of various nonwhite peoples is a powerful tool for undoing the damage done to whites who have been raised in a white supremacist culture. The corrective truth offered by the generosity of writers such as Alcoff, Mills, and Du Bois can be a bitter but salutary pill.

The critical race theorist and Caribbean philosophy scholar Lewis Gordon also uses the term *license* to capture the behavior of whites as unrestrained and unaccountable. His account of license is brief; primarily, he is uses it to demonstrate the inadequacy of the term *white privilege*, common among many antiracist educators. For instance, the rapacious acquisition of goods and labor in the early colonial period went beyond any sense of privilege; in truth, "whiteness here is an identity that extends beyond the realm of privilege. It demands a *license*."[13] Likewise, the centuries-long record of white atrocities against Black people in the Americas and the Caribbean and on the African continent was more like a "license to kill" than any version of a privilege.[14]

Thus, my use of *license* to capture Du Bois's conception of whiteness is in one sense much broader than Gordon's and, in another, somewhat narrower. White men, for example, do not have license to abuse other white men or to take their property. Gordon obviously knows this and does not imply otherwise, though his suggestion that whites in the early modern period "supposedly acquired a license to everything" must be read contextually: he means a license to everything not already under white ownership.[15] It is crucial to Du Bois's account that the moral holiday offered by white license extends only to behavior that targets people of color. It is broader than Gordon's notion in the sense that it captures more than behavior, also including attitudes and epistemic opacity.

Shannon Sullivan's work on whiteness focuses on the habituated actions and attitudes that facilitate whites' ability to understand themselves as presumptively good despite their history of atrocities.[16] Key among these habits is "ontological expansiveness"—whites' tendency not only to assume that they belong everywhere but also to act as if they have always inhabited every space that is fit for habitation.[17] Sullivan notes Charles Mills's account of the way in which places are marked according to the racial contract: civilized places are seen as white; uncivilized ones are inhabited by people of color. In fleshing out the unconscious tendency of whiteness to expand and claim, she explicitly makes use of Du Bois's 1920 assertion that whiteness precisely equals "ownership of the earth, forever and ever."[18] Sullivan relies on a number of his insights to emphasize the goodness that whites claim and the ignorance through which they cause harm. As she points out, "white people generally don't know how to live their racial identities in ways that promote racial justice. Even worse, their ignorance often poses as knowledge, making it all the more insidious."[19] This is clearly consonant with my discussion of Du Bois's views.

Ella Myers has carefully analyzed the conception of whiteness that Du Bois developed between 1920 and 1940.[20] She calls his account "whiteness as dominion," insightfully expanding on his comments in "The Souls of White Folk," which argue that whiteness is ownership of the world forever.[21] For Myers, this is a "pervasive, taken-for-granted interpretive schema" that presumes "nonwhite people and their lands as the a priori property of whites."[22] She calls this schema a "horizon of perception," borrowing language from Judith Butler and Hans-Georg Gadamer.[23] Myers points out that whites persist in their proprietary orientation because it constitutes something like a religion or faith, and she uses other terms, including *schema, horizon, gaze,* and *outlook* to "denote a multifaceted worldview, entailing both explicit belief and tacit presupposition, philosophical creed and visceral sensibility, and knowing commitment and default intuition."[24] In her view, Du Bois saw whiteness as dominion as a vestige of the Atlantic slave trade, given his emphasis, in *Black Reconstruction*, on the nature of ownership constructed by American laws that defined slavery as a property relation rather than exploitation.[25] By reading his account of chattel slavery in *Black Reconstruction* alongside his examination of whiteness in "The Souls of White Folk," Myers shows the causal link between slavery and modern whiteness as ownership of the world and nonwhite peoples.[26]

While Myers's account is evocative and consistent with mine, it is also incomplete. I disagree with her claim that Du Bois's worldview of whiteness is less epistemic and more hermeneutical than Mills's account of white ignorance.[27] In *Dusk of Dawn*, Du Bois insisted that whites' attachment to racial superiority and their resistance to contrary evidence was motivated by more than greed, that it was more than simple ignorance. As I have discussed throughout, whites' hesitation to see people of color as fully human rests on an almost unconscious suspicion that such recognition would endanger their white sense of self, not just their entitlement to space and place. Whiteness as worldview is more than a slanted hermeneutic or a damaged perception; for Du Bois, it pervades the experience of white individuals and groups and affects our behavior in ways that go beyond presumptions of control or ownership—although these elements are certainly part of white license.

According to Du Bois, the epistemic elements of whiteness do more than explain its survival. They underwrite a harmful comportment that outstrips a sense of dominion—as apt as that concept can be. I use the term *license* consciously to evoke a sense of licentiousness and the peculiar way of being in which white people do not need to conform to the usual rules or respect proportionality. In his novel *Long Division* (2013), Kiese Laymon has one of his characters sum up a particularly galling white behavior in this way: "You got to be a special kind of evil to spend your whole life getting more than you deserve, then turn right around and hate on folks for getting half of what you was born into. Just evil."[28] Du Bois rarely invoked evil as an explanation for whiteness, but his account was no less damning. The concept of dominion does not cover those moments when whiteness steps outside the bounds of civil states, projecting malice and holding hatred for others for who are getting half (or less) of the plenty that white people have been born with.

Recall the passage from "The Souls of White Folk" in which Du Bois observed the hatred white men have for Black folk who are out of place: in this case, a small Black woman sitting by herself in a Pullman car. Clearly, the man in the vignette feels he has dominion over who can sit where on a train because people like him have always made such rules. Even if the woman were sitting in a Blacks-only car, the white man could choose to harm her without fear. That is a feature of dominion, certainly, but the fact that the hatred is so deep and so unfounded (except through white license) demands explanation. One senses that whites' insistence on their own goodness requires them to imagine people of color as containers for all that is detestable in the world.

For Du Bois, these structures of whiteness, which determine individual life chances, group-based inequalities, and the public face of national and international institutions, challenge our common narratives about individuals' responsibility for their own destiny. He wrote powerfully about the struggle of Black folk to see themselves as fully human and pursue human lives within a comprehensive system of white supremacy. As the scholar Lucius Outlaw has noted, "the disparities and contradictions between the two—the high principles and rhetoric of grand promises, and the arrogant, indignant, legalized inhumanity intended to thwart colored folks' sharing the dreams of opportunity, let alone working to realize them—were painfully obvious, as was intended."[29] White license, especially white comportment, tend to transmit the message that those who are truly human get rights and those who are not flourishing must not be truly human. The contradiction, according to Outlaw, lies atop a surface of appearance but dissipates when one absorbs the intended implication.

WHITENESS AND HUMANITY

How can white folk change themselves and the culture they have built to minimize the injustice and injury that results from white identity in a system of white supremacy? Answering this question was not Du Bois's project, for his primary concern was not whites' well-being. At most, he saw such change as a side benefit to racial justice and the liberation of people of color. He knew that the suffering of whites under white supremacy is not comparable to the suffering of people of color, although their moral peril is greater.

Nonetheless, Du Bois believed that white persons could be transformed in some way by coming face to face with their own whiteness and its consequences. But how? Given that they are epistemically compromised by their racialization as white and that their very sense of being seems to depend on maintaining the artifice of their innocence, confronting the disaster of whiteness directly (or being confronted with it) will likely be ineffective, at best.

Du Bois's writings and activism confirm as much. Still, if whites do finally infer that their existence as white *is* a problem, they must, as Du Bois urged, push themselves to listen to the testimony of African Americans and others who have a clearer view of white supremacy and can explain its mechanisms.

In his recent compelling book, *White Reconstruction*, Dylan Rodríguez calls upon a wide spectrum of historical and theoretical work to demonstrate how "White Being,"[30] an aspirational construction of supremacy that masquerades as legitimate superiority, has emerged at key moments in U.S. history. White Being is often physiologically violent, acting through cultural means to dominate, and it is always animated by a "hollow ideology of force used to dominate nonwhites and appropriate global resources."[31] Rodríguez argues that the shape of White Being has changed over time, even showing up in the "formal disassembly of American apartheid"— that is, in the ongoing statecraft of white liberals who tout criminal justice reform and multicultural inclusion.[32] He notes that "anti-Blackness, racial-colonial violence, and domestic war . . . survive periods of reform" and contends that these relations of dominance are visible in and vital to such reforms, which maintain, over time, the differential life experiences and life chances of racialized groups.[33]

In short, Rodríguez sees white supremacy as a "violence of aspiration and logic of social organization that invents, reproduces, revises, and transforms changing modalities of social domination and systemic, targeted physiological and ecological violence."[34] Because white supremacy is never an accurate characterization of any underlying physiological or metaphysical superiority, White Being creates and mandates a wide array of constructions that support this aspiration. Echoing Du Bois's claim that Black humanity was briefly recognized after the Civil War, a conflict in which Black men were willing and able to kill others, Rodríguez quotes the scholar Sylvia Wynter's proposition that white supremacy requires Black folk to commit violence on themselves to appear more human.[35] White reconstruction, then, is a coalescence of such efforts to achieve not just the appearance of superiority but hegemony, which is always resisted by people of color. For example, Rodríguez argues that Jim Crow apartheid in the post-Reconstruction United States was not truly hegemonic, given the violence and disfranchisement necessary to sustain it.[36]

Rodríguez takes up Du Bois's foundational capacity to perceive the reality behind white contentions of motivations and objectives, which then primes his examination of the Freedmen's Bureau archive and his engagement with Du Bois's work on Reconstruction. In the record, he finds the consistent presumption that whites were "the assumptive subject of knowledge, politicality, sociality and modernity."[37] Not only were they the judges of whether and when the freed population might be ready to join white civilization, but they were the model against which nonwhite subhumans could be compared. Meanwhile, as Du Bois insisted, the white version of history remained indistinguishable from fiction, for it had been molded and polished to present whiteness as the telos of humanity and whites as the agents of civilization for these benighted refugees of primitive savagery. The notion of "white man's burden" demonstrates the superiority of whiteness, a willingness to lift up and "include" the historically marginalized that was only the latest in a long string of nominally humane gestures. Here, Rodríguez quotes Du Bois's famous remark that white folk are crowned as superior because they appoint the judge and jury and summon every witness.[38]

For Rodríguez, the "perpetual violence of white freedom and white entitlement to a presumption of bodily integrity" reproduces white supremacy as compulsory, especially when this entitlement is compared with and defined against the lack of any such entitlement for people of color.[39] This is (as I think Rodríguez would agree) consistent with Du Bois's portrayal of whites' heedless comportment: one need not be overly concerned with one's own physical safety when every state apparatus is lined up to prevent or punish harm to oneself. Moreover, social and political mores guarantee that whites' accidental or purposeful harm of nonwhites will be treated as a clumsy accident, a peccadillo. In his discussion of the Thirteenth Amendment's explicit provision for involuntary servitude as a criminal punishment, Rodríguez highlights the distance between whites' sense of belonging in the world and the precarity of nonwhite being. The historical record is transparent: "[The] Thirteenth Amendment inaugurates a state of permanent carceral war against Black people ... that unfolds in a generalized symbiosis with protracted conditions of racial-colonial conquest."[40] Rodríguez's reading of the Freedmen's Bureau archive is a harrowing revelation of the lengths to which postwar white politicians and administrators would go to recast white supremacy in the aftermath of Emancipation. The gradual withdrawal of resources and support from local Black governments, impoverished by centuries of slavery and the kleptocratic tendencies of local white power, is one of many instances demonstrating whites' intentional and occasionally desperate work to maintain supremacy while pretending to attend to racial equality.

A globalized heedless comportment thus remains, even in discursive regimes and institutional rearticulations that are couched in liberal multiculturalism. For Rodríguez, this is a key element of white reconstruction. The clueless interlocutors in *Souls of Black Folk* and *Dusk of Dawn* pretend that they are trying to reason with Du Bois or even exchange views between equals. Yet they all know that, in the end, he will have to accommodate himself to the individual and institutional instantiations of white supremacy. The duo may act as if they are voluntarily parting, but both know they are being separated by the rules of a private club or a legally mandated color line. As the works of Rodríguez and Du Bois make clear, the modalities of white social domination change over time, but its violent aspiration always finds expression through new or existing logics of social organization.[41]

In *The Abolition of White Democracy*, Joel Olson points out that the meaning of *white* and its implications have changed over time, especially since the civil rights movement and the end of de jure white supremacy. For him, as for Du Bois, whiteness is a historical artifact having more to do with power and its maintenance than with any social or cultural similarities. Olson ties whiteness to political power at its most transparent: the very claim to citizenship. As Du Bois argued in *Black Reconstruction*, most postwar white Americans could not conceive of African Americans as co-citizens in a political project, even with the existence of the Fourteenth Amendment. Olson shows how whites were able to maintain their illusion of themselves as committed to democracy despite explicitly working to exclude Black Americans from it.[42]

CONCLUSION

It is no surprise that Du Bois's work to make whiteness visible has become the foundation from which more recent theorists and activists have conceived and critiqued whiteness. Every theorist I mention in this chapter has continued his work of delineating the problem of white racial identity—with Rodríguez, who models his own thinking directly on Du Bois's *Black Reconstruction*, offering especially complex and illuminating arguments. Clearly, Du Bois's writings still resonate, and in many cases they surpass newer examinations of whiteness. His insight, analytical skills, and compassion allowed him to lay bare the crimes of whiteness while continuing to recognize the humanity of white people. Given the length of his career, his books offer a breadth and depth that are unmatched. We still have a great deal to learn from him.

Numerous other writers also speak cogently on issues of white supremacy. Among them is Aimé Césaire, whose *Cahier d'un retour au pays natal* concerns colonial relations, reminding us that most of the problems of colonized people can be traced to whiteness. To my mind, he stands with Du Bois in the acuity of his perceptions.[43] While other writers of the colonial experience might push against Du Bois's presumption that the white oppressor is always, first, a human being, I believe that a comparative survey would be tremendously productive. I also recommend Saidiya Hartman's *Wayward Lives, Beautiful Experiments*. It is a brilliant book for many reasons, one of which is its portrayal of Du Bois as a young sociologist in Philadelphia. Her evocation of the lives of young Black women in the early twentieth century brings life to barely glanced-at shadows in the archive and will resonate today with those who are experimenting in waywardness of many kinds.[44] White Americans should read it for insight into white saviorism, social science "data," and other points of white oppression; the focus of the book is on the power of Black women's creativity and agency despite all efforts to destroy them.

CONCLUSION

WHITE FOLK HAVE, at least since the beginning of the colonial era, comported themselves with the presumption that what they desire is theirs by right. Thus, after the Civil War, even though the emancipated were no longer legally slaves, the logic of white license dictated that they could and would still be bent to the white will. Jim Crow laws controlled where they could live, work, learn, spend money, and move about in public. By the end of the nineteenth century, the U.S. armed services were deployed in service of white material interests in the Caribbean, in Indochina, and during both world wars. Most wars involve the interests of capital, of course, but white supremacy has directed the projects of modern empire, as Du Bois prodigiously outlined in the lion's share of his writings. Moreover, because feeding a war machine depends on private contractors, who supply everything from guns and bullets to shoes and socks (even more now than in Du Bois's time), wars have always been good for large, white-owned, well-connected businesses. Recall President Dwight D. Eisenhower's farewell speech, in which he warned of the military-industrial complex and noted that America had developed a new industry in armaments, supplanting the old model of manufacturers who were "gearing up for war."[1]

Every day, we learn again that national and international legal, economic, political, and social policies and practices skew visibly to the benefit of white people. While not all of these people are wealthy and healthy, they are wealthier per capita than are other racially defined groups; and when they are not healthier, that is only because of the illnesses of excess. Even in what we repeatedly refer to as "the wealthiest nation on Earth," people of color have less access to healthcare, get less good care, and are more likely to live in areas of environmental danger. Our carceral system not only imprisons many, many more Black folk per capita than whites, but we build prisons in regions that are populated by whites. This means that we remove Black men and women from their neighborhoods and transfer them to distant, often rural communities. There, they can no longer vote, but they will be counted for purposes of local and national representation, in an unacknowledged echo of the universally condemned three-fifths rule from the time of legal slavery.[2] Meanwhile, though neither Du Bois nor I would ever suggest that holding other human beings in cages is a job that leads to human flourishing, whites in these regions benefit economically from prison jobs and the linked businesses that fill the needs and wants of corrections employees.

Had Du Bois lived longer, he no doubt would have contributed to the social theorizing that has worked to explain how systemic advantages for identifiable groups do not require the sort of conspiratorial offshore meetings of politicians, generals, and financiers portrayed in *The Black Flame* trilogy. Of course, such meetings may happen; but even without them, the workings of the market economy, along with a juridical system that creates arcane rules of evidence and civil procedure, ensures that the advantage will, for the most part, remain firmly ensconced among those who are already advantaged. As Du Bois wrote, "modern imperialism and modern industrialism are one and the same system; root and branch of the same tree. The race problem is the other side of the labor problem; and the black man's burden is the white man's burden."[3]

My work here is an effort to establish and support a quite different project for white people. In his novel *Cloudsplitter*, Russell Banks portrays John Brown as a white man who distrusts other white people.[4] This distrust appears not only in the context of trying to keep his various guerrilla campaigns against slavery secret but in his quotidian relations with white neighbors. In short, John Brown's worldview alienated him from white society. Banks and Du Bois both present him as a man who largely escaped the bonds of whiteness. While other writers often treat Brown as a fanatic who would rather kill proslavery white folk than engage in the lengthy and frustrating process of trying to change their minds and hearts, it is at least as likely that he was motivated by the urgency of ending slavery: enslaved Black Americans were owed immediate liberation, and their enslavers were evil enough to be owed nothing. In any case, imagining Brown's discomfort with white displays of heedless comportment and with the flawed epistemology of whiteness is a lesson in possibility. If some white Americans can give up the belief that the effects of white supremacy are not that bad and that life under white supremacy is fair enough, we may begin to see new ways of white being.

Du Bois's work offers us, if we will take up its invitation, a mirror in which white Americans can recognize their missteps and work to act otherwise. Abolitionism, the creative and many-faceted school of liberation that seeks to undo the narrowing gaze of whiteness and its violent enforcement of white desires, suggests a way out of the fraud constituted by whiteness as superiority—a fraud that Du Bois diagnosed. If we can take up his vision of a future lived otherwise, we may yet understand that what is need not be forever, that what is worth living for may yet be.[5]

Notes

Preface

1. According to *Politico*, Obama won "43 percent of white voters, 4 percentage points below Carter's performance in 1976 and equal to what Bill Clinton won in the three-man race of 1996. Republican John McCain won 55 percent of the white vote" (www.politico.com).
2. I was one of those facilitators.
3. This reaction also put to rest any early questions about Obama's racial identity: we could tell he was "really Black" by the way white America treated him. Legislators vowed to block every one of his legislative proposals and refused to move forward on a Supreme Court nomination made with nearly a year left in Obama's final term ("Republicans Vow No Hearings and No Votes for Obama's Supreme Court Pick," *Washington Post*, February 23, 2016).
4. For brilliant accounts of the construction of whiteness and its defense through violence and brutality, see Nell Painter, *The History of White People* (New York: Norton, 2011); and Carol Anderson, *White Rage: The Unspoken Truth of Our Racial Divide* (New York: Bloomsbury, 2017). It is ironic that whites have historically accused people of color of savagery, given that the number of people of color murdered by whites in the past four hundred years far outstrips the number of white people killed or harmed by people of color.
5. W. E. B. Du Bois, "The Conservation of Races," in *Writings* (New York: Library of America, 1986), 815–26.
6. Some theorists have objected to the phrase "school-to-prison pipeline," arguing that many schools are already effectively prisons, given their surveillance and disciplinary regimes.
7. Naomi Murakawa, *The First Civil Right: How Liberals Built Prison America* (New York: Oxford University Press, 2014), 11.
8. Aldon D. Morris, *The Scholar Denied* (Oakland: University of California Press, 2015), xvi.
9. Sara Ahmed, *Living a Feminist Life* (Durham, NC: Duke University Press, 2017), 6.
10. As a white writer, I have certainly felt this difficulty while working on this project.

Introduction

1. Eric Porter, *The Problem of the Future World: W. E. B. Du Bois and the Race Concept at Midcentury* (Durham, NC: Duke University Press, 2010), 14.
2. Here I am influenced by the late Charles Mills's discussion of the state of nature in his groundbreaking *The Racial Contract* (Ithaca, NY: Cornell University Press, 1997). Mills argues that the white supremacist conception of people of color is that they are always

in the state of nature—uncivilized and thus not protected by civil law as whites are. Du Bois would certainly agree, as I discuss in chapter 9. The irony, of course, is that it is actually white folk who act as if they are uncivilized.
3. For John Locke, the external authority of the state is required only because individuals will suffer honest disagreements over various facts in the state of nature, despite generally behaving according to the natural law (*Second Treatise of Government* [Cambridge, MA: Hackett, 1980], chap. 2).
4. W. E. B. Du Bois, *The Souls of Black Folk* (1903; Amherst: University of Massachusetts Press, 2018), 9.
5. Walter Johnson argues that the "language of 'dehumanization' is misleading because slavery depended upon the human capacities of enslaved people.... It depended upon their labor. And it depended upon their sentience. Enslaved people could be taught: their intelligence made them valuable" ("To Remake the World: Slavery, Racial Capitalism, and Justice," *Boston Review*, February 20, 2018; quoted in Clint Smith, *How the Word Is Passed* [Boston: Little, Brown, 2021], 67).
6. Du Bois, *The Souls of Black Folk*, 1–2.
7. W. E. B. Du Bois, *The World and Africa* (1939; New York: Oxford University Press, 2007), 26.
8. Mills, *The Racial Contract*; Charles Mills, "White Ignorance," in *Epistemologies of Ignorance* (Albany: State University of New York Press, 2007), 11–38.
9. Mills, *The Racial Contract*, 18.
10. W. E. B. Du Bois, *Color and Democracy: Colonies and Peace* (1945; New York: Oxford University Press, 2007).
11. W. E. B. Du Bois, *Black Reconstruction* (1935; New York: Free Press, 1992), 577. Theodore W. Allen notably took up Du Bois's concept of the blindspot. See Theodore W. Allen and Noel Ignatiev, "White Blindspot: The Original Essays on Combating White Supremacy and White-Skin Priviledge [sic]," c. 1969, Theodore W. Allen Papers, MS 1021, Special Collections and University Archives, University of Massachusetts Amherst Libraries.
12. W. E. B. Du Bois, *Dusk of Dawn* (1940; New York: Oxford University Press, 2007), 66.
13. Charles W. Mills, "Du Bois: Black Radical Liberal," in *A Political Companion to W. E. B. Du Bois*, ed. Nick Brommell (Lexington: University of Kentucky, 2018), 46.
14. See chapter 5.
15. David Blight, *Race and Reunion: The Civil War in American Memory*, rev. ed. (Cambridge, MA: Belknap, 2002), 256ff.
16. See, for example, *The Papers of Jefferson Davis*, http://jeffersondavis.rice.edu.
17. Du Bois, *Color and Democracy*, esp. 278ff.
18. For clear discussions of race as a social construction, see Naomi Zack, *The Philosophy of Race: An Introduction* (New York: Palgrave Macmillan, 2018), 123ff; and Paul C. Taylor, *Race: A Philosophical Introduction*, 3rd ed. (Cambridge, UK: Polity, 2022).
19. Our racial concepts immediately buckle under the application of the smallest weight. Discerning readers will note that the human species has its origins on the African continent. Thus, in a strict sense, none of us lacks African ancestry, and the African continent still has the planet's greatest genetic diversity. The modern race concept, having been developed long after some humans had evolved to have lighter skin (in order to absorb more vitamin D at different latitudes), ignores this fact.
20. Mills often uses *nonwhite* to refer to those marked out as subpersons by the racial contract. When Europeans have had political power, they have defined those with any identifiable non-European heritage as subpersons and nonwhite.
21. The advantage of the acronym BIPOC is that it emphasizes the particular catastrophe of settler practices in the Americas for Indigenous people and those transported to

the Americas as slaves. However, there is no consensus among nonwhite people as to whether this benefit outweighs the tendency of acronyms to obscure the numerous differences between those swept up in the category.

22. Du Bois, *The Souls of Black Folk*, 11.
23. Du Bois, *Dusk of Dawn*, 58.
24. Porter, *The Problem of the Future World*, 25.
25. David Levering Lewis, *W. E. B. Du Bois: Biography of a Race* (New York: Holt, 1993), 357.
26. Nahum Dmitri Chandler, "The Souls of an Ex-White Man: W. E. B. Du Bois and the Biography of John Brown," in *X—The Problem of the Negro as a Problem for Thought* (New York: Fordham University Press, 2014), 112–28.
27. Chad Williams, *The Wounded World: W. E. B. Du Bois and the First World War* (New York: Farrar, Strauss, and Giroux, 2023).
28. The context of *Darkwater*'s publication is discussed in David Levering Lewis, *W. E. B. Du Bois: The Fight for Equality and the American Century, 1919-1963* (New York: Holt, 2000), 13–16.
29. Du Bois briefly joined the Socialist Party, prompted by his admiration for Eugene Debs, and in *John Brown* (1909) strongly condemned the role of market capitalism in human suffering. See Lewis, *W. E. B. Du Bois: Biography of a Race*, 420–21.
30. Joel Olson, *The Abolition of White Democracy* (Minneapolis: University of Minnesota Press, 2004).
31. Porter, *The Problem of the Future World*, 29.
32. Porter, *The Problem of the Future World*, 4.
33. Du Bois, *Dusk of Dawn*, xxxiii.
34. Porter, *The Problem of the Future World*, 3.
35. Manning Marable, introduction, in *Darkwater*, by W. E. B. Du Bois (1920; Mineola, NY: Dover, 1999), vi.
36. Kimberlé Crenshaw, "Demarginalizing the Intersection of Race and Sex: A Black Feminist Critique of Antidiscrimination Doctrine, Feminist Theory, and Antiracist Politics," *University of Chicago Legal Forum* (1989): 139–67; Kimberlé Crenshaw, "Mapping the Margins: Intersectionality, Identity, and Violence against Women of Color," *Stanford Law Review* 43, no. 6 (1991): 1241–99.
37. My regret is tempered by the fact that such good work on Du Bois's gendered tendencies has already been done. See, for instance, Hazel Carby, *Race Men* (Cambridge, MA: Harvard University Press, 1998); Joy James, *Transcending the Talented Tenth: Black Leaders and American Intellectuals* (New York: Routledge, 1997); Farah Jasmine Griffin, "Black Feminists and Du Bois: Respectability, Protection, and Beyond," *Annals of the American Academy of Political and Social Science* 568, no. 1 (2000): 28–40; and Lauren Louise Anderson, "Du Bois in Drag: Prevailing Women, Flailing Men, and the 'Anne Du Bignon' Pseudonym," in *Citizen of the World: The Late Career and Legacy of W.E.B. Du Bois*, ed. Phillip Luke Sinitiere (Evanston, IL: Northwestern University Press, 2019).
38. Porter, *The Problem of the Future World*, 2.
39. Martin Luther King Jr., "Honoring Dr. Du Bois, 1929–1968," February 23, 1968, W. E. B. Du Bois Papers, MS 312, Special Collections and University Archives, University of Massachusetts Amherst Libraries.

CHAPTER 1: Early Interventions

1. W. E. B. Du Bois, *Dusk of Dawn* (1940; New York: Oxford University Press, 2007), 17.
2. Ibram X. Kendi, *Stamped from the Beginning* (New York: Nation Books, 2015), 264. Kendi

points out that this strategy is still in vogue among some Black activists, though it is clearly ineffective.
3. See, for example, Aldon Morris, *The Scholar Denied: W. E. B. Du Bois and the Birth of Modern Sociology* (Oakland: University of California Press, 2015), 21.
4. Josiah Nott was recognized as a leading scientist during his career, repeatedly offering his opinion that "Negro" people were inferior and had reached their highest level of civilization during North American slavery (George Fredrickson, *The Black Image in the White Mind* [1970; Middletown, CT: Wesleyan University Press, 1987], 79–80). Later, the insurance statistician Frederick Hoffman argued that "Negroes" were so physically inferior to whites that they would soon be extinct, a conclusion quickly accepted by American demographers (249–51). Du Bois wrote of living to see every one of Hoffman's assumptions contradicted (*Dusk of Dawn*, 50).
5. W. E. B. Du Bois, "Jefferson Davis as a Representative of Civilization" (1890), in *Writings*, ed. Nathan Huggins (New York: Library of America, 1986), 811.
6. W. E. B. Du Bois, *The Autobiography of W. E. B. Du Bois* (New York: International, 1968), 147.
7. Du Bois, "Jefferson Davis," 811. In *Darkwater*, Du Bois reported that during this speech he told his audience "certain astonishing truths" ([1920; Mineola, NY: Dover, 1999], 8).
8. Du Bois, *Autobiography*, 146.
9. David Levering Lewis, *W. E. B. Du Bois: Biography of a Race, 1868–1919* (New York: Holt, 1993), 101.
10. Shamoon Zamir, *Dark Voices: W. E. B. Du Bois and American Thought, 1888–1903* (Chicago: University of Chicago Press, 1995), 65.
11. See, generally, David Blight, *Race and Reunion: The Civil War in American Memory* (Cambridge, MA: Harvard University Press, 2001); and Karen L. Cox, *Dixie's Daughters: The United Daughters of the Confederacy and the Preservation of Confederate Culture* (Gainesville: University Press of Florida, 2019).
12. Audrey Smedley, *Race in North America: Origin and Evolution of a Worldview* (New York: Routledge, 2012).
13. Du Bois, "Jefferson Davis," 811.
14. See, for example, Roxanne Dunbar-Ortiz, *An Indigenous Peoples' History of the United States* (Boston: Beacon, 2014); and Ernesto Chavez, *The U.S. War with Mexico: A Brief History with Documents* (Boston: Bedford/St. Martin's, 2007).
15. Du Bois, "Jefferson Davis," 811.
16. Du Bois used *Teutonic* as a synonym for *Anglo-Saxon* (Zamir, *Dark Voices*, 49).
17. Indeed, white people often emerged with the sense that their violent campaigns had benefited their victims; for instance, consider the Indian schools, meant to "civilize" young Indigenous Americans, and claims that the Atlantic slave trade had Christianized the "African Heathen."
18. Du Bois, "Jefferson Davis," 812.
19. This analysis, while true to Hegel's discussion of the dialectical development of spirit, ignores his absurd dismissal of the African continent and its people, of which Du Bois was all too aware (Lewis, *Biography of a Race*, 139–40). See, for example, Babacar Camara, "The Falsity of Hegel's Theses on Africa," *Journal of Black Studies* 36, no. 1 (2005): 82: "Hegel . . . denigrates Africans whom he sees as children in the forest, unaffected by the movement of history." Du Bois explicitly targeted Eugène Guernier's proclamation: "Seule de tous les continents l'Afrique n'a pas d'histoire!" (Du Bois, *The World and Africa* [1947; Oxford: Oxford University Press, 2008], xxxii.)
20. Du Bois, "Jefferson Davis," 812.
21. Du Bois, "Jefferson Davis," 812.

22. Du Bois, "Jefferson Davis," 812–13.
23. Du Bois, "Jefferson Davis," 813.
24. Du Bois, "Jefferson Davis," 813.
25. To be clear, young Du Bois was operating almost entirely without empirical knowledge of African cultures. He gained access to anthropological evidence of African civilizations in 1906, when Franz Boas delivered a commencement address at Atlanta University (Lewis, *Biography of a Race*, 352). His argument seems beholden to lingering notions about the docility of the average enslaved African or African American. Still, before an audience of those with every reason to esteem the strong man, "culturally, politically, and economically the most powerful social group in America at that time" (Zamir, *Dark Voices*, 62), Du Bois insisted that the strong have heretofore advanced themselves in a manner that is anything but admirable. What could be more savage, less humane, than brutality toward the weaker and less well-armed? Standing before his audience as a representative of the "Submissive" man, he allowed his own humanity to stand as the proposition that the strong must temper and transform itself in order to "discern the totality of Truth" ("Jefferson Davis," 813).
26. Zamir provides access to the undergraduate Du Bois's sharp critique of white America in the unpublished "A Vacation Unique" (*Dark Voices*, 217–25).
27. Kant and Hegel are only two examples of brilliant and still influential philosophers who demonstrated failures of reason and deadly ignorance regarding African peoples. See Emmanuel Eze, ed., *Race in the Enlightenment* (Hoboken, NJ: Wiley-Blackwell, 1997).
28. Shannon Sullivan has coined the evocative phrase "ontological expansiveness" to refer to this tendency, which I will discuss in chapter 9 (*Revealing Whiteness: The Unconscious Habits of Racial Privilege* [Bloomington: University of Indiana Press, 2006], 10).
29. Du Bois, "Jefferson Davis," 813. Interestingly, "Ich Dien" is the motto on the prince of Wales's shield. Of course, in that context, the service is to "God and Country" and thus white supremacy.
30. W. E. B. Du Bois, *The Philadelphia Negro* (1899; Philadelphia: University of Pennsylvania Press, 1997).
31. Lewis, *Biography of a Race*, 170–74.
32. "Du Bois's suggestion in 'Conservation' that races exist as social and historical entities has made the essay the perfect point of reference for the contemporary debate" (Chike Jeffers, "The Cultural Theory of Race: Yet Another Look at Du Bois's 'The Conservation of Races,'" *Ethics* 123, no. 3 [2013]: 403–26, 405). An early argument, primarily between Lucius Outlaw and Kwame Anthony Appiah, set the terms of the debate; see, for example, Anthony Appiah, "The Uncompleted Argument: Du Bois and the Illusion of Race," *Critical Inquiry* 12 (1985): 21–37, esp. 23–30; and Lucius Outlaw, "Against the Grain of Modernity: The Politics of Difference and the Conservation of 'Race,'" *Man and World* 25 (1992): 443–68, esp. 460–66. See also Paul Taylor, "Appiah's Uncontested Argument: W. E. B. Du Bois and the Reality of Race," *Social Theory and Practice* 26, no. 1 (2000): 103–28. Aldon Morris offers an incisive and, I think, correct analysis of this debate in *The Scholar Denied*, 30–33.
33. W. E. B. Du Bois, "The Conservation of Races" (1897), in Huggins, *Writings*, 818.
34. Du Bois, "The Conservation of Races," 818.
35. Du Bois, "The Conservation of Races," 819.
36. Du Bois, "The Conservation of Races," 825.
37. Du Bois, "The Conservation of Races," 826.
38. *Plessy v. Ferguson*, 163 U.S. 537 (1896).
39. *Plessy v. Ferguson*, 163 U.S. at 551.
40. In his edited volume *W. E. B. Du Bois: The Problem of the Color Line at the Turn of the*

Century: The Essential Early Essays (New York: Fordham University Press, 2017), Nahum Dmitri Chandler convincingly argues that in order to study Du Bois's conception of the proper life work for Black American intellectuals at this time, "Conservation" and "Strivings of the Negro People," both published in 1897 but displaying quite different rhetorical strategies, must each be read through the lens of the other (7). As my project is a somewhat different one, I focus on this point from "Strivings" as it is presented in "Of Our Spiritual Strivings" in 1903's *The Souls of Black Folk* (see chapter 2).

41. W. E. B. Du Bois, *The Suppression of the African Slave-Trade to the United States of America, 1638–1870* (1896; Mineola, NY: Dover, 1999), 198.
42. Du Bois, *The Suppression of the African Slave-Trade*, 199.
43. Du Bois, *The Philadelphia Negro*, 394.
44. Lewis notes that Du Bois "knew that his sponsors held a theory about the race to be studied"—that crime and venality among its Black population were ruining Philadelphia. Moreover, he believed that he would be able to show that racism was the cause of Black criminality, which it was, and not the result of Black vice (*Biography of a Race*, 189).
45. Du Bois, *The Suppression of the Atlantic Slave-Trade*.
46. Du Bois, "Conservation," 819: "The other racial groups are striving, each in its own way, to develop [sic] for civilization its particular message, its particular ideal, which shall help to guide the world nearer and nearer that perfection of human life for which we all long, that 'one far off Divine event.'"
47. Joseph Conrad, *The Heart of Darkness* (New York: Blackwood's, 1902); Joseph Conrad, *Lord Jim* (New York: Blackwood's, 1900); Edgar R. Burroughs, *Tarzan of the Apes* (New York: McClurg, 1914).

CHAPTER 2: *The Souls of Black Folk*

1. Nahum Dmitri Chandler's *The Problem of the Color Line at the Turn of the Twentieth Century* collects these and other early essays and provides a trenchant analysis of the maturity and complexity displayed in these early pieces (New York: Fordham University Press, 2015).
2. David Blight and Robert Gooding-Williams, "Introduction," in *The Souls of Black Folk*, by W. E. B. Du Bois (1903; Boston: Bedford, 1997), 2.
3. Lawrie Balfour, *Democracy's Reconstruction: Thinking Politically with W. E. B. Du Bois* (Oxford: Oxford University Press, 2011), 121.
4. Patricia Wald, *Constituting Americans: Cultural Anxiety and Narrative Form* (Durham, NC: Duke University Press, 1995), 191.
5. Blight and Gooding-Williams, "Introduction," 23.
6. W. E. B. Du Bois, *The Souls of Black Folk* (1903; Amherst: University of Massachusetts Press, 2018), 5. Unless otherwise noted, this is my source for all quotations from *Souls*.
7. Rayford Logan, *The Negro in American Life and Thought: The Nadir, 1877–1901* (New York: Dial, 1954).
8. Glenda Gilmore, *Gender and Jim Crow* (Chapel Hill: University of North Carolina Press, 1996).
9. Blight and Gooding-Williams, "Introduction," 1.
10. David Levering Lewis, *W. E. B. Du Bois: Biography of a Race, 1868–1919* (New York: Holt, 1993), 277.
11. Dolan Hubbard, "Introduction," in *The Souls of Black Folk: One Hundred Years Later*, ed. Dolan Hubbard (Columbia: University of Missouri Press: 2006), 9.

12. Robert Gooding-Williams, *In the Shadow of Du Bois: Afro-Modern Political Thought* (Cambridge, MA: Harvard University Press, 2011); Stephanie J. Shaw, *W. E. B. Du Bois and "The Souls of Black Folk"* (Chapel Hill: University of North Carolina Press, 2015). Shamoon Zamir also reads *Souls* as indebted to Hegel but only in the first chapter. He notes that we can read the work as an inversion of the traditional slave narrative, given that the early chapters focus on Emancipation but the final chapter returns us to the voices of the enslaved, with a harrowing recounting of the Sorrow Songs (*Dark Voices: W. E. B. Du Bois and American Thought, 1888–1903* [Chicago: University of Chicago Press, 1995]).
13. George Yancy, "Dear White America," *New York Times*, December 24, 2015.
14. "What is weak or less successful in *The Souls of Black Folk* is but relative demerit in an ensemble of transcendent intellectual passion and numinous prose" (Lewis, *W. E. B. Du Bois: Biography of a Race*, 278).
15. Du Bois, *The Souls of Black Folk*, 2.
16. Du Bois regularly acknowledged the shortcomings of some Black folk within their communities: their shortsightedness, slothfulness, and tendency to spend rather than save. Yet he consistently found that their cause was a lack of white accountability and the power of white racism following Emancipation.
17. Here, I follow the work of David S. Owen, "Whiteness in Du Bois's *The Souls of Black Folk*," *Philosophia Africana* 10, no. 2 (2007): 116–17.
18. Du Bois, *The Souls of Black Folk*, 38–39.
19. *Souls* has been through at least 120 printings since 1903. See Henry Louis Gates, Jr., "The Black Letters on the Sign," in *The Souls of Black Folk*, by W. E. B. Du Bois (1903; Oxford: Oxford University Press, 2007), xiii.
20. We might also reflect on the extent to which the Black joy contained in the book is experienced in spite of and even in opposition to whiteness.
21. See, however, the letter from D. Tabak, reprinted in Du Bois, *The Souls of Black Folk* (Bedford edition), 260–61.
22. Du Bois, *The Souls of Black Folk*, 8.
23. Du Bois, *The Souls of Black Folk*, 9.
24. Du Bois, *The Souls of Black Folk*, 95.
25. Du Bois, *The Souls of Black Folk*, 3.
26. Keith Byerman, "W. E. B. Du Bois and the Construction of Whiteness," in Hubbard, *The Souls of Black Folk: One Hundred Years Later*, 164.
27. Du Bois, *The Souls of Black Folk*, v.
28. Byerman, "W. E. B. Du Bois and the Construction of Whiteness," 163.
29. "Let the ears of a guilty people tingle with truth" (Du Bois, *The Souls of Black Folk*, 257).
30. W. E. B. Du Bois, "The Souls of Black Folk," *Independent*, November 17, 1904; reprinted in Du Bois, *The Souls of Black Folk* (Bedford edition), 255.
31. W. E. B. Du Bois, "The Souls of Black Folk," *Independent*, November 17, 1904; reprinted in Du Bois, *The Souls of Black Folk* (Bedford edition), 255.
32. "The world was thinking wrong about race, because it did not know. The ultimate evil was stupidity" (W. E. B. Du Bois, *Dusk of Dawn* (1940; New York: Oxford University Press, 2007), 30).
33. Eric Porter, *The Problem of the Future World: W. E. B. Du Bois and the Race Concept at Midcentury* (Durham, NC: Duke University Press, 2010), 25.
34. Lewis, *W. E. B. Du Bois: Biography of a Race*, 227.
35. Du Bois, *The Souls of Black Folk*, 66–67, 240.
36. Shaw, *W. E. B. Du Bois and "The Souls of Black Folk."*
37. Zamir, *Dark Voices*, 146.

38. Gooding-Williams, *Shadow of Du Bois*, 101.
39. Gooding-Williams, *Shadow of Du Bois*, 101.
40. Lewis, *W. E. B. Du Bois: Biography of a Race*, 280.
41. W. E. B. Du Bois, *Black Reconstruction in America* (1935; New York: Free Press, 1998), 700.
42. Owen, "Whiteness in Du Bois's *The Souls of Black Folk*," 116–17.
43. Owen, "Whiteness in Du Bois's *The Souls of Black Folk*," 110.
44. Du Bois made these demands more explicit in "The Souls of White Folk," included in *Darkwater* (New York: Harcourt and Brace, 1920). See chapter 4.
45. To capture this dynamic, Gooding-Williams uses the phrase "political deontic status." Whites deny political deontic status to Black people: they do not recognize any political duties to Black people. Anything they give, will be given, say, out of the goodness of their hearts (*Shadow of Du Bois*, 75–76).
46. Byerman, "W. E. B Du Bois and the Construction of Whiteness," 164–65.
47. Bryan Stevenson, *Just Mercy* (New York: Spiegel and Grau, 2014), 101.
48. Du Bois, *The Souls of Black Folk*, v, 257.
49. Du Bois, *The Souls of Black Folk*, v, italics added.
50. Du Bois, *The Souls of Black Folk*, 257. Jessie Fauset, who later became Du Bois's colleague at the NAACP and was the author of several classic novels, wrote to him after reading *Souls* as a college student: "It hurt you to write that book, didn't it?" (Shaw, *W. E. B. Du Bois and "The Souls of Black Folk*," 159). Du Bois was not in the habit of revealing his own pain publicly, although, as I will discuss, his anger was often on well-controlled display.
51. Nathan Huggins, ed., *W.E.B. Du Bois: Writings* (New York: Library of America, 1986), 547. Interestingly, the sentence containing this phrase, "Let the ears of a guilty people tingle with truth, and seventy millions sigh for the righteousness which exalteth nations, in this drear day when human brotherhood is mockery and a snare," is parenthetical in every edition of *Souls* I have checked but for one: the University of Massachusetts Press edition marking the 150th anniversary of the text, reprinted from A. C. McClurg's first edition in 1903. (Du Bois, *The Souls of Black Folk*, (1903; Amherst: University of Massachusetts Press, 2018), iv.)
52. As noted, Byerman reads "The Forethought" as parodic: "a signifying performance that reveals its black author as a literary ventriloquist who imitates the white audience's genteel rhetoric as a means of subverting its claims to be the nation and to define the nation as inherently good" ("W. E. B. Du Bois and the Construction of Whiteness," 162).
53. Du Bois, *The Souls of Black Folk*, 60.
54. Hazel Carby, *Race Men* (Cambridge, MA: Harvard University Press, 1998), 18.
55. Carby, *Race Men*, 19.
56. W. E. B. Du Bois, "The Damnation of Women," in *Darkwater* (1920; Mineola, NY: Dover, 1993); Joy James, "Profeminism and Gender Elites: W. E. B. Du Bois, Anna Julia Cooper, and Ida B. Wells-Barnett," in James, *Transcending the Talented Tenth* (New York: Routledge, 1997), 35–59. James points out, for example, that Du Bois was well aware of Wells-Barnett's antilynching journalism and activism, but his autobiographical writings on antilynching "mostly ignore" her (48).
57. Du Bois, *The Souls of Black Folk*, 95. See also W. E. B. Du Bois, *The Philadelphia Negro* (1899; Philadelphia: University of Pennsylvania Press, 1996), 339: "The difficulties encountered by the Negro on account of sweeping conclusions made about him are manifold."
58. William James, letter, in Du Bois, *The Souls of Black Folk* (Bedford edition), 261. Nonetheless, James was impressed by the book; he sent a copy to his brother Henry, calling it "decidedly moving" (Lewis, *W. E. B. Du Bois: Biography of a Race*, 644, n. 62).

59. James, letter, 261.
60. Du Bois, *The Souls of Black Folk* (Bedford edition), 265; D. Tabak, "Letter from D. Tabak to W. E. B. Du Bois," ca. 1905, W. E. B. Du Bois Papers (MS 312), Special Collections and University Archives, University of Massachusetts Amherst Libraries.

CHAPTER 3: The Riddle of John Brown

1. W. E. B. Du Bois, *The Souls of Black Folk* (1903; Amherst: University of Massachusetts Press, 2018).
2. Thomas Dixon, *The Leopard's Spots* (New York: Doubleday, Page, 1902); Thomas Dixon, *The Clansman* (New York: Doubleday, Page, 1905); Thomas Dixon, *The Traitor* (New York: Doubleday, Page, 1907). These books, as well as D. W. Griffith's 1915 film *The Birth of a Nation* (an adaptation of *The Clansmen*), helped to create the stereotype of African Americans as savagely criminal and desirous of white women. The film's release spurred several violent acts, including at least one murder, and correlated with a steep increase in the number of lynchings. See David Levering Lewis, *W. E. B. Du Bois: Biography of a Race* (New York: Holt, 1993), 507.
3. Lewis, *W. E. B. Du Bois: Biography of a Race*, 276.
4. George Fredrickson, *The Black Image in the White Mind* (1971; Middletown, CT: Wesleyan University Press, 1987), 249–50.
5. Saima S. Iqbal, "Louis Agassiz, under a Microscope," *Harvard Crimson*, March 18, 2021.
6. Lewis, *W. E. B. Du Bois: Biography of a Race*, 444. See also A. C. McClurg, letter to W. E. B. Du Bois, June 10, 1903, W. E. B. Du Bois Papers (MS 312), Special Collections and University Archives, University of Massachusetts Amherst Libraries.
7. Lewis, *W. E. B. Du Bois: Biography of a Race*, 357. Turner may have been perceived as too controversial, but the editor would also have seen the absence of written biographical records as a serious stumbling block.
8. See David Roediger, "Introduction," in *John Brown*, by W. E. B. Du Bois (1909; New York: Modern Library, 2001), xii–xiii; and Lewis, *W. E. B. Du Bois: Biography of a Race*, 356–57.
9. Du Bois, *John Brown*, 202.
10. Du Bois's access to many of these archives would have been severely limited due to Jim Crow laws and policies, especially in the South. See David Levering Lewis, "Introduction," in *Black Reconstruction*, by W. E. B. Du Bois (1935; New York: Free Press, 1992), x.
11. Du Bois, *John Brown*, xxv.
12. See, for example, David S. Reynolds and Christopher Benfey, "An Exchange on John Brown," *New York Review of Books*, March 7, 2013.
13. Brown's story is complicated by his anonymous publication of a pamphlet titled "Sambo's Mistakes," which offers so-called "sensible" advice to enslaved Black folk.
14. In an 1846 letter to his father, Brown wrote: "When I think how very little influence I have even tried to use with my numerous acquaintances and friends in turning their minds toward God and heaven, I feel justly condemned as a most wicked and slothful servant" (Du Bois, *John Brown*, 20–21).
15. Du Bois, *John Brown*, xxv.
16. Lewis, *W. E. B. Du Bois: Biography of a Race*, 357.
17. Nahum Dmitri Chandler, *The Problem of the Negro as a Problem for Thought* (New York: Fordham University Press, 2014), 113.
18. Du Bois, *John Brown*, 40.
19. Du Bois, *John Brown*, 49.
20. Du Bois, *John Brown*, 46.

21. Du Bois, *John Brown*, 50.
22. Du Bois, *John Brown*, 53.
23. Du Bois, *John Brown*, 54.
24. Du Bois, *John Brown*, 58
25. Du Bois, *John Brown*, 57–60.
26. Du Bois, *John Brown*, 51.
27. Chandler, *The Problem of the Negro*, 126. See also my discussion of Linda Martín Alcoff's notion of white double consciousness in chapter 9.
28. Chandler, *The Problem of the Negro*, 113.
29. Du Bois, *John Brown*, 20.
30. Du Bois quoted Osborne Anderson's report about life at the farm near Harpers Ferry, where several men from different states and backgrounds worked and lived together in exceedingly close quarters. When nosy neighbors happened by, all of the guerillas had to squeeze into the same small attic room. "In John Brown's house, and in John Brown's presence, . . . no hateful prejudice dared intrude its ugly self—no ghost of distinction found space to enter" (*John Brown*, 178).
31. Chandler, *The Problem of the Negro*, 113.
32. Chandler, *The Problem of the Negro*, 182. Russell Banks, in his epic *Cloudsplitter*, suggests that Brown avoided friendships with whites, finding it difficult to trust that they would understand the humanity of Black people (New York: HarperCollins, 1998).
33. Du Bois, *John Brown*, 178.
34. Du Bois, *John Brown*, 57. See also David S. Reynolds, *John Brown: Abolitionist* (New York: Vintage, 2005), 128.
35. Du Bois, *John Brown*, 41.
36. Book of Hebrews 13:3, KJV.
37. Du Bois, *John Brown*, 10. See also Reynolds, *John Brown*, 33.
38. Du Bois, *John Brown*, 10.
39. Consider Frantz Fanon's analysis of white supremacist colonial exploitation in *Les damnés de la terre* (Paris: Maspero, 1961).
40. Edward E. Baptist, *The Half Has Never Been Told: Slavery and the Making of American Capitalism* (New York: Basic Books, 2014), 210–11.
41. Du Bois, *John Brown*, 139.
42. Chandler, *The Problem of the Negro*, 181.
43. In each of his three autobiographies, Frederick Douglass addressed the toll on the slaveholder's character. The following quotation is characteristic: "The slaveholder, as well as the slave, was the victim of the slave system. Under the whole heavens there could be no relation more unfavorable to the development of honorable character than that sustained by the slaveholder to the slave" (*The Life and Times of Frederick Douglass, Written by Himself* [1893; New York: Citadel, 1983], 34).
44. Du Bois, *John Brown*, 42.
45. Du Bois, *John Brown*, 42.
46. When Oedipus is able to answer, the sphinx dies.
47. In 1920, Du Bois titled one of the poems in *Darkwater* "The Riddle of the Sphinx" (see chapter 4). To my knowledge, no one has yet examined all of his references to the riddle or what role it played in his thinking.
48. Du Bois, *John Brown*, 67–68.
49. Du Bois, *John Brown*, 202. The inability to see due to blinding radiance seems to refer to Plato's allegory of the cave; see chapter 6.
50. See, for example, Herbert Aptheker, *American Negro Slave Revolts* (1943; New York: International Publishers, 1963).

51. According to the traditional theory, most of Brown's violence would not be justified under criminal law because only immediate threats can be met by violence. While I am not making an argument for his legal innocence here, I do note that the law of a state that upholds slavery is probably inadequate to evaluate morally the actions of those trying to tear down that institution. For a summary of the history of this and related doctrines, see D. A. H. Miller, "Self-Defense, Defense of Others, and the State," *Law and Contemporary Problems* 80, no. 2 (2017): 85–102.
52. Du Bois, *John Brown*, 204.
53. Du Bois, *John Brown*, 203.
54. Certain Black Americans who had the opportunity to join Brown's campaign at Harpers Ferry also did not do so, either because of strategic concerns (Frederick Douglass) or because of illness (Harriet Tubman). They, obviously, are another matter, given that they had already risked themselves repeatedly to save others and try to end the institution.
55. Du Bois, *John Brown*, 208, 209. For a fuller account of the interrogation, see Reynolds, *John Brown*, 329–31.
56. The M'Naghten Rule refers to the common law standard for determining a defendant's possible legal culpability in an insanity plea. See Sanford Kadish, Stephen Schulhofer, and Rachel E. Barkow, *Criminal Law and Its Processes, Cases and Materials* (Boston: Aspen, 2022), 949ff.
57. Brown's appointed lawyers initially pled insanity, against his wishes. See Du Bois, *John Brown*, 216.
58. Reynolds and Benfey, "An Exchange on John Brown."
59. Du Bois, *John Brown*, 213.
60. Du Bois, *John Brown*, 213.
61. More than one historian credits Brown with having sparked the Civil War, including Reynolds.
62. Chandler, *The Problem of the Negro*, 122.
63. Du Bois, *John Brown*, 3.
64. Du Bois, *John Brown*, 3.
65. Brown's intention in the raid on Harpers Ferry was to take the fight against slavery "into Africa," which he believed would become the name of the American South once enslaved people were accepted as full citizens of the United States. See Terry Bisson, *Fire on the Mountain* (1988; Oakland, CA: PM Press, 2009). On Timbuctoo, see Nichole Christian, "Recalling Timbuctoo, a Slice of Black History," *New York Times*, February 19, 2002.
66. Du Bois, *John Brown*, 225. Du Bois refers here to early hints of eugenics and the social Darwinism against which he was struggling.
67. Du Bois, *John Brown*, 225.
68. Du Bois, *John Brown*, 228; Rayford Logan, *The Negro in American Life and Thought: The Nadir, 1877–1901* (New York: Dial, 1954).
69. Du Bois, *John Brown*, 230.
70. Du Bois, *John Brown*, 232–33.
71. Du Bois, *John Brown*, 234.
72. Du Bois, *John Brown*, 234.
73. Roediger, "Introduction," xxii.
74. Lewis, *W. E. B. Du Bois: Biography of a Race*, 335.

186 | NOTES TO PAGES 63–65

CHAPTER 4: *Darkwater's* Faith in Humanity

1. Manning Marable, "Introduction," in *Darkwater: Voices from within the Veil*, by W. E. B. Du Bois (1920; Mineola, NY: Dover, 1999), v.
2. Marable, "Introduction," vi.
3. David Levering Lewis describes this catastrophe as "a tidal wave of homicides, arson, mayhem, and organized racial combat sweeping up from the Deep South and Longview, Texas, into Washington, D.C., across the country to Chicago, and, dipping down to Knoxville, Tennessee, rolling on finally over Omaha, Nebraska" (*W. E. B. Du Bois: Biography of a Race, 1868–1919* [New York: Holt, 1993], 579.
4. Marable, "Introduction," vii.
5. "The Negro in America," *Times Literary Supplement* [London], November 4, 1920.
6. Marable, "Introduction," vi.
7. As I mentioned in chapter 3, Linda Martín Alcoff writes about the promise of white double consciousness as a mechanism for white antiracists (*The Future of Whiteness* [Cambridge: Polity, 2015], 168–71).
8. David Levering Lewis, *W.E.B. Du Bois: The Fight for Equality and the American Century, 1919–1963* (New York: Holt, 2000), 20.
9. Herbert Aptheker, ed., *Writings by W. E. B. Du Bois in Periodicals Edited by Others* (Millwood, NY: Kraus-Thomson, 1982), 25–29. In a letter to Du Bois, Hamilton Holt, then managing editor of *The Independent*, apparently suggested an essay with a similar title (April 20, 1910, W. E. B. Du Bois Papers [MS 312], Special Collections and University Archives, University of Massachusetts Amherst Libraries). Also see Reiland Rabaka, "The Souls of White Folk: W. E. B. Du Bois's Critique of White Supremacy and the Contributions to Critical White Studies," *Ethnic Studies Review* 29, no. 2 (2006): 1–19, 8.
10. The *Oxford English Dictionary* traces the use of *whiteness* as a human quality:

> Light skin-colour, esp. in a person of European origin or descent; the state or condition of being white (see white adj. 5a), conceived in terms of racial or cultural identity. Also with capital initial.
>
> 1597 A. Hartwell in tr. D. Lopes Rep. Kingdome of Congo To Rdr. sig. *3v The heate of the Sunne is not the cause of Whitenesse or Blacknesse in the Skinnes of men.
>
> 1680 tr. J.-B. Tavernier Coll. Several Relations & Treat. vi. 17 The Tunquineses . . . are . . . of an Olive Complexion, very much admiring the whiteness of the Europeans.
>
> 1735 Prompter 10 Jan. (single sheet) What wild imaginary Superiority of Dignity has their pale sickly Whiteness to boast of, when compar'd with our Majestick Glossiness!
>
> 1756 R. Rolt New & Accurate Hist. S.-Amer. i. ii. 26 People, differing from the Europeans in whiteness, and the Africans in blackness . . . , and being a medium between both.
>
> 1871 C. Darwin Descent of Man II. ii. xix. 346 The negroes rallied Mungo Park on the whiteness of his skin and the prominence of his nose.
>
> 1922 S. G. Millin Adam's Rest 42 In South Africa . . . A poor white belongs to a type characterised by dubious antecedents, dubious whiteness, dubious respectability, dubious earning capacity.
>
> 1968 Daily Times-News (Burlington, N. Carolina) 18 May 4 a/3 Characteristics don't come from blackness or whiteness, but they come from a man's conditioning, or his cultural background.
>
> 2000 Teaching Tolerance Fall 16/2 Together they are experiencing a collective meltdown over the realities of race and their own Whiteness.
>
> 2007 Independent 17 Aug. 36/6 Why should I, or any other mixed-race person, be compelled to regard 'whiteness' as our dominant identity?

See *OED Online*, December 2021, www.oed.com. As is clear from the entry, the consideration of whiteness as a meaningful identity, connoting traits other than skin color, was not seen until 1922 and then only in South Africa.

11. Du Bois, *Darkwater*, 18.
12. Du Bois, *Darkwater*, 17.
13. Du Bois, *Darkwater*, 22, quoting "Harris" (perhaps a reference to Alice Seely Harris).
14. Edgar Rice Burroughs's *Tarzan of the Apes* (New York: McClurg, 1914) and its sequels are the most famous of this genre. It is something of an irony that the publisher of *The Souls of Black Folk* also published the Tarzan series.
15. Du Bois, *Darkwater*, 19.
16. Du Bois, *Darkwater*, 19.
17. The level of brutality displayed in white violence against people of color, most often African Americans and Native Americans, overwhelms my phrase *heedless comportment*. For now, I am hesitant and unwilling to explore this phenomenon, as it is outside my scope, but it is certainly not irrelevant to my inquiry or to Du Bois's. See Saidiya Hartman, *Scenes of Subjection: Terror, Slavery, and Self-Making in Nineteenth Century America* (Oxford: Oxford University Press, 1997), which makes a persuasive argument that recounting episodes of torture against African Americans, especially those who were enslaved, is not often a worthwhile exercise, as it tends to feed the white appetite for the suffering of Black people.
18. Du Bois, *Darkwater*, 22, emphasis in original.
19. Lewis, *W. E. B. Du Bois: Biography of a Race*, 555–56; W. E. B. Du Bois, "Close Ranks," *The Crisis* 16, no. 3 (1918), 111–14.
20. Du Bois, *Darkwater*, 25.
21. The point Du Bois would later make in *Black Reconstruction* (1935; New York: Free Press, 1992)—of a "public and psychological wage" secured through white racial identity in exchange for a healthy labor movement—was already part of his analysis in 1920. See chapter 5.
22. Du Bois, *Darkwater*, 24.
23. W. E. B. Du Bois, *Dusk of Dawn* (1940; New York: Oxford University Press, 2007), 34.
24. Invasion and conquest have likely been around as long as human beings have. However, the imperialism of white nations in the modern era is subject to particular evaluation—in part because of the development of conceptions of universal human rights and moral values that became the foundation of western political and moral theories in that era. Various authors have articulated both the material differences in the rapacious conquest by white nations and the moral irony of their inability to apply revolutionary moral theories to newly discovered humans. See, for example, Audrey Smedley, *Race in North America: Origin and Evolution of a Worldview* (New York: Routledge, 1993).
25. Charles W. Mills argues that white supremacy governs white political and moral relations with people of color (*The Racial Contract* [Ithaca, NY: Cornell University Press, 1999], 109ff).
26. Du Bois, *Darkwater*, 17
27. Du Bois, *Darkwater*, 20.
28. Du Bois, *Darkwater*, 33.
29. Mills, *The Racial Contract*, 13.
30. Mills, *The Racial Contract*, 16.
31. Du Bois, *Darkwater*, 52.
32. Du Bois, *Darkwater*, 57.
33. Du Bois, *Darkwater*, 57.

34. Du Bois, *Darkwater*, 130.
35. Du Bois, *Darkwater*, 143.
36. Du Bois, *Darkwater*, 144. Du Bois was generous to suggest that there is some symmetry in the hate that results from the Veil. However, if Black folk do hate white folk as a group, that hatred is more justified than the hatred that flows in the opposite direction. In other words, whites hate Black folk because they do not know them; Black folk hate what white folk have actually done because they know them all too well.
37. Matthew Hughey offers a history and analysis of the creation of "The Souls of White Folk" in "'The Souls of White Folk' (1920–2020): A Century of Peril and Prophecy," *Ethnic and Racial Studies* 43, no. 8 (2020): 1307–32.
38. Du Bois, *Darkwater*, 17. This echoes Du Bois's assertion in *The Souls of Black Folk* that, after the episode in which his visiting card was refused by the young white newcomer, he "lived above [the Veil] in a region of blue sky and great wandering shadows" (1903; Amherst: University of Massachusetts Press, 2018), 2.
39. Du Bois, *Darkwater*, 17.
40. Du Bois, *Darkwater*, 17. This perspective was not unique to Du Bois. James Weldon Johnson wrote, "The colored people of this country know and understand the white people better than the white people know and understand them" (*The Autobiography of an Ex-Colored Man* [1912; New York: Norton, 2015], 14.) Du Bois's line showed up in the 1910 version "The Souls of White Folk," printed in *The Independent*, August 10, 1910.
41. Du Bois, *Darkwater*, 17. I address this complex map of human consciousness in chapter 6.
42. "It is not permissible that the authors of devastation should also be innocent. It is the innocence which constitutes the crime" (James Baldwin, "Letter to My Nephew," *The Progressive*, December 1, 1962).
43. Du Bois, *Darkwater*, 18.
44. Du Bois, *Darkwater*, 18–19. Written in 1920, the comment on Japan is meant only to invoke America's xenophobia.
45. Du Bois, *Darkwater*, 30–31.
46. Marable, "Introduction," vii.
47. See, for example, Marilyn Frye, "A Note on Anger," in *The Politics of Reality* (Freedom, CA: Crossings Press, 1983); Audre Lorde, "On the Uses of Anger," in *Sister Outsider* (Freedom, CA: Crossings Press, 1984); and Maria Lugones, "Hard-to-Handle Anger," in *Pilgrimages/Peregrinajes: Theorizing Coalition against Multiple Oppressions* (Lanham, MD: Rowman and Littlefield, 2003).
48. Du Bois, *Darkwater*, 19.
49. Du Bois, *Darkwater*, 19.
50. Du Bois, *Darkwater*, 19.
51. Du Bois, *Darkwater*, 20.
52. Du Bois, *Darkwater*, 20.
53. Du Bois exhibited excellent intellectual understanding of the inequity of gender oppression even as he was unable to live into a commitment to gender equality. This is not surprising, as many of us share that tendency. Joy James brilliantly unpacks Du Bois's complex commitments around gender in "Profeminism and Gender Elites: W. E. B. Du Bois, Anna Julia Cooper, and Ida B. Wells-Barnett," in *Transcending the Talented Tenth: Black Leaders and American Intellectuals* (New York: Routledge, 1997), 35–59.
54. Interestingly, Du Bois appeared to believe that gender roles would be more durable. To me, this is plausible, even if one believes that gendered roles are also socially constructed. They may be more natural but also more difficult to relinquish and less dependent on the audience of others.

55. Du Bois, *Darkwater*, 155.
56. Du Bois, *Darkwater*, 41.
57. Du Bois, *The Souls of Black Folk*, 3.
58. Stanley Kramer's 1958 film *The Defiant Ones* has a similar theme: two convicts come to trust each other when they are given the opportunity to escape from a chain gang but remain shackled to each other during that escape.
59. Du Bois, *Darkwater*, 158.
60. "The Comet" appears alongside works by George Schuyler, Octavia Butler, and Steven Barnes in *Dark Matter*, an anthology of speculative fiction of the African diaspora (ed. Sheree R. Thomas [New York: Warner Books, 2000]).
61. Du Bois, *Darkwater*, 28, emphasis in original.
62. Du Bois, *Darkwater*, 34.
63. Du Bois, *Darkwater*, 34.
64. Marable, "Introduction," vi.
65. Du Bois, *Darkwater*, 47.
66. Du Bois, *Darkwater*, 60.

CHAPTER 5: *Black Reconstruction*

1. "No body of thought rivals that of W. E. B. Du Bois for an understanding of the dynamics, indeed dialectics, of race and class in the US" (David Roediger, *The Wages of Whiteness: Race and the Making of the American Working Class* [New York: Verso, 1991], 11–12).
2. See, for instance, Eric Foner, *Reconstruction: America's Unfinished Revolution, 1863–1877* (New York: Harper and Row, 1988).
3. David Levering Lewis, "Introduction," in *Black Reconstruction*, by W. E. B. Du Bois (1935; New York: Oxford University Press, 2007), xxvi.
4. See, for instance, Nell Painter, *The History of White People* (New York: Norton, 2011); and Tyler Stovall, *White Freedom: The Racial History of an Idea* (Princeton, NJ: Princeton University Press, 2021).
5. W. E. B. Du Bois, *Black Reconstruction* (1935; New York: Free Press, 1992), 141. Unless otherwise noted, I am citing from this edition in the text. There is a chilling scene in the recent remake of *Roots* (episode 4) in which the situation of formerly enslaved Black folk who remained on southern plantations at the end of the Civil War becomes all too clear. The scion of a slaveholding family informs Black soldiers who have returned victorious at the end of the Civil War: "We will redeem this country and put you people back where you belong. It's just natural law" (Bruce Beresford, dir., June 2, 2016, History Channel).
6. See, for instance, Nicholas Lemann, *Redemption: The Last Battle of the Civil War* (New York: Farrar, Strauss, and Giroux, 2007).
7. David Levering Lewis, *W. E. B. Du Bois: The Fight for Equality and the American Century, 1919–1963* (New York: Holt, 2000), 360.
8. Carol Anderson, *White Rage: The Unspoken Truth of Our Racial Divide* (New York: Bloomsbury, 2016); Lemann, *Redemption*; Douglas Blackmon, *Slavery by Another Name: The Re-Enslavement of African Americans from the Civil War to World War II* (New York: Random House, 2008).
9. Du Bois, *Black Reconstruction*, 166.
10. Du Bois, *Black Reconstruction*, 189.
11. Du Bois, *Black Reconstruction*, 189.
12. Du Bois, *Black Reconstruction*, 405.
13. See, for instance, Leon Litwack, *Been in the Storm So Long* (1980; New York: Vintage,

2010): "The key provisions were those which defined [anyone formerly enslaved] as an agricultural laborer, barred or circumscribed any alternative occupations, and compelled [them] to work. [In sum, the codes did not recognize the freed people as] entitled to equal protection under the law" (366).

14. Du Bois, *Black Reconstruction*, 167.
15. Du Bois, *Black Reconstruction*, 239.
16. Du Bois, *Black Reconstruction*, 17.
17. Du Bois, *Black Reconstruction*, 20.
18. Du Bois, *Black Reconstruction*, 239. This line echoes Du Bois's criticism of Booker T. Washington's program for Black uplift; his focus on the importance of civil rights and social equality for the maintenance of human rights might have originated with his study of the demands of the abolition democrats.
19. More than one historian has suggested that we would better understand the reality of the past and present United States by admitting that the South actually won the Civil War. See, for instance, Heather Cox Richardson, *How the South Won the Civil War* (New York: Oxford University Press, 2020).
20. 109 U.S. 103 (1883).
21. Loïc Wacquant, "From Slavery to Mass Incarceration," *New Left Review* 13 (January-February 2002), 41-60; Blackmon, *Slavery by Another Name*; Michelle Alexander, *The New Jim Crow: Mass Incarceration in the Age of Colorblindness* (New York: New Press, 2010).
22. See, generally, Brenda Wineapple, *The Impeachers: The Trial of Andrew Johnson and the Dream of a Just Nation* (New York: Random House, 2019).
23. Du Bois, *Black Reconstruction*, 298-300.
24. Du Bois, *Black Reconstruction*, 82. It is painful to imagine the courage and cunning of those who fled enslavement and reached friendly forces, only to be returned to their enslavers and, presumably, punished for the attempted escape.
25. Du Bois, *Black Reconstruction*, 150.
26. Du Bois, *Black Reconstruction*, 150.
27. Du Bois, *Black Reconstruction*, 102-3.
28. Du Bois, *Black Reconstruction*, 420.
29. Du Bois, *Black Reconstruction*, 428.
30. Du Bois, *Black Reconstruction*, 549-50.
31. Du Bois, *Black Reconstruction*, 125.
32. Du Bois, *Black Reconstruction*, 705.
33. Du Bois, *Black Reconstruction*, n.p.
34. Du Bois, *Black Reconstruction*, 7.
35. Du Bois, *Black Reconstruction*, 377.
36. Du Bois, *Black Reconstruction*, 370.
37. Roediger, *The Wages of Whiteness*, esp. 11-13.
38. See, for instance, Herbert Hill, "Racism within Organized Labor: A Report of Five Years of the AFL-CIO, 1955-1960," *Journal of Negro Education* 30, no. 2 (1961): 109-18.
39. Du Bois, *Black Reconstruction*, 39.
40. Du Bois, *Black Reconstruction*, 167.
41. Du Bois, *Black Reconstruction*, 275.
42. Du Bois, *Black Reconstruction*, 242.
43. Du Bois, *Black Reconstruction*, 52.
44. Du Bois, *Black Reconstruction*, 52.
45. Du Bois, *Black Reconstruction*, 52.
46. Linda Martín Alcoff writes of staying at the Lee House at the University of Virginia

and notes also that Washington and Lee University retains its name (*The Future of Whiteness* [Cambridge: Polity, 2015], 178ff). The recent removal of some statues of Lee and other Confederate heroes suggests a faltering of this dynamic; see, for instance, "Charlottesville Removes Robert. E. Lee Statue at Center of White Nationalist Rally," *New York Times*, July 9, 2023. However, only time will tell whether such removals will be remembered as isolated episodes or as part of a longer trajectory toward racial justice.

47. Christina Sharpe, *In the Wake: On Blackness and Being* (Durham, NC: Duke University Press, 2016) 7. In the cited chapter, Sharpe reports the sudden deaths of two members of her family, one by murder. Her analysis includes work by Joy James and João Costa Vargas showing that extralegal Black death is always an integral part of what is called justice in the United States.
48. According to a 2019 study by the Pew Research Center, 56 percent of white Americans agreed that being white in America is an advantage, and 70 percent of Black respondents agreed (www.pewresearch.org). In a poll taken a year later, 58 percent of whites believed that being white is an advantage, and 83 percent of Black respondents agreed. Tellingly, only 30 percent of white Americans said that they were moved by events during the summer of 2020, including the murder of George Floyd, to take any action to try to "understand racial issues" in the United States. (www.ipsos.com).
49. As I will discuss in chapter 9, Du Bois laid the groundwork for the tremendous work done by Charles W. Mills on white ignorance (*The Racial Contract* [Ithaca, NY: Cornell University Press, 1997]). Also see Charles W. Mills, "White Ignorance," in *Epistemologies of Ignorance*, ed. Nancy Tuana and Shannon Sullivan (Albany: SUNY Press, 2007). Here, Mills is explicit regarding Du Bois's metaphor of the Veil as a key invocation of white ignorance about Black humanity (18).
50. Du Bois, *Black Reconstruction*, 630.
51. W. E. B. Du Bois, *Dusk of Dawn* (Oxford: Oxford University Press, 2007), 11.
52. Du Bois, *Black Reconstruction*, 606.
53. "Back toward Slavery" is the title of chapter 16 in *Black Reconstruction* (670).
54. Anderson, *White Rage*, 31–32.
55. Du Bois, *Black Reconstruction*, 631.
56. Du Bois, *Black Reconstruction*, 319–20.
57. Roediger, *The Wages of Whiteness*, 13, citing Du Bois, *Black Reconstruction*, 27–30.
58. James Baldwin, *The Fire Next Time* (New York: Random House, 1993), 5.
59. W. E. B. Du Bois, *Darkwater: Voices from within the Veil* (1920; Mineola, NY: Dover, 1999), 18.

CHAPTER 6: *Dusk of Dawn* and the Triumph of Unreason

1. W. E. B. Du Bois, *Dusk of Dawn: An Essay toward an Autobiography of a Race Concept* (1940; New York: Oxford University Press, 2007), xxxiii. Unless otherwise noted, I cite from this edition.
2. Du Bois, *Dusk of Dawn*, xxxii.
3. Draft of two chapters of *Dusk of Dawn*, 1940–42, box 1, folder 2, W. E. B. Du Bois Papers (Sc MG 109), Schomburg Center for Research in Black Culture, Manuscripts, Archives and Rare Books Division, New York Public Library.
4. David Levering Lewis, *W. E. B. Du Bois: Biography of a Race, 1868–1919* (New York: Holt, 1993), 158–59.
5. W. E. B. Du Bois, *Dusk of Dawn*, xxxiii.
6. This trip formed the basis for Du Bois's unpublished epistolary novel, "A World Search

for Democracy" (1937), W. E. B. Du Bois Papers (MS 312), Special Collections and University Archives, University of Massachusetts Amherst Libraries.
7. Du Bois, *Dusk of Dawn*, 1.
8. Du Bois, *Dusk of Dawn*, 2.
9. Du Bois, *Dusk of Dawn*, 2.
10. Du Bois, *Dusk of Dawn*, 2.
11. Du Bois, *Dusk of Dawn*, 2–3.
12. Du Bois, *Dusk of Dawn*, 32.
13. Du Bois, *Dusk of Dawn*, 34.
14. A. Morris, *The Scholar Denied: W. E. B. Du Bois and the Birth of Modern Sociology* (Oakland: University of California Press, 2015), 76.
15. Du Bois, *Dusk of Dawn*, 43.
16. Du Bois's son Burghardt died of diphtheria in 1899; his daughter, Yolande, was born in 1901 and was living on campus with her parents in South Hall during the 1906 riot (Lewis, *Biography of a Race*, 335).
17. Du Bois, *Dusk of Dawn*, 48.
18. Du Bois, *Dusk of Dawn*, 49.
19. Du Bois, *Dusk of Dawn*, 49.
20. Du Bois, *Dusk of Dawn* 50. In his early works, Du Bois insisted that Africans and their descendants were capable of great culture but had not yet produced it and needed the opportunity to do so ("Conservation," *The Negro* [1915], *passim*). See also Stephanie J. Shaw, *W. E. B. Du Bois and "The Souls of Black Folk"* (Chapel Hill: University of North Carolina Press, 2015).
21. This period is discussed at length by Stephen Jay Gould, *The Mismeasure of Man* (New York: Norton, 1986). See also Joseph Graves Jr., *The Emperor's New Clothes: Biological Theories of Race at the Millennium* (New Brunswick, NJ: Rutgers University Press, 2003).
22. Du Bois, *Dusk of Dawn*, 65.
23. Du Bois, *Dusk of Dawn*, 66.
24. Du Bois, *Dusk of Dawn*, 66.
25. In Plato's *Republic*, he compares the human experience of reality to the perceptions of those trapped in a cave, where the shadows of reality are cast upon the cave wall for prisoners to see. They believe that they are seeing the true nature of things. However, one who is able to escape the cave might travel into the sunlight and, after a time of adjustment, be able to see truth as it really is (514a–20a). The story serves as a metaphor for the use of philosophical thinking to see beyond daily illusions.
26. Du Bois, *Dusk of Dawn*, 66.
27. Du Bois, *Dusk of Dawn*, 66.
28. Joel Olson, *The Abolition of White Democracy* (Minneapolis: University of Minnesota Press, 2004), 24.
29. Du Bois, *Dusk of Dawn*, 89–90.
30. Du Bois, *Dusk of Dawn*, 92.
31. Du Bois, *Dusk of Dawn*, 114.
32. Du Bois, *Dusk of Dawn*, 143.
33. Du Bois, *Dusk of Dawn*, 147.
34. Du Bois, *Dusk of Dawn*, 147.
35. Du Bois, *Dusk of Dawn*, 159–60. See also David Levering Lewis, *W. E. B. Du Bois: The Fight for Equality and the American Century, 1919–1963* (New York: Holt, 2000), 425–26.
36. Du Bois, *Dusk of Dawn*, 159.

37. Eric Porter, *The Problem of the Future World: W. E. B. Du Bois and the Race Concept at Midcentury* (Durham, NC: Duke University Press, 2010), 21. See also Morris, *The Scholar Denied*, 31–32.
38. Du Bois, *Dusk of Dawn*, 66.
39. Du Bois, *Dusk of Dawn*, 66.
40. Du Bois, *Dusk of Dawn*, 71.
41. Du Bois, *Dusk of Dawn*, 71.
42. Du Bois, *Dusk of Dawn*, 75.
43. Du Bois, *Dusk of Dawn*, 78.
44. Du Bois, *Dusk of Dawn*, 80.
45. W. E. B. Du Bois, *Dusk of Dawn*, c. 1940, W. E. B. Du Bois Papers (MS 312), Special Collections and University Archives, University of Massachusetts Amherst Libraries (hereafter cited as *Dusk of Dawn* ms.)
46. Du Bois, *Dusk of Dawn*, 82–83. See also Du Bois, *Dusk of Dawn* ms. Between drafts, Du Bois apparently played a bit with the lists of qualities germane to each identity category.
47. Du Bois, *Dusk of Dawn*, 3.
48. Sander L. Gilman and James M. Thomas, *Are Racists Crazy? How Prejudice, Racism, and Antisemitism Became Markers of Insanity* (New York: New York University Press, 2016).
49. Du Bois, *Dusk of Dawn*, 66.
50. Du Bois, *Dusk of Dawn*, 66–67.
51. Du Bois, *Dusk of Dawn*, 66.
52. Du Bois, *Dusk of Dawn*, 69.
53. Du Bois, *Dusk of Dawn*, 69.
54. Du Bois, *Dusk of Dawn*, 72.
55. Du Bois, *Dusk of Dawn*, 73.
56. Du Bois, *Dusk of Dawn*, 74.
57. Du Bois, *Dusk of Dawn*, 76.
58. Du Bois, *Dusk of Dawn*, 77.
59. Du Bois, *Dusk of Dawn*, 77.
60. Du Bois, *Dusk of Dawn*, 87.
61. Du Bois, *Dusk of Dawn*, 96.
62. Du Bois, *Dusk of Dawn*, 97.
63. "[White ignorance] will often be shared by nonwhites to a greater or lesser extent because of the power relations and patterns of ideological hegemony involved" (Charles Mills, "White Ignorance," in *Race and Epistemologies of Ignorance*, ed. Shannon Sullivan and Nancy Tuana [Albany: State University of New York Press, 2007], 22).
64. Du Bois, *Dusk of Dawn*, 11. One wonders why nearby Amherst and Williams colleges were not seen as options, but, again, the answer likely involves the inability of his benefactors to imagine Du Bois among large numbers of white students.
65. Du Bois complicated his childhood and adolescence a bit in his posthumous *The Autobiography of W. E. B. Du Bois* (New York: International, 1968), 105ff.
66. Du Bois, *Dusk of Dawn*, 76.
67. Du Bois, *Dusk of Dawn*, 76. Du Bois's use of the first-person plural here is a bit of poetic license.
68. Marilyn Frye offers a useful observation in this regard: "Any serious moral or political challenge to a whitely person must be a direct threat to her or his very being" (*Willful Virgin* [Freedom, CA: Crossroads, 1992], 157).
69. Porter, *The Problem of the Future World*, 17.

70. Later scholars have suggested that Du Bois's vision in *Dusk* hewed too closely to the biological essentialism of an earlier time. See Chike Jeffers, "The Cultural Theory of Race," *Ethics* 123, no. 3 (2013): 403–26.
71. Du Bois, *Dusk of Dawn*, 142.
72. Du Bois, *Dusk of Dawn*, 151.
73. Du Bois, *Dusk of Dawn*, 155.
74. W. E. B. Du Bois, *Black Reconstruction* (1935; New York: Free Press, 1992), 370.
75. Porter, *The Problem of the Future World*, 43.
76. Porter, *The Problem of the Future World*, 44.

CHAPTER 7: The Postwar Collapse of Whiteness

1. Nahum Dmitri Chandler, *W. E. B. Du Bois: The Problem of the Color Line at the Turn of the Twentieth Century* (New York: Fordham University Press, 2015), 14.
2. The power of the new organization seemed to lie with the Security Council, which was dominated by "white Europe and America" (W. E. B. Du Bois, "The World and Africa" and "Color and Democracy: Colonies and Peace," ed. Henry Louis Gates [1947, 1945; New York: Oxford University Press, 2007], 247).
3. Information about the long-term effects of the atomic bombs was effectively censored by the U.S. government for a year after their use. The journalist John Hersey was the first to report from Japan about the aftermath; see "Hiroshima," *The New Yorker*, August 31, 1946. The story of the censorship and Hersey's reporting is told in Lesley M. M. Blume, *Fallout* (New York: Simon and Schuster, 2021).
4. For years, Du Bois had hoped to publish a book exploring the astonishing courage and brilliance of Black troops in World War I. Chad Williams's *The Wounded World: W. E. B. Du Bois and the First World War* (New York: Farrar, Strauss, and Giroux, 2023).
5. Du Bois made this argument in "The African Roots of War," *Atlantic Monthly* 115, no. 5 (1915). However, he briefly stepped back from this critique when he saw potential for Black service in the Allied military as a means of improving the political and social status of African Americans. By the time *Darkwater* was published, he had concluded that white supremacy would continue to serve colonialism as well as domestic racial violence. See, for example, Bill V. Mullen, *W. E. B. Du Bois: Revolutionary across the Color Line* (London: Pluto, 2016).
6. See, for example, Mike Davis, *Late Victorian Holocausts: El Niño Famines and the Making of the Third World* (London: Verso, 2001).
7. On the connection of Nazi ideology and American white supremacy, see, for example, James Q. Whitman, *Hitler's American Model* (Princeton, NJ: Princeton University Press, 2017).
8. Herbert Aptheker, *The Literary Legacies of W. E. B. Du Bois* (White Plains, NY: Kraus International, 1989), 283.
9. Du Bois, *Color and Democracy*, 241.
10. Du Bois, *Color and Democracy*, 254.
11. See, for instance, S. H. Plunkett and J. J. Kimble, *Enduring Ideals: Rockwell, Roosevelt, and the Four Freedoms* (New York: Abbeville, 2018).
12. Du Bois, *Color and Democracy*, 252.
13. Mike Davis notes that British policies "in Africa forced the local labor force to live in precarious shantytowns on the fringes of segregated and restricted cities" (*Planet of Slums* [London: Verso, 2007], 52). In African and Asian colonies, the imperial governments were so committed to not seeing these slums that they refused to provide basic infrastructure, including sewage or sanitation. As a result, many of these cities remain

deeply segregated with tremendous disparities of health and welfare, half a century after independence.
14. "We know how the lure of profit from rich, unlettered, and helpless countries has tempted great and civilized nations and plunged them into bloody rivalry" (Du Bois, *Color and Democracy*, 250).
15. Du Bois, *Color and Democracy*, 246.
16. Du Bois, *Color and Democracy*, 250.
17. David Levering Lewis, *W. E. B. Du Bois: The Fight for Equality and the American Century* (New York: Holt, 2000), 503–4.
18. Du Bois, *Color and Democracy*, 247.
19. Du Bois, *Color and Democracy*, 247.
20. Du Bois, *Color and Democracy*, 248.
21. Gerald Horne, introduction, in Du Bois, *Color and Democracy*, 240.
22. Du Bois, *Color and Democracy*, 251.
23. Lewis, *W. E. B. Du Bois: The Fight for Equality*, 504.
24. Du Bois, *Color and Democracy*, 252.
25. "[John] heard stealing toward him the faint sweet music of the swan" (W. E. B. Du Bois, *The Souls of Black Folk* [1903; Amherst: University of Massachusetts Press, 2018], 239).
26. W. E. B. Du Bois, "A World Search for Democracy," c. 1937, W. E. B. Du Bois Papers (MS 312), Special Collections and University Archives, University of Massachusetts Amherst Libraries. See also Lisa McLeod, "Du Bois's 'A World Search for Democracy': The Democratic Roots of Socialism," *Socialism and Democracy* 32, no. 3 (2018): 105–24, 110.
27. Du Bois's concern here echoes his letter to Woodrow Wilson in 1918, which reminded the president, as he traveled to Versailles, that African Americans would be present in Paris to remind other delegates that the champion of democracy, the United States, contained 12 million "souls whose consent to be governed is never asked" (*Autobiography* [1968; New York: International, 2003], 271). See also Mullen, *W. E. B. Du Bois*, 49–50.
28. Du Bois, *Color and Democracy*, 288.
29. Du Bois, *Color and Democracy*, 293.
30. Du Bois, *Color and Democracy*, 295.
31. Du Bois, *Color and Democracy*, 295.
32. Du Bois, *Color and Democracy*, 302.
33. See W. E. B. Du Bois, *The Negro* (New York: Holt, 1915); and W. E. B. Du Bois, *Black Folk: Then and Now* (New York: Holt, Rinehart, and Winston, 1939). Both volumes analyze available historical data from various regions of the continent and include Du Bois's commentary on the implications for Black humanity worldwide.
34. W. E. B. Du Bois, *The World and Africa* (1939; New York: Oxford University Press, 2007), 163.
35. Du Bois, *The World and Africa*, 3.
36. Du Bois, *The World and Africa*, xxxiv.
37. Joy James, "The Profeminist Politics of W. E. B. Du Bois with Respects to Anna Julia Cooper and Ida B. Wells Barnett," in *W. E. B. Du Bois on Race and Culture*, ed. Bernard Bell, Emily R. Grosholz, and James B. Stewart (New York: Routledge, 1996), 141.
38. Du Bois, *The World and Africa*, 185.
39. "The African slave trade of the sixteenth and seventeenth centuries gave birth to the Industrial Revolution of the eighteenth and nineteenth" (Du Bois, *Black Folk*, 127).
40. Du Bois, "The African Roots of War." See also W. E. B. Du Bois, "The Hands of Ethiopia," in *Darkwater* (1920; Mineola, NY: Dover, 1999): 32–42.

41. Du Bois, *The World and Africa*, 21.
42. Du Bois, *The World and Africa*, 23.
43. Du Bois, *The World and Africa*, 26.
44. Du Bois, *The World and Africa*, 1.
45. Du Bois, *The World and Africa*, 1.
46. Du Bois, *The World and Africa*, xxvi.
47. Du Bois, *The World and Africa*, 67.
48. Du Bois quotes Eugène Guernier's proclamation, "Seule de tous les continents l'Afrique n'a pas d'histoire!" (Of all the continents, Africa has no history!) (*The World and Africa*, xxxii).
49. Du Bois, *The Negro*, xi.
50. Some of Du Bois's most trenchant comments on Hitler appear in his novel *Worlds of Color* (1961; New York: Oxford University Press, 2007), 33–37. In "A World Search for Democracy," his protagonist, visiting Germany in 1936, finds the country "orderly" and says this "is not reassuring." By this time the nation was already awash in propaganda about German superiority and the Jewish menace.
51. Du Bois, *The World and Africa*, 15.

CHAPTER 8: The Promise of the Black Flame

1. W. E. B. Du Bois, *The Ordeal of Mansart* (1957; New York: Oxford University Press, 2007), 229–30.
2. Gayatri Spivak, "Du Bois in the World: Pan-Africanism and Decolonization," *boundary2* (2018), https://www.boundary2.org.
3. See, for example, Robin D. G. Kelley, *Hammer and Hoe: Alabama Communists during the Great Depression* (1990; Chapel Hill: University of North Carolina Press, 2015); Gerald Horne, *Black and Red: W. E. B. Du Bois and the Afro-American Response to the Cold War* (Albany: State University of New York Press, 1985); and Kate Baldwin, *Beyond the Color Line and the Iron Curtain: Reading Encounters between Black and Red, 1922–1963* (Durham, NC: Duke University Press, 2002).
4. Eric Porter, *The Problem of the Future World: W.E.B. Du Bois and the Race Concept at Midcentury* (Durham: Duke University Press, 2010), 3. Porter has avoided the tendency to trivialize the later Du Bois, as have more recent scholars. See, for instance, Phillip Luke Sinitiere, ed., *Citizen of the World: The Late Career and Legacy of W. E. B. Du Bois* (Evanston, IL: Northwestern University Press, 2019); and Phillip Luke Sinitiere, ed., *Forging Freedom in W. E. B. Du Bois's Twilight Years: No Deed but Memory* (Jackson: University Press of Mississippi, 2023).
5. Spivak, "Du Bois in the World." Spivak prefaces the quoted sentence with this remark: "Du Bois had worked to take Africanity beyond the unique separator of enslavement. He took into account, as indeed did Marx, that in colonialism, slavery became an instrument (however out of sync) of the self-determination of capital. This allowed him to write it into the world-historical discourse of Marxism, rewriting the color line, by way of colonialism, into brown, red, and yellow."
6. The trilogy is mentioned once in David Levering Lewis's *W. E. B. Du Bois: The Fight for Equality and the American Century, 1919–1963* (New York: Holt, 2000), 545.
7. H. L. Gates, Jr., The Black Letters on the Sign, in Du Bois, *Mansart Builds a School*, xv.
8. It is tempting to replay such historical moments and speculate just what minor changes might have led to a more just and honorable outcome. Alternate history is a small but lively literary genre. (Terry Bisson's *Fire on the Mountain* [Binghamton, NY: PM Press, 1988] is a good example.) An alternate history of Reconstruction by Du Bois might have been a satisfying project for him and a great gift to Americans.

9. Later in the trilogy, Du Bois refers to Mrs. Breckinridge as Claire; I will continue to call her Clarice to avoid confusion.
10. Du Bois, *The Ordeal of Mansart*, 18.
11. W. E. B. Du Bois, *Mansart Builds a School* (1959; New York: Oxford University Press, 2007), 87.
12. Du Bois, *Mansart Builds a School*, 88.
13. Du Bois, *Mansart Builds a School*, 37.
14. Du Bois, *Mansart Builds a School*, 116.
15. Du Bois, *Mansart Builds a School*, 83.
16. The notion of pathology, as I use it here, in no way implies that white Americans lack culpability for the ongoing consequences of white supremacy. It is a feature of Du Bois's account of white epistemic and moral failure that white Americans must work to end white supremacy despite the psychological barriers they have inherited. See Joel Olson, "W. E. B. Du Bois and the Race Concept," *Souls* 7, nos. 3–4 (2005): 118–28; John Shuford "Four Du Boisian Contributions to Critical Race Theory," *Transactions of the Charles S. Peirce Society* 37, no. 3 (2001): 301–37.
17. Du Bois, *Mansart Builds a School*, 177.
18. W. E. B. Du Bois, *Worlds of Color* (1961; New York: Oxford University Press, 2007), 20.
19. Du Bois, *Worlds of Color*, 200.
20. Du Bois, *Worlds of Color*, 210–11.
21. To the best of my recollection, Susan has one substantive scene in a book that is well over five hundred pages. As I will discuss later in the chapter, when her two older sons are drafted into the U.S. Army to serve in World War I, she cries out, "They're taking my babies to fight for their country; what country? They have no country; they are stuck pigs in a dirty pen!" When Mansart tries to quiet her protests, she continues: "Why did you make me bear children to die for white folks?" His response to this legitimate heartbreak is unfortunately muted (Du Bois, *Mansart Builds a School*, 27). The gender politics of the trilogy are fascinating, but they are not free of sexism or misogyny. Thanks to Dawn Potter for reminding me to name Susan as well as Sojourner.
22. Du Bois, *The Ordeal of Mansart*, 5.
23. Du Bois, *The Ordeal of Mansart*, 11. Wade Hampton is a historical figure, a Confederate general who was elected governor of South Carolina in 1876 and led a faction known as the Redeemers. In 1879, he was elected to the U.S. Senate and served for two terms. See Rod Andrew, *Wade Hampton: Confederate Warrior to Southern Redeemer* (Chapel Hill: University of North Carolina Press, 2008). Today the community named after him—Wade Hampton, South Carolina—is 81 percent white (http://www.census.gov).
24. Du Bois, *The Ordeal of Mansart*, 123.
25. Du Bois, *The Ordeal of Mansart*, 123. The genealogy of the Scroggs family become somewhat confused over the course of the trilogy. Nothing turns on these minor inconsistencies; but, like Mrs. Breckinridge's floating name, they highlight the lack of resources available to Du Bois in his later years.
26. Du Bois, *The Ordeal of Mansart*, 149.
27. Du Bois, *The Ordeal of Mansart*, 150.
28. 347 U.S. 483 (1954); 349 U.S. 294 (1955).
29. W. E. B. Du Bois, *The Autobiography of W. E. B. Du Bois* (1968; New York: International, 2003), 333.
30. Du Bois, *Worlds of Color*, 210.
31. Du Bois, *The Ordeal of Mansart*, 81.
32. Du Bois, *Mansart Builds a School*, 146
33. Du Bois, *Worlds of Color*, 155. Writing of Truman's rise to the presidency, Du Bois said,

"It was a fantastic and awful commentary on naïve American belief that any man—at least any white man—could do anything; a belief which might one day ruin the world" (*Mansart Builds a School*, 144).
34. Du Bois, *Mansart Builds a School*, 27.
35. W. E. B. Du Bois, "Close Ranks," *The Crisis* 16, no. 3 (1918), 111–14. See the discussion of this article in David Levering Lewis, *W. E. B. Du Bois: Biography of a Race* (New York: Holt, 1993), 555–57.
36. Du Bois, *Worlds of Color*, 1.
37. Heather McGhee has produced reams of research demonstrating that white Americans are so determined to ensure that Black Americans are not given access to basic goods, including decent schools, health care, and public swimming pools, that they are willing to sacrifice their own well-being to ensure Black deprivation (*The Sum of Us: What Racism Costs All of Us and How We Can Prosper Together* [New York: Penguin Random House, 2022]).
38. Du Bois, *Worlds of Color*, 14–16.
39. Du Bois, *The Ordeal of Mansart*, 10.
40. Du Bois, *The Ordeal of Mansart*, 73.
41. Du Bois, *The Ordeal of Mansart*, 72.
42. Du Bois, *The Ordeal of Mansart*, 73.
43. Du Bois, *The Ordeal of Mansart*, 117.
44. Du Bois, *The Ordeal of Mansart*, 117.
45. Betsy may be modeled on the famous Elizabeth Freeman, or Mum Bett, an enslaved woman who, through ingenuity, successfully sued for her freedom in western Massachusetts in 1780. Du Bois, who grew up in Great Barrington, was well acquainted with this legend, and he even suggested that Freeman had married into the Black Burghardt family. See Ben Z. Rose, *Mother of Freedom: Mum Bett and the Roots of Abolition* (Waverley, MA: Treeline, 2009); and Lewis, *W. E. B. Du Bois: Biography of a Race*, 14.
46. Du Bois, *The Ordeal of Mansart*, 8.
47. Du Bois, *The Ordeal of Mansart*, 34.
48. Du Bois, *The Ordeal of Mansart*, 147.
49. Du Bois, *The Ordeal of Mansart*, 147.
50. Du Bois, *The Ordeal of Mansart*, 150.
51. Du Bois, *The Ordeal of Mansart*, 25.
52. Du Bois, *The Ordeal of Mansart*, 62.
53. Du Bois, *Autobiography*, 333.
54. Du Bois, *Mansart Builds a School*, 44.
55. Du Bois, *Mansart Builds a School*, 44.
56. Du Bois, *The Ordeal of Mansart*, 147.
57. Edwards, introduction, xxv.
58. Edwards, introduction, xxv.
59. Edwards, introduction, xxv.
60. According to Keith Byerman, the trilogy is "cast in the form of novels"; they are "a blending of history, fiction, social commentary, political criticism, and autobiography" (*Seizing the Word: History, Art, and Self in the Work of W. E. B. Du Bois* [Athens: University of Georgia, 1994], 138). I find this view is a bit uncharitable; I think they are fine novels that need revision and an effective editor.

CHAPTER 9: Moral Reconstruction

1. W. E. B. Du Bois, *The Philadelphia Negro* (1899; Philadelphia: University of Pennsylvania Press, 1996), 394; "If [whites'] policy in the past is the parent of much of this condition, and if to-day by shutting black boys and girls out of most avenues they are increasing pauperism and vice, then they must hold themselves largely responsible for the deplorable results." Also see W. E. B. Du Bois, *Mansart Builds a School* (1959; New York: Oxford University Press, 2007), 133–145.
2. Eduardo Bonilla-Silva, *Racism without Racists: Colorblind Racism and the Persistence of Racial Inequality in America* (2003; Lanham, MD: Rowman and Littlefield, 2003/2017).
3. Charles W. Mills, *The Racial Contract* (Ithaca, NY: Cornell University Press, 1999).
4. Charles W. Mills, "W. E. B. Du Bois: Black Radical Liberal," in *A Political Companion to Du Bois*, ed. Nick Brommel (Lexington: University Press of Kentucky, 2018), 43.
5. Mills, "W. E. B. Du Bois: Black Radical Liberal," 44.
6. Mills, "W. E. B. Du Bois: Black Radical Liberal," 46.
7. Mills, "W. E. B. Du Bois: Black Radical Liberal," 48.
8. Charles W. Mills, "The Illumination of Blackness," in *Antiblackness*, ed. Moon-Jie Kung and João H. Costa Vargas (Durham, NC: Duke University Press: 2021), 35.
9. Linda Martín Alcoff, *The Future of Whiteness* (Cambridge: Polity, 2015), 1.
10. Alcoff, *The Future of Whiteness*, 135.
11. Alcoff, *The Future of Whiteness*, 112.
12. Alcoff, *The Future of Whiteness*, 140.
13. Lewis Gordon, *Freedom, Justice, and Decolonization* (New York: Routledge, 2021), 20.
14. Lewis Gordon, *Fear of Black Consciousness* (Farrar, Strauss, and Giroux, 2022), 104–5.
15. Gordon, *Freedom, Justice, and Decolonization*, 19.
16. Shannon Sullivan, *Revealing Whiteness: The Unconscious Habits of Racial Privilege* (Bloomington: Indiana University Press, 2006). See also Shannon Sullivan, *White Privilege* (Cambridge: Polity, 2019).
17. Sullivan, *Revealing Whiteness*, 144, and *passim*.
18. Sullivan, *Revealing Whiteness*, 122.
19. Shannon Sullivan, *Good White People* (Albany: State University of New York Press, 2014), 3.
20. Ella Myers, "Beyond the Psychological Wage: Du Bois on White Dominion," *Political Theory* 47, no. 1 (2018): 6–31.
21. Myers, "Beyond the Psychological Wage," 7.
22. Myers, "Beyond the Psychological Wage," 8.
23. Myers, "Beyond the Psychological Wage," 22.
24. Myers, "Beyond the Psychological Wage," 29, n. 82.
25. Myers, "Beyond the Psychological Wage," 10.
26. In fact, in Du Bois asserts that "the philosophy which assigns to the white race alone the hegemony of the world" is the child of the African slave trade and of the expansion of Europe during the nineteenth century (*The Negro* [1915; Philadelphia: University of Pennsylvania Press, 2001], 233.)
27. Myers, "Beyond the Psychological Wage," 30, n. 83.
28. Kiese Laymon, *Long Division* (2013; New York: Scribner's, 2021), 90.
29. Lucius Outlaw, *On Race and Philosophy* (New York: Routledge, 1996), xi.
30. "White Being is the militarized, normative paradigm of human being that inhabitants of the ongoing half-millenial civilizational project have involuntarily inherited as a violent

universal" (Dylan Rodríguez, *White Reconstruction: Domestic Warfare and the Logics of Genocide* [New York: Fordham University Press, 2020], 7–8).
31. Rodríguez, *White Reconstruction*, 15.
32. Rodríguez, *White Reconstruction*, 6.
33. Rodríguez, *White Reconstruction*, 6.
34. Rodríguez, *White Reconstruction*, 7.
35. Rodríguez, *White Reconstruction*, 9.
36. Rodríguez, *White Reconstruction*, 10.
37. Rodríguez, *White Reconstruction*, 66.
38. Rodríguez, *White Reconstruction*, 68.
39. Rodríguez, *White Reconstruction*, 62.
40. Rodríguez, *White Reconstruction*, 63.
41. Rodríguez, *White Reconstruction*, 7.
42. Joel Olson, *The Abolition of White Democracy* (Minneapolis: University of Minnesota Press, 2004).
43. Aimé Césaire, *Journal of a Homecoming / Cahier d'un retour au pays natal*, trans. N. Gregson Davis (1939; Durham, NC: Duke University Press, 2017).
44. Saidiya Hartman, *Wayward Lives, Beautiful Experiments: Intimate Histories of Riotous Black Girls, Troublesome Women, and Queer Radicals* (New York: Norton, 2019).

Conclusion

1. Dwight D. Eisenhower, speech, January 17, 1961, in *Public Papers of the Presidents*, https://avalon.law.yale.edu.
2. Michelle Alexander, *The New Jim Crow: Mass Incarceration in the Age of Colorblindness* (New York: New Press, 2012), 240.
3. W. E. B. Du Bois, "The Negro Mind Reaches Out," in *The New Negro, An Interpretation*, ed. Alain Locke (New York: Boni, 1925), 385.
4. Russell Banks, *Cloudsplitter: A Novel* (New York: HarperCollins, 1998).
5. W. E. B. Du Bois, *Autobiography* (1968; New York: International, 2003), 423.

Index

Abolition of White Democracy, The (Olson), 169
abolition-democracy, 83–86
African Americans. *See* Black Americans
Agassiz, Louis, 25, 47
Alcoff, Linda Martín, 162–63
American Blindspot, 117
American Negro Academy, 19, 25, 26
American Negro Slavery (Bowers), 83
Anderson, Carol, 95
Anderson, Osborne, 48, 53, 184n30
antisemitism, use of, 126
Appiah, Anthony, 105
arrogant, irrevocable license (conception of whiteness): in *Black Flame* trilogy, 142–54; *Black Reconstruction* and, 86–94; epistemic opacity, 7–8, 89–92; of Europeans, 122–23; hostility to postwar civil rights, 86–89; maintaining bitterness, 92–94; overview, 4–5; in readings of Du Bois, 157–59; resilient presumption of innocence, 3, 8–10; *The Souls of Black Folk* and, 34–37; summarizing, 2–3
Atlanta Constitution, 150
Atlanta University, 4
Autobiography (Du Bois), 20–21

Baldwin, James, 72
Banks, Russell, 172
Bargain of 1876, 93–94
Basic American Negro Creed, 105
Belgium, damage done by, 65, 67
BIPOC, acronym, 176n21
Black Americans: conception of African character, 23–24; and defeat of Reconstruction, 86–89; and mechanism of white supremacy, 70–71; population as problem, 34–37; and Veil metaphor, 40–41
Black Codes, 84

Black Flame, The (trilogy): accomplishment of, 156; character of Du Bignon, 139–40; dramatizing fate of formerly enslaved, 138–39; glimpsing at world of Sam Scroggs, 140; harm to white people in, 155–56; historical context behind, 135–36; opening of, 137–38; overview of trilogy, 137–41; progression of, 141; scholarly examination of, 135; speaking directly to reader, 134; themes found in, 136–37; tragedies in, 140; white license in, 142–54
Black radical liberalism, 160–61
Black Reconstruction (Du Bois), 8–9, 41, 69, 113–14, 161, 164, 169; American Blindspot, 117; and arrogant, irrevocable license of whiteness, 86–94; diving into white supremacy, 82; and flaws of Reconstruction, 94–96; Johnson-Douglass meeting, 86; overview, 81–83; Oxford edition of, 81; perception as revisionist history, 82; "To the Reader," 89–90; scope of, 83; and tragedy of Reconstruction, 83–86
Blight, David, 31, 32, 33
Boas, Franz Boas, 179n25
Bonilla-Silva, Eduardo, 159
Bowers, Claude G., 83
Breckenridges. See *Black Flame, The* (trilogy)
Britain, 123
Brown v. Board of Education of Topeka, 145–46
Brown, Henry Billings, 27
Brown, John: addressing Black Americans, 48–49; being "no longer white," 53–54; and connection between Africa and North America, 60–62; demonstrating moral vision of, 48; evolution of plans of, 51; life in brief, 49–51; presence in "Vision of the Damned, The" (Du Bois), 54–56; in *The Souls of Black Folk*, 47–49;

Brown, John (continued) and sphinx riddle, 56–60; transcending demands of whiteness, 53; vignette of unusual destiny of, 54; whiteness, 51–54
Burroughs, Edgar R., 30

Cahier d'un retour au pays natal (Césaire), 170
Carby, Hazel, 44
cave, metaphor, 103, 115–16
Césaire, Aimé, 170
Chandler, Nahum Dmitri, 27, 49, 52–53, 55–56, 57
China, 124
Civil Rights Cases of 1883, 85
Civil War, 69, 95
civilization, collapse of, 130–31
Clansman, The (Dixon), 47
Cloudsplitter (Banks), 172
"Collapse of Europe, The" (*World and Africa*), 128–29
colonialism, moral catastrophe of, 121–22
Color and Democracy: Colonies and Peace (Du Bois), 118–20; accomplishment of, 127; on colonialism, 121–22; conception of, 121; "Democracy and Color," 126; echoing *The Souls of Black Folk*, 125–26; European arrogant, irrevocable license, 122–23; inequalities favoring white and wealthy, 126–27; United Nations structure, 123–25; on use of antisemitism, 126
"Colored World Within, The" (*Dusk of Dawn*), 112–13
"Comet, The" (essay), 76–78
"Concept of Race, The" (*Dusk of Dawn*), 101–3
Confederacy, 22
Conrad, Joseph, 30
"Conservation of Races, The" (speech), 25–28, 102
contemporary theories, whiteness, 159–66
Crisis, The, 155
critical race studies, 112
Crummell, Alexander, 25, 40, 41

"Damnation of Women, The" (essay), 64
Dana, Richard Henry, Jr., 53
Dark Princess (Du Bois), 134
Darkwater: Voices from within the Veil (Du Bois), 7–8, 97; aims in writing, 64; "Of Beauty and Death" (essay), 69–71; "Comet, The" (essay), 76–78; denouncing, 63–64; heedless comportment in, 65–67; manifestation of white ignorance, 67–72; overview of, 63–64; presumed white innocence, 72–76; representation of Du Bois in, 64; "Souls of White Folk," 41, 62, 64–65, 68, 71–76, 78–80, 165–66; theme echoing in, 78–80; white psyche in, 64
Darwin, Charles, 61
Davenport, Charles, 25
Davis, Jefferson, 9–10, 20–24
Davis, Jim. *See* "Comet, The" (essay)
Debs, Eugenes, 177n29
Dieman, Roger Van, 5; and epistemic opacity, 110–13; and resilience of white innocence, 113–16; white friendship and, 106–8
Dixon, Thomas, 47
dominion, whiteness as, 164–65
double consciousness, 37–38
Douglass, Frederick, 48, 50, 53; meeting with Johnson, 86
Dowell, Josie, 44
Du Bignon, Jean. *See Black Flame, The* (trilogy)
Du Bois, W. E. B., access to anthropological evidence of African civilizations, 179n25; acknowledging shortcomings of Black folk, 181n16; analysis of white southern workers, 90–91; See also *Black Flame* trilogy, 134–56; See also *Black Reconstruction*, 81–96; book overview of, 11–17; and colonialism, 121–22; on competition for colonial resources, 123; "Conversation of Races, The" (speech), 25–28; conversing with Roger Van Dieman, 106–8; See also *Darkwater: Voices from within the Veil*, 63–80; death of son of, 40; demonstrating disordered nature of white thinking, 103–4; See also *Dusk of Dawn: An Essay toward an Autobiography of a Race Concept*, 97–117; early interventions of, 18–30; on exhausting work of being Black, 109–10; "Jefferson Davis as Representative of Civilization" (speech), 20–24; legacy of, 157–70; life experience of, 99–100; on longevity of slavery, 59; modest

assignment for white America, 26–27; as pioneer of whiteness studies, 41–42; and postwar collapse of whiteness, 118–33; professional career of, 100–101; project of racial justice, 19; referring to white world as "other world," 42; See also *Souls of Black Folk, The,* 31–46; on structures of whiteness, 159–66; tracing conception of whiteness of, 1–3; on United Nations, 123–25
Dumbarton Oaks, 118, 123–25
Dunning, William A., 83
Dusk of Dawn (Du Bois), 161; "Apology," 98; "Colored World Within, The," 98, 104, 112–13; "Concept of Race, The," 101–3; contents of, 97–99; epistemic opacity in, 7–8, 108–13; Eric Porter reading of, 116–17; final chapters of, 104–6; heedless comportment in, 5–6, 106–8; philosophical writing prompted by, 105–6; "Plot, The," 99–100; and resilient presumption of innocence, 10; "Science and Empire," 100–101; white innocence in, 113–16; "White World, The," 103–4, 106–8, 112

East Africa, 66
Economic and Social Council, 124
Edwards, Brent, 156
Eisenhower, Dwight D., 171
epistemic opacity (arrogant, irrevocable license), 3, 7–8, 158; in *Black Flame* trilogy, 143–45, 148–49; and defeat of Reconstruction, 89, 91–92; in *Dusk of Dawn,* 108–13
epistemic shortcomings, revealing, 69–70
Europeans, arrogant, irrevocable license of. See *Color and Democracy.*

feminist theory, 112
First World War, 125, 130
Fisk University, 102
Fourteenth Amendment, 27, 169
Freedmen's Bureau, 83, 168
Frémont, John C., 86
Fugitive Slave Act, 56

Gates, Henry Louis, Jr., 136
Gift of Black Folk, The (Du Bois), 81
Gooding-Williams, Robert, 31, 32, 33, 41

Gordon, Lewis, 163
Grady, Henry, 150. See also white license (in *Black Flame* trilogy)
Great Barrington, Massachusetts, 43, 99, 114–15, 198n45
Great Depression, 132

"Hands of Ethiopia, The" (Du Bois), 68, 77, 79
Harlan, John, 27
Harpers Ferry, 48, 52–53, 58–59, 184n30, 185n55, 185n65
Hartman, Saidiya, 170
Heart of Darkness (Conrad), 30
heedless comportment, 2, 5–6, 169; in *Black Flame* trilogy, 143–45, 147; in *Darkwater: Voices from within the Veil,* 65–67; in *Dusk of Dawn,* 106–8
Hegel, G. W. F., 23, 129
Hitler, Adolf, 126
Hoffman, Frederick, 47
Holocaust, 132–33
horizon of perception, schema, 164–65
Horne, Gerald, 125
Hose, Sam, 4–5
Hubbard, Dolan, 33
Hudson, David, 50

"Illumination of Blackness, The" (Mills), 161–62
Independent, The, 65
Indian wars, 21
Industrial Revolution, 129
innocence: illusion of, 15; presumption of, 72–76; resilience of, 113–16; white innocence, 8, 83, 115, 154, 158

James, William, 46
"Jefferson Davis as Representative of Civilization," speech, 20–24
Jim Crow, 6, 22, 32, 40, 82, 89, 95, 112, 120, 133, 139, 141, 171
John Brown (Du Bois), 12, 63; final chapter of, 61; genealogy of, 48–49; penultimate chapter of, 58; reviews of, 61–62; slaveholder epistemology, 90. See also Brown, John
Johnson, Andrew, 21, 83, 91; meeting with Douglass, 86

INDEX

Jones, John, 40, 44
Journal of Race Development, 65
Just Mercy (Stevenson), 43–44

Kendi, Ibram X., 18

Laymon, Kiese, 165
Lee, Robert E., 58, 92–93
legacy (of Du Bois), 169–70; Black radical liberalism, 160–61; contemporary theories of whiteness, 159–66; humanity and whiteness, 166–69; overview, 157–59
Leopard's Spots, The (Dixon), 47
"Lesson for Americans" (*Suppression*), 28–29
Lewis, David Levering, 33, 41, 47, 64
Lewis, Sinclair, 99
liberalism, changing attitude toward, 116–17
license, term, 4, 163–64
Lincoln, Abraham, 86–87
Locke, John, 4, 176n3
Logan, Rayford, 32
Long Division (Laymon), 165
Lost Cause, 9, 21
Lowndes County, Alabama, studying agriculture in, 101

Mamdani, Mahmood, 131
Mandates Commission, 125
Mansart, Manuel. See *Black Flame, The* (trilogy)
Mansart, Tom. See *Black Flame, The* (trilogy)
Mansart Builds a School (Du Bois), 134
Mansarts. See *Black Flame, The* (trilogy)
Marable, Manning, 63–64
McClurg (publisher), 48
McDowell, Irvin, 86
Mills, Charles, 7–8, 68, 113, 159–62
Morris, Aldon, 101
Murphy, William, 88
Myers, Ella, 164–65

National Association for the Advancement of Colored Persons (NAACP), 63, 66, 104–5, 123
Native Americans, 187n17
Negro, term, 25
Negro problem, 79–80, 107

New York City draft riots of 1863, 87
New York Times, 33
Niagara Movement, 138
nonwhite, term, 176n20
North Africa, 66
North Atlantic Treaty Organization, 131
Nott, Josiah, 178n4

Obama, Barack, 175n1, 175n3
oblivious performance, whiteness, 37–43
Oedipus Rex (Sophocles), 56–60
"Of Beauty and Death" (essay), 69–71
"Of Our Spiritual Strivings" (*Souls of Black Folk*), 36
"Of the Coming of John" (*Souls of Black Folk*), 43
"Of the Culture of White Folk" (essay), 65
"Of the Meaning of Progress" (*Souls of Black Folk*), 44
"Of the Passing of the First-Born" (Du Bois), 40
"Of the Training of Black Men" (*Souls of Black Folk*), 36–37
"Of Work and Wealth" (Du Bois), 68
Olson, Joel, 103, 169
Ordeal of Mansart, The (Du Bois), 134
Owen, David S., 41–42
ownership of the world, phrase, 67

people of color, 1, 3, 175n4; arrogant, irrevocable license and, 4; and *Black Reconstruction*, 92, 93–95; and *Darkwater*, 65–68, 70, 72, 75, 78; and Du Bois early interventions, 19, 28; epistemic opacity and, 7; essential and common humanity of, 106; John Brown and, 51, 61; and moral reconstruction, 158–59, 162–68, 171; and postwar collapse of whiteness, 122, 124, 127, 132; and promise of *Black Flame* trilogy, 135–36, 143, 145–46, 151–52, 155; resilient presumption of innocence and, 8–10; and *The Souls of Black Folk*, 31, 39, 46; term, 10–11; and triumph of unreason, 97, 100, 102, 106, 109, 113, 115–17
pessimism, of *The Souls of Black Folk*, 43–45
Phenomenology of the Spirit, The (Hegel), 23
Philadelphia Negro, The, 25, 29, 100, 158; rhetorical style of, 31

INDEX | 205

Porter, Eric, 2, 39, 105, 116–17, 135
Problem of the Future World, The (Porter), 2
profit management, global nature of, 130
public and psychological wage, 89

Quest of the Silver Fleece, The (Du Bois), 48, 134

Race Traits and Tendencies of the American Negro, The (Hoffman), 47
Racial Contract, The (Mills), 68, 159
racial identity, metaphysics, 105–6
racism without racists, model, 159
Reconstruction, 82; analysis of white southern workers, 90–91; "color problem" contributing to failure of, 90; exploring economics following, 137; factors to defat of, 88–94; flaws of, 94–96; Lincoln approach to compensation, 86–87; Northerners giving up on, 95–96; as rational response, 84; and subjugation of emancipated, 84–86; tragedy of, 83–86; white attitude during, 87; white leadership during, 83
Reed, Adolph, Jr., 2
resilient presumption of innocence (conception of whiteness), 3, 8–10, 113-16
"Riddle of the Sphinx, The" (*John Brown*), 56–60, 73
Rodríguez, Dylan, 167–69
Roediger, David, 62, 81, 90
Russia, 123

Schadenfreude, 68
Scroggs, Sam. See *Black Flame, The* (trilogy)
Second Treatise on Government (Locke), 4
Second World War, 158
segregation, effect on white people, 155–56
Sharpe, Christina, 93
Shaw, Stephanie J., 40
slavery, 6, 8, 13, 21; abolition of, 13, 35, 84; American slavery, 54–55, 178n4; and concept of free state, 81–82; confronting moral status of, 59; epistemology, 90–92, 96; Lincoln perceiving, 86–87; and suppression of African slave-trade, 28–29; and tragedy of Reconstruction, 83–86
Souls of Black Folk, The (Du Bois), 81, 97, 110, 114–15; on African Americans' special relationship with Africans, 60–61; arrogant, irrevocable license of whiteness in, 34–37; chapter 1 of, 34–37; as document of primordial condition, 41; double consciousness in, 37–38; and epistemic opacity, 7–8; essays in, 32–33; "Forethought, The," 38; and heedless comportment, 5–6; as Hegelian account, 40–41; interpretation rewarded to, 33; "Of the Coming of John," 43; "Of the Meaning of Progress," 44; pessimism of, 43–45; poetic tone in, 39; rhetorical style of, 31–32; riddle of John Brown in, 47–62; "Strivings of the Negro People" in, 27–28; success of, 45–46; and uplift suasion, 18–19; Veil and, 37–43; on white supremacy, 32
souls of Black folk, understanding, 35
"Souls of White Folk, The" (Du Bois), 41, 62, 64–65, 68, 165–66; engaging with white ignorance in, 71–72; predicting violent uprising in, 78–80; and white innocence, 72–76
Spanish-American War, 65
speeches: "Conversation of Races, The," 25–28; "Jefferson Davis as Representative of Civilization," 20–24
Sphinx, riddle of, 56–60
Spivak, Gayatri, 134
Stevenson, Bryan, 43–44
"Strivings of the Negro People" (essay), 27
Stuart, J. E. B., 58
Submissive Man, 23–24
Sullivan, Shannon, 164
Summer, Charles, 82
Suppression of the African Slave-Trade to the United States of America (Du Bois), 28–29, 31, 59, 96; rhetorical style of, 31

Tabak, D., 46
Tarzan the Ape Man (Burroughs), 30
Thirteenth Amendment, 168
Traitor, The (Dixon), 47
Truman, Harry, 119, 154
Truth, Sojourner, 56
Twain, Mark, 99

United Nations, criticisms of, 123–25
untermenschen, term, 68
uplift suasion, 18, 26

U.S. Constitution: Fourteenth Amendment, 27, 169; Thirteenth Amendment, 168
U.S. Labor Commission, 101
U.S. Supreme Court, 27

Veil, 67, 122, 152, 188n36; "behind the Veil," 32, 35, 40, 42, 44; breaking through, 109; casting off, 57; cave allegory as revisiting, 103; as continuing function of whiteness, 41–42; *Dusk of Dawn* passage on, 10; intimation of, 44; metaphor of, 7–8; *Souls of Black Folk* and, 37–43; viewing life within, 38; violence and, 69; whiteness as underlying mechanism of, 40–44, 70–71
Villard, Oswald Garrison, 74–76, 155
Voting Rights Act of 1965, 95

Wages of Whiteness, The (Roediger), 81
Washington, Booker T., 48
Wayward Lives, Beautiful Experiments (Hartman), 170
Western Europe, 120, 123, 128, 131
white, changing meaning of, 169
White Being, 167–69
white friend, conversing with, 69–70
white license (in *Black Flame* trilogy): breaking down opening scene, 142; and *Brown v. Board of Education of Topeka*, 145–46; commitment to moral innocence, 153–54; echoing *Black Reconstruction*, 148; monolithic obstacles, 152; public psychological wage, 151–52; revealing white comportment, 143–45; white ignorance and lack of contact, 149–51; witnessing global consequences, 147–48; World War I impact, 146–47
white man's burden, 168
white people, harm to, 155–56
white privilege, term, 163
White Reconstruction (Rodríguez), 167
white supremacy, 3, 68; bringing harm to white people, 155–56; humanity and, 166–69; origins of, 98; presumed naturalness of claims to, 131–32; strong man attitude, 23; in terms of wealth and power, 133; theory on triumph of, 159–61
"White World, The" (*Dusk of Dawn*), 103–4, 106–8, 112

whiteness, 171–73; addressing in "To the Reader" (*Black Reconstruction*), 89–90; analysis of white southern workers, 90–91; in *Black Flame, The* (trilogy), 142–54; cognitive opacity of, 161; colonialism and, 121–22; contemporary theories of, 159–66; as dominion, 164–65; Du Bois on crux of, 162–63; *Dusk of Dawn* portraying, 106–8; habituated actions and attitudes facilitating, 164; harm to white people, 155–56; and humanity, 166–69; ignorance manifestations, 67–72; irony of, 175n4; irreconcilable ideals of, 108–13; and John Brown, 51–54; maintaining bitterness, 92–94; moral ignorance, 66; null-consciousness and, 37; oblivious performance of, 37–43; postwar collapse of, 118–20, 132–33; potential to overcome, 162–63; presumed innocence, 72–76; resilience of innocence in, 113–16; taunting, 71–72; tracing as human quality, 186n10; and tragedy of Reconstruction, 83–86; uncertain future of, 162–63; untrustworthy agents, 42–43; Veil as continuing function of, 41–42; wealth and real estate, 68–69; white friendship, 106–8
Wilberforce University, 25
Wise, Henry, 58
World and Africa, The (Du Bois), 6, 119–20, 132–33; "Collapse of Europe, The," 128–29; demonstrating entitlement in, 128; on international peace, 128–29; on perfection of human culture, 130–32; on presumed naturalness of claims to white supremacy, 130; as record of unsustainability, 129–30; as urgent reinterpretation, 127–28; on white humanity continuation, 129
World War I. *See* First World War
World War II. *See* Second World War
world wars, 122–23, 128–31, 171
Worlds of Color (Du Bois), 134
Wynter, Sylvia, 167

Yancy, George, 33

Zamir, Shamoon, 21, 41